DREAMGIRL

DREAMGIRL
MY LIFE AS A SUPREME

MARY WILSON

With Patricia Romanowski and Ahrgus Juilliard

ST. MARTIN'S PRESS / NEW YORK

Design by M. Paul

Library of Congress Cataloging-in-Publication Data

Wilson, Mary, 1944–
    Dreamgirl : my life as a Supreme.
    1. Wilson, Mary, 1944–   2. Singers—United States—Biography.
3. Supremes (Musical group)   I. Title.
ML420.W553A3 1986   784.5′5′00924 [B]   86-13811
ISBN 0-312-21959-8

First Edition
10 9 8 7 6 5 4 3 2 1

Dedicated
to
my mom, Johnnie Mae Wilson, whose eyes have always shown love,
to
my aunt and uncle, I.V. and John L. Pippin,
and to the memory of
Florence "Blondie" Ballard

There is one person who must be thanked apart from all the rest, the person who is responsible for pulling this book together and making it happen. Thank you, Patty Romanowski.

ACKNOWLEDGMENTS

I am grateful to God for giving me the opportunity to live the life of a Supreme. This story has all the elements of a classic opera, the comedy, the tragedy, and finally the will to survive. And like all good theater the stage must be shared with a multitude of co-stars, supporting cast, and bit players. I must sing their praises.

Once the Primettes came into being, Milton Jenkins did everything in his power to make our dreams come true; I am only sorry he didn't reap the benefits of his initial hard work. Jesse Greer, Richard Morris, and John O'Den are among the many who saw the same bright potential and tried to help us achieve our goals.

Throughout those early days we had the support of the Primes, including Eddie Kendricks, Kel Osborne, and the late Paul Williams.

Berry Gordy, Jr., orchestrated and directed the whole fairy-tale. I would have no story to tell if it were not for Berry making us his "girls."

My deepest gratitude must go to John L. Pippin, my aunt I.V., my cousin Josephine, and Jackie Burkes for traveling down Memory Lane with me to the days when I was just little Mae-Mae in a starched dress and pigtails.

Florence Ballard's sisters, Barbara, Pat, and Maxine were invaluable in helping me piece together Florence's life after the Supremes.

There are too many members of the Motown family to name in this small space. But I want to especially mention Janie "Money" Bradford, who spent hours laughing and reminding me of the "good old days," and Thomas "Beans" Bowles, Choker Campbell, Joe Hunter, and Teddy Harris, who helped me reminisce about the Motown days. And, of course, we must also remember the likes of James Jamerson, Benny "Papa Zita" Benjamin, and Hank Cosby, just a few of the musicians who provided the sound that inspired so many voices to sing their hearts out.

Brian and Eddie Holland and Lamont Dozier's music gave the

Supremes the perfect vehicles to ride. I thank you, gentlemen. Among our early songwriter/producers were also Freddy Gorman and Smokey Robinson.

The Temptations have always been some of my staunchest allies, especially Melvin Franklin (who always believed in me) and Richard Street. And let's not forget Joe Billingslea of the Contours, Bobby Rogers of the Miracles, Gladys Horton of the Marvelettes, Rosalind Ashford of the Vandellas, Clarence Paul, Joe Shaffner, Kim Weston, who continues to encourage the young voices of Detroit to sing out, Cholly Atkins, who made the moves possible, and his beautiful wife, Maye "Mom" Atkins, Esther Edwards who tried to lead us down the straight and narrow path of life, Maurice King and Gil Askey for their musical support and guidance, Nate McAlpine, Norris Patterson, Eddie Bisco, Winnie Brown, Shelly Berger, Don Foster, Weldon McDougle, and Sylvia Moy, just to name a few of the people who laughed, cried, and relived our past.

Dick Clark helped to launch the Supremes and he continues to be one of Motown's greatest supporters and admirers. I also would like to thank so many of the other artists on the Dick Clark tour who shared their memories of those crazy tours with me, especially singer Mike Clifford.

Mark Bego was the first to help me try to compile my memoirs and I thank him for setting me on the right path. Bart Andrews and Sherry Robb of Andrews and Robb Agency were the first to set the wheel in motion so that this book could become a reality.

Because of the grace of God, the Supremes have touched many lives, so it is with great passion that I thank our many fans, who have shared our dream and made it a reality. Without the help of the fans, this manuscript could never have come into being. The clippings, photos, and stories they provided were an invaluable part of its creation. I must thank Carl Feuerbacher, president of the Supremes fan club, who at his own expense has continued to publish the monthly newsletter and gather materials and information for *Dreamgirl*, and also Tom and Barbara Ingrassia and the many fans who helped. His help and continued support is worth more than words can ever express. Allen Poe, my godson and personal assistant, gave me a supporting hand throughout the writing of this book and I shall not forget it.

I must also thank my New York research team, Jim Lopes, and—again—Mark Bego, John Christe, Edmund Greer, Tony Turner, and

Mark Case, my Los Angeles research team, David Horii and John Wyman, my Detroit research team, Martha Harris and Alice Fletcher, and my European research team.

To my attorney, Robert P. Kragulac, Esq.: Thanks for keeping me afloat and my corporation together.

Esther Gilmore's busy fingers transferred hours of chatter into legible transcripts. Constance Pappas Hillman gave me access to her library and Brother Prince was a patron when I needed him. Each of these people is an integral part of the book.

A thank-you to Ahrgus Juilliard, who sat and worked with me for a year and a half, pulling my diaries, scrapbooks, transcripts, and thoughts together for this book. Thanks, girl.

And a special thank-you to Pedro Ferrer, my ex-hubby, for telling me to get started on writing this book.

None of this could have been possible without my main sister, Hazel Bethke Kragulac, who since 1972 has been much more than my secretary, friend, and Executive Assistant.

But most of all I give my sincerest gratitude to Bob Miller, my editor, who has encouraged and supported me for the past few years as I labored through this manuscript. Bob never lost sight of our ultimate goal and he never lost faith that we'd achieve it.

God bless you all.

Mary Wilson
Los Angeles, California
1986

PREFACE

Since the Supremes' last official farewell concert in 1976 at London's Drury Lane Theater, with Scherrie Payne and Susaye Green, I have pursued a solo career. It was strange at first. I had sung almost all my life, but after Berry Gordy had designated Diane Ross as the sole lead vocalist of the original Supremes, I assumed my position in the background, knowing that my turn would come again.

When it finally did, fourteen years later, I was scared to death but exhilarated. I took my show on the road from 1977 to 1979, touring the world and working only occasionally in the United States. It's amazing how many performers will stay in the States and suffer at the hands of a fickle record industry while all over the world there are hundreds of thousands of fans dying to see them and buy their records. I went to those far-off, exotic places and started over again. I met some wonderful people over there, but each time I'd come home I would inevitably run into someone who would ask, "Are you still singing?" Worse yet, many people assumed I was broke, probably living in some tawdry apartment, wearing a frayed, ancient floor-length sequined gown, looking through old scrapbooks of my Motown days, like some sort of pop-music Miss Havisham with a wedding cake made of gold records.

In fact, throughout the seventies, I not only reestablished my own career but got married, had three children, and continued traveling, working anywhere between nine and eleven months a year. I also began studying acting and singing with several teachers, and have spent twelve years with my voice teacher, Guiseppe Belestrieri.

In 1979 I recorded my first solo album, *Mary Wilson* (Motown), from which was released the single "Red Hot." I felt ready to return to the States and make my American solo debut. I was booked into the New York, New York club in Manhattan, and the audience included friends from the music business as well as fans, the rich and the famous. The critics didn't think I was so hot, but the kindest among them at least gave me credit for having courage. This disappointment sent me back to Europe, where I vowed I'd learn to sing lead again. It had taken ten years of singing "oohs" and "aahs" in the background for me to lose my confidence; it would take me some time to get it back.

That year Motown released me from my contract after I recorded four contemporary pop tunes in London. The release marked the close of a huge chapter in my life. I'd been with Motown for twenty years, and in that time I'd seen almost every dream I could imagine as a young girl come true. But now I was on my own.

I decided to write my memoirs, and had just started contacting all my old friends, relatives, and colleagues when a friend suggested I see a new Broadway musical called *Dreamgirls*. By the second act I was crying because while many of the incidents depicted in the play could have happened to any of a number of female singing groups, I knew in my heart that this story rang far truer than the producers could have imagined. There were bits and pieces of my life—and the lives of my two best friends—up there. I was awed at the powerful influence of the Supremes legacy. And I was more determined than ever that the real story be told.

I have no desire to expose or indict anyone. I want to tell the true story behind the rise and fall of the greatest female pop group of all time—a real-life Cinderella story and a tragedy deeper than anyone ever knew: my life as a Supreme.

PROLOGUE

It had now been nearly five hours since the taping of Motown's twenty-fifth-anniversary special, "Motown 25," began. At the rate things were going, I could see this was going to last until midnight, but I didn't mind. I was happy to be back among my friends: the Four Tops, the Temptations, Marvin Gaye, Stevie Wonder, Martha Reeves, Smokey Robinson—people I'd worked with for years at Motown. I was also proud, knowing that within just moments, I would be standing onstage with my friends Diane Ross and Cindy Birdsong for our first reunion in over thirteen years. I just tried to relish every second. Next on the show were DeBarge, High Inergy, and a clip of Rick James, followed by Smokey Robinson and Linda Ronstadt's duets on "Ooo Baby Baby" and "The Tracks of My Tears." The segment ended on two lighter notes—a film of Motown staffers, many of whom had been with the company from the start, singing the company song Smokey wrote years ago (with lines like, "We're a swinging company . . .") and Richard Pryor's comic medieval fable about the young warrior Berry's quest for gold records in the kingdom of Hitsville. We were "three fair maidens from the Projects of Brewster." How far from that I was now, but, thinking minutes ahead to the reunion, I knew that I was going home.

Adam Ant started singing his version of the Supremes' first number-one hit, "Where Did Our Love Go." I was as surprised as everyone else backstage to see him doing our song. "Why is *he* doing that?" people asked over and over. Ant was typical of the British New Wave rockers, with his makeup, chains, feathers, and earrings. Our eyes were glued to the monitor when suddenly we heard the audience screaming. Ant grinned until he saw what the commotion was all about. The camera cut to stage right, and we saw Diane in a short black satin skirt and silver-beaded jacket moving toward Ant, doing a bump and grind. For a second, Ant was caught off guard, but he moved toward her and danced along with her as much as he could before she disappeared again.

People in the room were mortified.

"I can't believe Diane would do that!"

"The Supremes were always so classy, why would she act like that?"

"How could she just jump up there while someone else was performing?"

The wings were filling with people, all trying to get the best view of the reunion. There were some more clips of us, including our last appearance with Diane on Ed Sullivan's show on December 14, 1969. Diane was walking up the aisle, toward the stage. Once she got on-stage, she took the white fox stole she'd flung over her shoulder and tossed it to the floor as the crowd gave her a standing ovation. The applause got louder, and I was surrounded by Nick Ashford, Valerie Simpson, Richard Pryor, Martha Reeves, and some of my friends from the Temptations. Suddenly I heard Diane reciting the first lines to Nick and Valerie's "Ain't No Mountain High Enough":

"If you need me, call me . . ."

Knowing Diane as they did, my friends backstage were encouraging me to do something when I got out there:

"Step on that fur, Mary!" Richard Pryor urged me, half-teasing.

"Kick it!" shouted a female voice.

I knew where they were coming from, and I had a little laugh over it, but I was soon swept up in the moment. Suddenly, everyone got quiet and Diane began speaking. She said she would be there forever if she started to talk about her life with Motown. Then she said a strange thing:

"But Berry had always felt that he's never been appreciated . . ."

When the camera picked out Berry Gordy, Motown's founder and president, it seemed to me, from the look on his face, that he was puzzled by her remarks. Then Diane said, "It's not about the people who leave Motown"—of which Diane was one—"but it's about the people who come back, and tonight everybody came back." At that moment I thought of all the people, like my dear friend Florence Ballard, who couldn't come back. Diane's words prompted a standing ovation, and she gave Berry the high sign. He responded in kind, then turned his palms upward, as if to say, "I let you go."

The applause died down as the opening notes of "Someday We'll Be Together" filled the room. "Mary, Cindy," Diane said as she looked to the wings. Cindy entered from stage right to more applause. After Cindy reached Diane's side, I sauntered out from stage left, doing my slowest Detroit strut, just like we used to do in the Projects. The crowd roared. When Diane looked at me, she stopped singing. She hadn't reached the bridge of the song, so I couldn't understand why she stopped. Thinking that perhaps she'd temporarily forgotten the words, I picked up the lead, certain that Diane would come back in on the next line and everything would be fine. After a few seconds, Diane introduced us again.

"This is Cindy Birdsong," and *"That's* Mary Wilson," she said, pointing at me. There was more applause, and then Diane started moving toward the edge of the stage. Before the show, I'd told Cindy to follow my every move. We'd had no rehearsal and there was no telling what could happen. When Diane took a couple of steps forward, we took a couple of steps forward. Diane moved up again, and we moved up again, all the while singing, "Someday—we'll be together . . ." But on the third surge forward, Diane suddenly turned and pushed me. The audience gasped. In a flash I saw something in her eyes that told me she knew she'd crossed the line. Of course, this was later cut from the tape. When Diane saw that I would ignore her behavior, she hung back, so that on the tape you see me and Cindy standing in front of her. Within seconds Smokey was onstage, and we weren't even halfway through the song. Many observers would correctly guess that he had been sent out on a rescue mission.

Before we knew it, other performers were filling the stage. There was Harvey Fuqua and the Tempts. Melvin Franklin of the Tempts came over to hug me. Then Michael Jackson came on, almost tripping over Miracles guitarist Marvin Tarplin in his rush to get to Diane. Richard Street and Marvin Gaye were onstage hugging me, followed by Dick Clark and the Commodores. I glanced over to see Martha Reeves and Stevie Wonder sharing a microphone, and I thought about how close we all were. Then I realized that Stevie wanted to have the microphone all to himself.

Before the next song, "Reach Out and Touch (Somebody's Hand)," started, Diane tried to take control of the stage, shouting, "Stand back! Everybody stand back!" I could tell she was angry, and she even tried to push people back, but there were too many of us, and we all pretty much ignored her.

The stage was getting crowded, and I was still singing. I stopped and beckoned the audience to stand. Diane made another short speech, a tribute to Berry. When she finished, I called up to Berry, "Berry, come on down!"

The next thing I knew, Diane forced my left hand down, pushing the microphone away from my mouth. Looking me right in the eyes, she said loudly, "It's been taken care of!" On the tape all you see of this episode is Diane turning around and calling out to Berry, "How long will it take you to get down here, Blackie [her nickname for him]? Well, come on."

Once Berry got onstage, Diane stood at the edge hopping up and down like a little girl, waiting for her turn to kiss him. He went to everyone, kissing or hugging each as was appropriate. He thanked Diane after he kissed her, and then he and Michael Jackson embraced. As he stood there with us, Diane was behind him, poking him in the head and pinching his rear end like she would when we were teens.

After Berry and Marvin embraced, Berry came to me. We hugged and kissed, then he whispered in my ear, "You finally learned how to sing, huh?" I held his hand and raised his arm into the air.

The next thing I knew, Diane ran to the back of the stage and climbed the orchestra platform, so that she was standing high above the rest of us. When the song ended, the producers asked us all to stay onstage so that a photographer from *Life* magazine could take our picture. In seconds, Diane had scurried down from her perch and pushed her way to the center of the stage. She grabbed for Stevie Wonder and kissed him. When the photo ran, sure enough, she was smack in the middle.

In the earlier days, Diane would do things like this, but never in public. We were best friends and I would ignore her antics. But tonight of all nights, why did it have to be this way? This was to be a joyous reunion. Even people whose parting with Motown had been less than amicable had returned with nothing in their hearts but love. Part of the Supremes' magic and appeal came from the fact that we were a fantasy, a dream come true. Our personal problems were kept under wraps. Over the years, I'd gotten a pretty good idea of how the public viewed the Supremes, Florence's dismissal, and Diane's leaving the group. And deep in my heart, I knew people were anxious to see a cat fight. That Diane had so foolishly given them that satisfaction hurt me deeply. Her actions seemed to say that the Supremes were unimportant, when in fact we both knew that the Supremes had changed our lives forever.

I returned to my dressing room hurt and angry. What a terrible way to end an evening, a career, a friendship. We had always been there for each other; Diane and I knew each other like books. She has done many things to hurt, humiliate, and upset me, but, strangely enough, I still love her and am proud of her.

Similarly, I will always hold Berry Gordy in the highest esteem, no matter what he does. As young performers, we brought him the raw materials of success, but he saw our potential and made it all work. Berry and I may have our differences, but the bottom line is that he, Diane, and I are inextricable parts of one another's lives.

These thoughts ran through my mind as four security guards escorted me across the street to the Pasadena Plaza Mall. The gala celebration was in full swing, and I was welcomed and comforted by my friends there. I felt the old camaraderie and love that brought me here. I didn't see Diane for the rest of the night.

And the historic Supremes reunion?

"Guests at Motown's twenty-fifth-anniversary bash are still buzz-ing about the finale. . . ."
—*Los Angeles Herald Examiner*

"Ross [did] some elbowing to get Wilson out of the spotlight."
—*People*

"Not once were they introduced as the Supremes, much to the audience's dismay."
—*US*

As always, the press had the last word, and the public knew everything —or at least they thought they did. But the Supremes' story was never that simple, and the whole truth has never been told.

Until now.

CHAPTER 1

I was born on March 6, 1944, in Greenville, Mississippi, a small, quiet Southern town near the Mississippi Delta. It was, I've been told, a hot, humid day in March when my mother, Johnnie Mae Wilson, began her labor. Though she was thirty, she'd married only recently. I was her first child. She was so afraid of the pain that she told her mother that she didn't want to have me; it hurt too much. Though Grandmama knew that my mother's labor was unusually hard and going too slowly, she was exasperated. A college-educated woman who'd given birth to all seven of her children at home, my grandmother couldn't understand why Johnnie Mae didn't just get on with it.

My father, Sam Wilson, had left to work on the riverboat, and my grandmother awaited anxiously the midwife's arrival. Home births were common here, yet few women would even think of bearing a child without a midwife present. In rural areas like Greenville, where medical care was far away and too expensive for most people, the midwife's knowledge and experience could be a woman's only comfort. Today no midwife could be found.

When the midwife finally arrived hours later, the house was cleared. She and Grandmama tried everything. Though darkness had fallen and the night air was mercifully cool, both women worked up a sweat.

"This baby should have been here a long time ago," said the midwife. Grandmama could only shake her head when the midwife suggested that my mother be taken to the hospital; my father could not afford it. That settled, she and the midwife returned to coaxing and coercing my mother along. Before it was all over, Grandmama lost her motherly tact: "You fool! You can't let that baby stay inside of you! It's got to come out!"

A little past midnight, I was finally born. I now wonder if my first appearance in life was somehow indicative of the path my life would later take. Even at my birth, I was a fence-sitter.

Grandmama and the midwife cleaned the room and changed the linens. When they heard Daddy's footsteps coming up the stairs, they realized that no one had chosen a name for me. After they'd placed me in his trembling arms, they asked him for his suggestions.

"She's so cute," he said, smiling, "I would like to name her after one of my old girlfriends: Mary."

Few women would have stood for that, but my mother loved the name, so she wasn't worried about its inspiration.

That my life began so unremarkably makes what would happen to me years later all the more amazing. My parents were in many ways typical of their time and place. Greenville was an unusual Southern town where blacks, whites, and Asians lived together peacefully. My father, who was twenty years older than my mother, was a butcher; my mother did not work.

My mother was tall and slender, with skin the color of polished ebony and a deceptively shy manner. Seemingly soft and delicate, she always appeared frail, partly as a result of cultivated feminine charm, and partly due to a minor, chronic childhood illness that had led her mother and her siblings to be overprotective of her. Grandmama hovered over her. While the five younger children—Preston, Rufus, Monever, Margaret, and I.V. (a corruption of the name Ivory)—attended school regularly in Moorehead, Mississippi, Johnnie Mae was kept home. Grandmama surely meant well, but as a result my mother would be nearly illiterate for the rest of her life. Despite this, my mother always had a wisdom about people, and she had a love of life that I have inherited from her. Whenever anyone treated her badly, she would forgive them. She believed that people were basically good, that no matter what happened, anyone would eventually be redeemed.

Grandmama's parents were slaves, but she attended college shortly after the turn of the century and was an intelligent and progressive woman. She married four, maybe five, times; no one is really sure. Grandmama struggled to raise a well-mannered, hardworking, God-fearing family. They adhered to all the traditions of the region and local culture, attending the local Baptist church regularly. Summers would find the children out picking cotton to earn extra money. As the four daughters grew to womanhood, they longed to live in the city, where people said there were better jobs, nicer houses, and more men. My mother may have been the most eager of all to leave, but before she could pull up stakes, Sam Wilson came to town.

He was tall, fair, good-looking, and suave—a real charmer. He didn't talk much, so even though he was a friend of my Aunt Margaret's husband, no one could vouch for his background. Even years later, my mother's family would know very little about my father. He was from Louisiana—probably New Orleans. Most of his family were dead; he'd spent some time in jail—why was never clear.

Mother's family immediately distrusted Sam. It was obvious that he loved the fast life. Although he had a trade, he couldn't hold a job, had long been a drifter, and, worst of all, he was a compulsive gambler. To proud and religious people like my mother's kin, Sam Wilson was just plain weak. My mother was always the quietest and most reserved of her siblings, but when it came to Sam, nothing they said could change her mind. She loved him.

That my mother's family came to accept my father is more a testament to their warmth and generosity than to any drastic change in his attitude. The little bedroom with the four-poster mahogany bed where I was born, was the struggling couple's first home. Grandmama always had a full house and a big heart. She was the center of a loving family that, despite differences, would always unite against hard times and trouble.

After the whole family moved to Greenville, a town about ninety miles from the state capital of Jackson, they came to regard Moorehead as a real hick town. There were so many more opportunities in Greenville. But like all fathers, mine wanted to make a better life for us, so when I was about a year old we moved to Saint Louis, a town known for its loose women, hot music, and a scarcity of legitimate employment. My mother knew the score. She demanded that my father leave Saint Louis, and he did. Next, we moved to Chicago, where, while living on the tough South Side, my father managed to do fairly well. He was working regularly, but even when he was on his best behavior my mother worried. As the old blues song goes, "When the eagle flies on Friday"—in other words, when Daddy got his paycheck—unless my mother "caught it" as soon as he got home, it would surely have flown away, spent on gambling and good times, before Monday morning rolled around.

My father tried everything he could to be a good provider, but soon he was back to his old ways. Holding a steady job, from which he could earn a pittance at best, was just too slow for him. There was fast money—and lots of it, he believed—to be made gambling. He could only be happy living the fast life, and he made no bones about it. My mother worried constantly about me and my baby brother Roosevelt. She hadn't minded being the main breadwinner in the early days of their marriage; she knew her man didn't like to work, and she got by working in Greenville and Moorehead. But living in the big city, far from friends and family, was something else. Despite her misgivings, my mother had followed him to Chicago; now she was stranded. Her youngest sister I.V. and her husband John L. Pippin came to see what they could do to help.

I.V. was ten years younger than my mother. A petite woman, I.V. was fine-featured and beautiful, but had a will of iron. John L., at over six feet, towered above his wife, but there was no mistaking who was the boss, at least most of the time. John L. was a man of integrity and sound judgment. He was reasonable, patient, kind, and generous. Every woman in my mother's family considered him the ideal husband. The Pippins had just purchased a lovely home on the outskirts of Detroit, near Dearborn, for $7,100 on a GI loan. After two years of marriage they were childless. They felt their taking me back to live with them would relieve some of my mother's burden. She was frightened, down to her last few dollars, and still without a job. She promised reluctantly that she would consider it.

No matter how much my mother loved me, her life was beyond her control and periodically complicated by my father's unpredictable appearances and disappearances. Any money that my mother might have squirreled away in his absence, Sam Wilson would surely squander upon his return. She loved him, but she loved us too. I hardly remember my father at all from this period. My only image of him—in a handsome light-colored suit posed in front of a shiny convertible—comes from a treasured photo.

And so in 1948, when I was three years old, Aunt I.V. and Uncle John L. drove me back to the little house at 3800 Bassett Street in Detroit, and my mother returned to Mississippi, where she would live with Grandmama and baby Roosevelt for the next several years.

I was only three then, too young to know what was going on, much less understand it. In fact, within a few years I would forget my real parents altogether, and call I.V. and John L. "Mom" and "Daddy." What I remember now most from my first few weeks in my new home was the house itself. Though it was typical of thousands of development houses built to accommodate young GIs and their families, compared to the dark apartment I grew up in, it seemed like a mansion. The three-bedroom house was filled with heavy, dark furniture, and on each piece were perched several stiffly starched, elaborately crocheted doilies. I had my own bedroom, decorated in blue with frilly ruffled curtains and a satin bedspread. Being in an immaculate new house surrounded by trees and soft green lawns seemed wonderfully alien.

Like many cities then, Dearborn was all white. Blacks could work and shop there, but they couldn't live there. Our neighborhood, just outside Dearborn, was working class and middle class, but all black. Like most people in the area, Daddy worked in the auto industry, at Chrysler; Mom worked for Hudson's Dry Cleaners. They were almost affluent by most standards, and our house was full of wondrous things: a new Eureka vacuum cleaner, freezer chests, a beautiful radio that was as big as a refrigerator. We were the first family on the block to own a television, and every year Daddy bought a shiny new Chrysler for himself and a stylish Chevrolet for Mom.

To ensure that our family wanted for nothing, Daddy always held down two jobs, working at Chrysler and then moonlighting, doing things like running a small gas station, so he had little time for leisure. When he did have time to spare, he liked fixing up things around the house, or sitting in the dark-wood-paneled basement recreation room he'd built and listening to his collection of 78-rpm R&B records by Nat "King" Cole, Sarah Vaughan, Glenn Miller, Duke Ellington, Cab Calloway, LaVern Baker, Brook Benton, and Joe Williams. It was through listening to these wonderful records that I fell in love with music—everything from jazz to Doris Day. John L. also liked to give parties, so the basement had a wet bar and red upholstered barstools. I.V.'s job left her exhausted at the end of the day, too, but both believed that having a nice home and the means to provide for themselves and help others was worth all the effort.

I.V. was a stylish dresser whose expansive collection of different colors of fingernail polish and fashion magazines, such as *Vogue*, kept me occupied for hours. She wanted me to always look my best and spared no expense on my clothing. My dresses were always ruffled or pleated, crisply pressed and starched and always worn over drifts of dainty white petticoats. My favorites were the frilly multicolored nylon "party dresses" for special occasions. I wore little black patent-leather shoes and lace-trimmed anklets, and my long thick hair was neatly braided and adorned with ribbons and bows. As far back as I can remember, I felt like a miniature fashion plate.

Large parts of our neighborhood were still under development, and some areas were almost like the country. Passing fruit orchards on our way to and from school, my little friends and I would pick all the peaches and apples we could carry, along with bunches of wild grapes that seemed to grow everywhere. We could play across the highway at Pepper Creek. Though I was basically a very dainty little girl, I loved to make mud pies and catch snakes and toads—which I would bring home to unappreciative parents.

Any seemingly idyllic existence has its share of drawbacks, and mine was no different. I dreaded having my hair fixed, and the daily ritual of I.V. hurting me as she tried to comb through that wild, tangled mess and me crying my eyes out came to exemplify my relationship with her. Looking back I see in this daily trauma the beginnings of several personality traits, such as a fear of authority and a reluctance to speak out. Though the tiny voice deep inside me told me that I was strong, I also knew that I was powerless to change my situation. Like all children, I viewed my parents—and I thought John L. and I.V. were my parents—as perfect, and I lived for their love. Their approval meant everything to me; their anger could throw me into confusion and self-doubt.

I learned very early on to quietly please and pacify I.V. however I could. This was especially difficult at times because I.V. Pippin had little patience for anyone or anything, and becoming an "instant mother" certainly must have tried what little patience she did have to the limit. I.V. was a no-nonsense woman and an almost fanatical perfectionist. The house had to be immaculate, her clothes had to be the finest, and her family had to reflect the highest qualities at all times. Given all this she—and I—were very lucky that she'd married John L. A more wonderful father simply doesn't exist. When I.V. would lose her temper with me, he would intervene on my behalf. After an incident, he'd take me aside and say, "She doesn't have much patience, you know."

I admit that I often hated her for forcing me to do everything exactly right, or do it over, or finally get a spanking. Now I realize that she meant well but was basically incapable of being flexible. When things were running smoothly, she was warm and loving, though always strict. When she insisted that everything be done her way, it wasn't out of meanness, but because she wanted me to grow up to be the best that I could be. She feared that I may have inherited what she viewed as my mother's "faults," like her lack of desire for education. Though I felt the brunt of her anger many times, I know that the values I.V. taught me have stood by me throughout my life and have given me confidence and poise and the will to survive. I still work hard and strive for perfection, though perhaps not to I.V.'s extreme standards.

I was five years old before I had any extensive contact with whites. In 1949 I started kindergarten at the Boynton School. My school in southwest Detroit was integrated. Most of my teachers were white. My first teacher, Mrs. Shufeldt, encouraged me to join the school glee club. When we participated in a citywide choir competition at the Ford Auditorium, I felt like the luckiest six-year-old in town. I loved to sing, and would take as many singing classes as I could throughout school. Making other school trips showed me that there was a great big world out there beyond Bassett Street.

By the age of eight, and with just a couple years of I.V.'s training, I was mother's little helper. I.V. was trying to instill in me a sense of cleanliness and pride in housekeeping. She couldn't know then that my greatest ambition was to never have to do housework when I grew up. She outlined my responsibilities for me and didn't give an inch. Each and every piece of stylish furniture, every floor and window had to sparkle. If I made even the smallest mistake or failed to polish the tiniest crevice, she'd say, "Go get me the belt," and I tearfully obeyed. After several years I came to fear I.V. Why was she beating me? Once my fear of her looming over me was so strong that I forgot my ABCs.

"Now, I.V., you're being too rough on that girl," John L. would say calmly. "So just calm down and talk to her." I couldn't understand why he didn't just make her stop, but he didn't.

My fear was manifested in a bed-wetting problem that lasted until I was about nine years old. Of course the problem, which was created by the beatings in the first place, was only aggravated by the beatings I received for wetting the bed. Scared to death that I.V. would ever find my bed sheets soiled, I awoke earlier than the rest of the household. If my bed was wet, I would run down into the cold basement and wash the sheets and remake my bed before I.V. woke up.

Finally my parents sought medical advice. Though most parents probably would do this today, in the early fifties bed-wetting was re-

garded as primarily a discipline problem. The doctor, a kindly pedia-
trician, assured my parents that my bed-wetting was nothing out the
ordinary. After a physical checkup showed nothing wrong, the doctor
said, "Mrs. Pippin, most children do this when they are under stress."

"Stress?" sniffed I.V. "She's not under any stress!"

I knew differently, but what could I say? I felt like a common
criminal. It was all the more confusing to me because John L. would
try to reason with me instead of yelling or hitting. "Mae Mae," he'd
say, calling me by my pet name, "why don't you get up at night and
go to the bathroom?"

"I will, Daddy," I promised, my head bent in shame.

I.V. wasn't a child beater in the usual sense of the term. She was
from the old Baptist school of "Spare the rod, spoil the child." She
didn't spank me all that often, but since I was bad so rarely, I thought
she could have reprimanded me verbally instead. If only she could see
what was happening to me.

Thank God for daydreams. I could always escape by mooning
away about my fabulous future as a movie star. I loved any kind of
fantasy—fairy-tales, radio shows, and movies. Before we got the television, I would watch the radio while listening to *The Shadow* or *The
Lone Ranger*. I loved horror movies, mysteries, adventures, like Erroll
Flynn swashbucklers, and, of course, musicals. Even my friends noticed that when I was seeing, listening to, or talking about a show or a
story or a dream, I would be transported. For those precious moments, it was all very real to me. I would sit around for hours, waiting
at the front picture window for my mother's return, planning and
dreaming and visualizing myself in these fantasies. John L. would be
home, napping before leaving for his night job, so I was as good as
alone.

I loved Christmas. Every year, Hudson's department store would be
remade into a winter wonderland, complete with Santa Claus, rein-
deer, little gingerbread houses peopled with elves, and every Christmas decoration imaginable. Once I stepped into the store, I believed
I was at the North Pole. Even when I was old enough to know better,
I could still believe in my dream.

Christmas was especially important to our family. Our tree was
always one of the prettiest on the block, and I would beg my parents
to keep it up for the whole year. Many times John L. Pippin was Santa
Claus to every child belonging to kin. If my Aunt Monever didn't have

the money, she could always depend on the Pippins' generosity. One of my favorite Christmas gifts was a set of miniature walnut dining-room furniture and a beautiful porcelain tea set. John L. and I.V. didn't buy me the toy versions of these things, but expensive, smaller-scale reproductions of the real things they treasured.

One spring day after school, I came home and assumed my usual position, sitting in front of the large picture window in our dining room. Every day I would patiently wait there until it was time for me to set the table for dinner.

When I spotted a little girl who lived down the street, I suddenly felt lonely, and waved to her to join me in the house. For some reason, John L., who should have been home napping, was out so I had the house to myself.

We were playing house and I suggested we have a real tea party with my tea set. We raided the refrigerator, helping ourselves to a large, juicy slice of watermelon, a bottle of soda pop, and some home-made cookies. Then I got a brilliant idea: Why not make this the most elegant tea party ever? "Girl," I said, "let's dress up in some of my mama's clothes."

My friend looked at me wide-eyed. "Won't your mama be mad at us?"

"She won't even know. We'll just wear them for the tea party and then hang them back up."

It was no problem fitting into I.V.'s petite clothes; on our tiny bodies, the hems just grazed the ground. She was one of the smartest dressers around. Over the past few months she had been accumulating a fabulous new wardrobe of brightly colored dresses especially for the long-overdue second honeymoon she and John L. would be taking in New York City. Naturally, she didn't skimp on quality, and for months her new outfits were the main topic of conversation. *Vogue* was I.V.'s bible, and once she was convinced that New York was a city for hats, she bought a straw hat for each outfit.

In our quest for glamour, we of course put on the prettiest and best outfits first. With our invited guests—two dolls—we sat slurping the watermelon and sipping strawberry pop. Within minutes, our "gowns" were covered with sticky, bright pink stains, prompting the next great solution: change clothes. And so we happily proceeded through the entire closet, making sure to wear the matching gloves, shoes, hats, and bags, and to parade up and down the block so every-one could see.

As if started out of a dream, I realized that I.V. and John L. would be home any minute and the clothes were a disaster. If we just hung the clothes back in the closet as neatly as possible, no one would be the wiser. Or so we hoped. Although I knew that these clothes were filthy and that I would be found out, I went along with it.

As I hid down the street, I worried about what was happening at home. I.V. opened her closet, as she did every night, to admire her new wardrobe. Within seconds John L. was running up the stairs and to find I.V. screaming, "Somebody's robbed us! Somebody has come in and robbed us!" One look at the evidence and he was convinced but puzzled. Everything was filthy, but nothing was missing.

John L. hurried down to the basement, where he kept his expensive phonograph, a couple of freezers, and some other valuables. After checking everything, he was relieved to see that nothing had been taken. Finally they realized what must have happened. And it didn't take them too long to know who did it.

When John L. asked a neighbor if she'd seen me, she said no, but made sure to mention how cute I had looked strutting up and down the sidewalk. Then I heard the call—"Mae-Mae, get your butt in here!"—and I knew it was the voice of doom. I had never heard him sound so angry. He had never spanked me; he always told I.V. that spanking wasn't the way. I hoped he would remember that. But with one look, I could see that they both wanted to kill me. All John L. said was, "Get the belt, Mary."

He almost never called me Mary, which made it all the more frightening. Just the thought of this huge man whipping me made me weak. As I carried the belt to him, it felt like a chain of iron.

"I.V. has been planning this trip for a long time," he said through clenched teeth. "And now we can't go because she doesn't want to go, and I will hear about this trip for another year or maybe two. That's why I whipped your ass." With that, he left the house.

For the next couple of weeks my parents made me feel that I was the only person in the house. John L. was right: I.V. did refuse to go on the trip and carried on about it for the next year. I thought she was just being mean; the clothes could have been cleaned where she worked for little or nothing. But that wouldn't have satisfied her. What I didn't know until years later was that I.V. and John L. were having problems with their marriage. I was too young then to see John L. and I.V. as people. After all, they were very young, newly married instant parents. Then, though, all I could think of was the trouble I had caused. I meant no malice. Like most children—even the best children—I lived in the moment and saw no further than the fun I was having. Based on what I saw as my parent's anger over the incident, I concluded that I must have been terribly bad, and I vowed that I would never cause this kind of trouble again. From this I learned a lesson that stayed with me for the rest of my life: to maintain peace, no matter what the cost.

CHAPTER 2

The summer of 1950 began like every summer I could remember, with me looking forward to the annual visit from my favorite aunt, Johnnie Mae. She was tall and pretty, and always especially nice, lavishing gifts of clothes and candy upon me, and smothering me with soft kisses and lingering hugs. I was instantly drawn to her. It felt so natural to me, so different from my own mom.

This year's visit was somehow different. Aunt Johnnie Mae stayed longer than usual this time, and there was tension in the house. I remember coming home and seeing them—Mom, Dad, and Johnnie Mae—huddled together around the dining-room table, talking in harsh, abrupt whispers.

One day, while I was outside playing, our neighbor Ruby Mae approached me. "I heard your mother is coming to live with you."

"What do you mean?" I asked, surprised. "I live with my mother already."

"No, child, I.V. ain't your mama. Johnnie Mae is."

"You're wrong," I said, summoning up all the courage a six-year-old could muster. "Johnnie Mae is my aunt, not my mother."

"No, no," Ruby Mae persisted. "Johnnie Mae is your mother."

Her words rang in my ears as I walked home, trying to convince myself that Ruby Mae was wrong. It was impossible. My real mother was I.V., and that was that. But no matter what I told myself, once I got home I began to look at my parents and Aunt Johnnie Mae differently.

A few days later, Johnnie Mae took me aside. She tried to explain to me as gently as she could that she was my real mother. Her voice and manner were so soft that the meaning of her words just didn't seem to penetrate. When I resisted what she had said and refused to believe it—which must have hurt her terribly—she didn't get angry, the way I knew I.V. would have. She tried only to comfort me, but nothing could help. My whole world had been turned upside down. I'd trusted these people, and they had lied to me.

Crying uncontrollably, I ran out of the house. I don't know how many times I walked up and down the block, crying my eyes out, convinced that all grown-ups were crazy.

By this time, Johnnie Mae had officially moved in with us. My younger brother Roosevelt and sister Cathy, or Cat, were still living in Greenville with Grandmama. Though in later years I could recall specific incidents from my childhood with my mother, I had forgotten her, my father, and baby Roosevelt. I still had not completely accepted Johnnie Mae as my mother, but I loved being around her because she made me feel safe.

A couple of months after she moved in, Johnnie Mae suddenly became ill. She was in a great deal of pain, sometimes so severe that she was unable to get around without help. I was too young then to know that she was suffering a miscarriage, but I did feel her great sadness. For a while our roles reversed, with me taking care of and comforting her. We were now closer than ever; she was really my mother.

One day I heard my mother fighting with John L. and I.V.

"I never said you could have Mary. I just said you could keep her until I was on my feet again."

"Johnnie Mae," John L. said, fuming, "you know we had an agreement that Mary was ours. You promised that she was ours."

"No, I didn't!"

"Yes, you did. You said—" John L. stopped when he spotted me on the other side of the room. "Mary," he said firmly, "go outside."

By this time John L. and I.V. had their own daughter, Pat, but that did not diminish their love for me. I know they tried to do what was best for me. Though I.V. was my mother's baby sister, she regarded Johnnie Mae as someone in need of constant protection. They didn't think my mother was in a good position financially; they worried about how she would take care of me. She took work living with an affluent white family and was home with us only on weekends. Up until then, John L. and I.V. were certain that I would be with them forever. To this day, Daddy (as I still call John L.) says that Mom promised them that they could keep me.

Despite all the anger and hurt, our family remained close. Eventually Roosevelt and Cat were brought up from Mississippi to live with my mother and me permanently. With their arrival, the quiet little house on Bassett Street became noisy and overcrowded. I so loved taking care of Pat that I ignored my two blood siblings, at least at the beginning. I turned up my nose at them; they seemed so country, and not as refined as I thought my other little friends were. I also loved Pat, who was like the most perfectly beautiful living doll. But soon enough I grew to love Roosevelt and Cat, too. They were rambunctious and cute, and, like our mother, open and happy.

As much as I loved my mother and the kids, I never wanted to leave the Pippins' home; it was *my* home. But seven people were too many. I knew we had to move. Still, I wondered if I'd done something to make the Pippins not love me anymore. I had always been a good girl; at least I had tried to be. My parents had given me everything I'd ever wanted, so I should have been perfect. But some people thought that was just my problem: maybe they gave me too much.

My mother took the three of us to live with her other sister, my Aunt Monever. We moved into Monever's row house in southwest Detroit. I.V. had helped Monever get a job working at Hudson's Dry Cleaners. Things seemed to be working out for us at last. Now the only children left with Grandmama and Big Daddy—Grandmama's latest husband—were Monever's two daughters, my older cousins Josephine, or Jo, and Christine.

My mother and aunts made plans for us to spend the summer of 1953 in Mississippi with my grandparents. This summer sojourn would become an annual event for the three sisters. Sometimes we'd all travel down by car, sometimes we'd take a train, and once everyone went on a Greyhound bus. There would be bags of food for all of us. John L.'s mother would bake pastries, fry up loads of chicken, and make us her specialty—fried apple pies.

We looked forward to this trip for weeks. I had gone almost every year for a couple of weeks with I.V., but this time would be different —I was going to spend the whole summer there. I would see my grandparents and finally get to know my real father, whom I barely remembered. Though certain kids would probably experience this as a trauma, I saw it as a great adventure.

While my mother struggled to keep us all together in Detroit, my father had returned to Mississippi. At age sixty, after years of roaming, he was trying to change his life. He began working steadily at a factory and was finally settling down when he lost his leg in an accident on the job. He could never work again. He moved in with Grandmama and Big Daddy, and they took care of him until he recovered from his operation. Though Sam Wilson had hardly been an ideal son-in-law, he was still my mother's husband, and her family was the only one he had.

Sam Wilson lived near my grandparents in a tiny house on Wilson Street. People there had named the street after him because his was the only house on it. Although he hadn't spent much time with his children over the years, we felt that he really did love us. He was so proud; he took us around and introduced us to all the shopkeepers in Greenville, treated us to ice cream cones, and gave us spending change.

Moving from the Pippins' house on Bassett Street did not separate me from John and I.V.; I would visit them on weekends and keep in touch with my good friends like Jackie Burkes. Jackie was my very best friend. We spent hours together, daydreaming, talking about boys, or sitting down in John L.'s basement, singing along to records such as LaVern Baker's "Jim Dandy," or Hank Ballard's "Annie Had a Baby." It would be years before I lived in a real house again and could enjoy the lush life of suburbia. We left Aunt Monever's and moved from one small apartment to another. Despite my mother's hard work, one day we found ourselves living on welfare. We had hit bottom.

Moving to the Brewster Projects in 1956 was a turning point in my life. It was a new complex of government-owned apartment buildings and older row houses on the east side of Detroit, within walking distance of downtown. There were about eight fourteen-story buildings grouped all together, each surrounded by patches of grass, and a brightly painted playground.

Many people would have considered a move into the Projects to be a step down. But for me, having already stepped down from a middle-class neighborhood to various apartments in the inner city, this was a step back up. I felt like I'd just moved into a Park Avenue skyscraper. The minute we kids finished helping cart our humble furnishings up to our second-floor apartment, we ran outside to explore the new world that was our home.

Hundreds of kids—from infants to young adults—lived in the Projects. It was quite crowded compared to suburbia, but I loved it; the more the merrier. The Projects were also a great school of life. You had to learn to get along with all kinds of people. I looked forward to every new day. I was not an A student, but I.V. had instilled in me the desire to learn and an equally strong fear of failure, so I did well enough. The social aspects of school were also very important to me. Only we kids could comprehend the significance of knowing and spreading the latest gossip, which our parents considered nonsense.

One negative aspect of living in Detroit then was the street gangs. If you were wise enough not to belong to a gang but unlucky enough to be cornered by one, you were in trouble. The vicious mob psychology sometimes scared otherwise good kids into joining gangs just for the protection. I never joined anything, not even clubs, but managed to ensure my own protection by being a gang leader's girlfriend. I was very young, and thought he was cute. Later I was befriended by a tough and unpopular girl, but only after she had beaten me up. After that, I was accepted by the other kids in the Projects. I didn't have an "attitude"; I was just open and friendly, and probably not very threatening.

I was in the fifth grade when they began busing us from the Projects to Algers Elementary School in 1956 to integrate the public schools. Among my new classmates was Carolyn Franklin, the daughter of the Reverend C. L. Franklin, whose New Bethel Baptist Church my family attended.

The New Bethel Baptist Church was probably the most famous church in Detroit. It was a huge, beautiful church, and the Reverend Franklin was certainly one of the most engaging speakers around. He would deliver his sermons, starting out speaking softly, then shouting dramatically before breaking out in song. Many women became quite excited during these presentations, and they would shout, "Preach, Reverend Franklin, preach!" As the tensions mounted, they'd be rocking back and forth in the pews, saying, "Yes, Jesus. Yes, Lord." There were several women in starched white nurses' uniforms, and they would go over to the most hysterical churchgoers and fan them. Roosevelt and I loved going to church. We would sit back and bet which of these middle-aged women was going to "get happy" first. As we watched the rocking get faster as the Reverend's sermon got more intense, we'd pick who we were betting on.

"Look! It's gonna be the woman in the pink! Look at her," I'd say.

"No," Roosevelt would reply, "the one in the red. See how fast she's going?"

Finally, it would just get to be too much, and several of the female worshipers would jump up, throw off their hats, toss away their purses, and scream. Once they'd calmed down, a nurse would accompany them back to their pews, and then it would start all over again.

Carolyn and her older sisters, Aretha and Erma, sang in the church's choir and often took solos. I remember being impressed by Aretha's piano playing as well. In Detroit, the Franklin girls were local celebrities. Unbeknownst to anyone in her family, Carolyn had formed her own singing group.

It had never occurred to me that I might want to be a singer. All of my fantasies revolved around becoming an actress; then maybe I'd sing too, but for now I sang just for pleasure. That all changed when I discovered the great new rock 'n' roll I heard played on DJ Frantic Ernie Durham's show on station WCHB. When I saw Frankie Lymon and the Teenagers—a very clean-cut young black quintet—singing on Ed Sullivan's television show one Sunday night, the die was cast. I wanted to sing, and I decided that getting into Carolyn's group would be the best way to start.

I made it a point to hang around Carolyn's area of the playground. She was a big wheel in the school, despite her petite size. She was always the center of attention, and her friends towered over her as she held court in the schoolyard. Although her tough attitude intimidated me, I finally got the courage to start a conversation with her. Having steered our chat to the subject of singing, I said nonchalantly, "I hear you guys have a group here. I'd like to maybe practice with you all, or join."

"You sing?" Carolyn asked, surprised.

"Oh yeah," I replied offhandedly. "I've been singing all my life, and I just decided that I want to join a group."

Carolyn just smiled. Hovering nearby was a very fair-skinned redhead named Alice. She was giving me the once-over and I could tell she hated me on sight. I knew Alice would make things difficult for me; still I met up with Carolyn every day, no matter who was around. Finally my audition was set.

When the big day arrived we were all standing on the school auditorium stage. I was thrilled to be there, but my stomach was in knots. If I passed, Carolyn would let me perform with them in the upcoming school talent show. We were going to sing a current hit, which Carolyn had chosen and for which she'd devised separate parts and harmonies. Even at the age of eleven or twelve, Carolyn showed promise as an arranger. Carolyn gave us the downbeat and we began singing a cappella. I had to concentrate so hard just to keep my knees from shaking and stay on my part. I was nervous enough, but then I realized that Alice was deliberately trying to drown me out. Before the song was over, Alice was shouting, "This girl can't sing! She messed up the harmony!"

"I did not! You're just starting trouble!"

"Girl, you can't sing!"

Before I knew it, I had shoved Alice halfway across the stage. She retaliated with even greater force, and the brawl was on. Out of the corner of my eye, I saw Carolyn staring in shocked dismay while the other girls tried to separate Alice and me.

I was not a fighter, but I would fight to be part of a group. I knew I had screwed up, but it was because of stage fright. I was sure that I would have passed my audition if Alice hadn't sabotaged it. In the end I had to admit that I had failed. Before this, I hadn't realized how much difference there was between singing solo or in a choir and singing in a doo-wop-style group.

At this time, these groups were all the rage, and every local street-corner was occupied by trios, quartets, and quintets of kids teaching themselves the intricate harmonies they picked up off current hit records by the Platters, the Drifters, the Coasters, the Cleftones, the Flamingos, Mickey & Sylvia, Elvis Presley, and others. We all loved Little Richard, Chuck Berry, and Sam Cooke, and my personal favorites included the McGuire Sisters, Doris Day, and Patti Page. By 1956 every major city's black ghetto housed hundreds of young singing hopefuls, the vast majority of whom, I thought, were living in the Brewster Projects. Very few of them would ever consider solo careers, and most were parts of vocal groups. Kids who played instruments were rare, and those who did were either playing with a church group or had their sights set on far more respectable occupations than entertaining.

Some groups used the roof for a stage, others used the hallways in the Projects buildings. Because of their smooth hard walls and echo, these spots were prized for their acoustics. The lucky kids had access to parent-free apartments, which served as rehearsal studios between the last school bell and dinner time.

Competition among members of rival groups and their fans could be fierce. They were competing for attention, competing for a choice space to sing in, competing for some kind of recognition in a place that didn't offer too much hope to any of them. You didn't need any formal training; all you needed was heart and the courage to take some chances and do something with whatever God gave you that would make your singing different or better. Friends, neighbors, and pass-ersby made up a critical and vocal audience. If you didn't have a good sound, or if the group wasn't up to par, the audience and your rivals would ask you—in quite unflattering terms—to vacate the spot. The more cherished the spot—say, a building stairwell—the tougher it was to keep it.

Since Elvis Presley and other stars had made R&B and rock 'n' roll big business, more than a few struggling youngsters saw singing as a ticket out. Though the average person might automatically think of anyone living in public housing as being deprived, we barely knew the meaning of the word. Our parents constantly reminded us that we were far better off than they had been at our age, and the camaraderie and freedom we felt as kids contributed to making mine perhaps the first generation of black youths to believe their individual potential was unlimited. Sadly, some would learn differently, but at that moment the sky was the limit. And there were few other legitimate ways of making it as big as you could make it in music, if you were lucky.

The images of our idols inspired our young dreams. The success of outrageous rockers like Little Richard and Chuck Berry, smooth singers like Sam Cooke and Clyde McPhatter or sexy guys like Jackie Wilson gave us something to aspire to. And I loved the Shirelles. We were also relating to the original teen rebel, James Dean, and we wore leather jackets and blue jeans; a red bandana carefully hung from the back pocket completed the picture. For the guys, emulation of white teens required processing their hair, a tedious and unpleasant chore most were glad to give up when it went out of style. But back then the look was everything, especially since few could afford the ultimate accessory—a motorcycle.

Around this time, nightclubs were becoming more popular than ever. Many of our parents frequented these places nightly, and the entertainment and music offered in some of them is legendary. One of Detroit's most popular spots was the Flame Show Bar, which pre-sented most of the current jazz greats and popular singers, such as Dinah Washington, Sam Cooke, Nat "King" Cole, and Sarah Vaughan. No matter where you went or what your age, music seemed to be everywhere in Detroit.

Over the next couple of years, I stayed with the school glee club, but it just wasn't enough. It was 1958, and in the seventh grade, at age fourteen, I felt quite grown-up. With my friends Betty and Olivia, I would go downtown to see the latest Alan Freed rock 'n' roll movie. We would leave our houses looking very innocent, then sneak on nylon stockings and heels. When we weren't at the movies, we were roller-skating or playing the machines in the arcade next to the Arcadia rink. I remember skating, timidly keeping to the rail, and watching Aretha Franklin whiz by. She didn't just skate: she bopped. In the arcade was a place where you could record an acetate of your voice. I made a record of me singing a song called "I'm Sorry."

This year, a new girl moved into our neighborhood. Her name was Diane Ross. Her building was sort of catty-corner from mine, but because she went to the junior high in her old neighborhood, I saw her only after school. She had a crush on one of my friends, Tommy Rogers, so she came into our circle through him. But our cliques included dozens of kids. You could know someone and maybe you went to see a movie with them every so often, but you wouldn't exactly be close friends. That was my relationship with Diane then. But even though I didn't know her well, I admired her enthusiasm about things.

One day in 1958 I impulsively signed up to sing in the talent show as a solo. After I realized what I'd done, I wondered where I'd got the nerve. I had no idea what song I would sing, though I was pretty sure it would be a rock 'n' roll song, or how—or even if—I could sing it a cappella. At the eleventh hour I was struck by inspiration. I would mime, or lip-synch, to the Teenagers' hit "I'm Not a Juvenile Delinquent," which I'd seen them perform in one of my favorite rock 'n' roll movies, Alan Freed's *Rock! Rock! Rock!*

As the moment of my debut neared, I peered down at the oversized leather jacket hanging from my small shoulders, wiped my sweaty palms on my tight stovepipe pants, and adjusted the red doorag wrapped around my head. In this outfit, which I'd borrowed from Roosevelt at the last minute, I came out of my normally shy self and projected the cocksure attitude of a neighborhood punk, even though the song I'd chosen to perform was about being well-mannered.

I heard my name announced and, as if in a trance, I strutted across the stage in an exaggerated swagger to the beat while I sang "live" to the record. Once I started, there was no stopping. A couple hundred kids were yelling and hooting for me. The spontaneous and enthusiastic applause at the finish made my heart soar.

I stayed and watched the rest of the show from the wings. One of the girls who went on after me was a neighbor, Florence Ballard. I would see her walking around the neighborhood and think that she was such a pretty girl, with her fair skin, auburn hair, long legs, and curvaceous figure. In those days, a large bustline was considered a prerequisite of female beauty, and compared to the rest of us, Flo looked like a movie star. Even without makeup, Flo's face was perfect, her big brown eyes perfectly balanced with her full, sensuous lips and valentine-pointed chin. Because her hair was relatively light, everyone called her "Blondie."

That night, her voice was magnificent as she sang a classical piece. It may have been "Ave Maria," a song I know she sang in school. When she finished, the audience applauded loudly. I felt very happy for her. We traded congratulations and hugged, jumping up and down, like teenage girls do. We started talking about how much we loved singing, and the words just poured out. We didn't even notice that the show had ended and we were the only ones left in the place.

As we walked home, we discussed every possible detail of our performances. We promised each other that if either of us were ever asked to join a singing group, she would call the other. After lingering outside my building for a while, we reluctantly said good-bye. There was a bond between us. We could not have known that it would last a lifetime.

CHAPTER 3

Soon after our meeting at the talent show, Flo and I became good friends. Once offstage, I was still the same shy little girl, and Flo, as always, seemed streetwise and much older than her years. Flo seemed so sure and so confident, and I really admired her for that. About six months had passed since the talent show. I would see Flo around, and we would talk, but I had forgotten about the promises we had made to bring each other into a group.

The eighth of thirteen children born to Jesse and Lurlee Ballard, Flo was a true product of the Motor City. Her father, like so many blacks from the rural South, took the train north to Detroit in 1929. Her mother was a buxom young woman with fair skin and pretty eyes. She always wore her waist-length hair in a long braid down her back. Soon after she and Jesse got together, their first child was born. As a young man Jesse had dreamed of finding a job up North and leaving the South behind forever. He landed a job with Chevrolet, and Lurlee soon followed her husband to the big city. Being with him was the only way she would ever escape the stifling atmosphere of Rosetta, Mississippi, so she happily left to join her husband.

Most of the Ballard children grew up in what they referred to as the "big house" on MacDougal Street, which their parents had moved into in the early fifties. Though their house was not really far from where I grew up, our paths never crossed, and we did not meet until after the Ballards moved to the Projects following the birth of their last child.

The Brewster Projects were where the family shared some of its fondest memories. Because of their many children, the Ballards were assigned one of the attached row houses, a two-story affair with enough bedrooms so that they were a little crowded but not as cramped as many of the other families. There were few luxuries in the ghetto; even so, this move marked a major advancement over what the Ballard children might have had if their parents had remained down South.

The burden of Mr. Ballard's daily job and the constant worry that he might one day be unable to feed his family never diminished his positive attitude and warm disposition. His children saw that with the move to the Projects, their father seemed to relax. He spent hours on end singing and playing the guitar for his kids, and he taught Flo to sing. Flo would tease him, saying that someday he would be a star. Years later, his daughters would reminisce about their father. "He'd get to playing that old guitar, and he'd just go down to the ground," Flo would say. "Boy, Daddy could play," her sister Barbara would add.

Mrs. Ballard took pains to see that her children were safe and secure. There was real love and caring in that family, and their affection for one another went beyond what most people think of as "close." I envied Flo having so many brothers and sisters, especially the older ones. I longed to have a sibling mentor, someone to show me how to do my nails or to talk with about boys. Coming from a smaller and much quieter family, I was taken aback at first by how loud and boisterous the Ballard kids could be when they were all together. But before long I grew comfortable there, and in time the Ballards' house would seem like my second home.

Though they'd lived in Detroit for many years, the Ballards all retained a "country" attitude and lifestyle. One advantage of this was that no matter what happened, they all stuck together. Problems were not discussed outside the family, and if one of the Ballards was after you for something, you knew they all were. Family always came first. All the kids were close, no matter how many years' difference there was between their ages. Bertie, the eldest daughter, was twenty years older than Flo, and Flo had five younger brothers and sisters. I eventually learned all of their names: Bertie, Cornell, Jesse, Jr., Gilbert, Geraldine, Barbara, Maxine, Flo, Billy, Calvin, Pat, and the baby, Linda. One of Flo's younger brothers, Roy, had been killed at the age of three in a freak accident. That tragedy and Jesse Ballard Sr.'s death from cancer in 1959 reinforced Mrs. Ballard's conviction that her children must be shielded from danger at all costs.

I was in the eighth grade, going through my usual school routine one day in early 1959, when Flo ran up to me in the hallway. Between her gasps for breath, I could see she was grinning from ear to ear. She grabbed my arm and asked excitedly, "Mary, do you want to be in a singing group with me and two other girls—"

"Yes!" I replied before she even finished the question. It didn't occur to me to ask what the group was about, or who was in it, or anything. The only word I heard Flo say was "singing," and that was enough for me.

From what little I knew of Flo then, I could see how excited she was. Generally a low-key type, Flo was now pressing my arm so hard it almost hurt. We agreed to meet after school on the playground.

By the time the last bell sounded, I felt like I had survived the longest school day of my life. Once school ended, I rushed to our meeting place, but Flo wasn't there. Five and then ten minutes passed, and I began to wonder if Flo was going to show at all. Did Flo change her mind about me joining the group? Did something happen on her way over? Or did she just forget about me? I said a silent prayer that nothing had happened to change our plans. And I waited. When I finally realized that I was one of the last kids left in the schoolyard, I slowly headed for home.

I'd gotten only a few yards down the sidewalk when Flo ran up from behind, redfaced. She'd had to finish a few things in school; she apologized. Then the excitement returned to her voice as she filled me in with the details of her original proposition.

She had been approached by a member of a male vocal trio called the Primes and their manager, Milton Jenkins, about forming a "sister" group to perform with his clients. Two other girls had already been recruited. The Primes were a classic vocal group, but their repertoire extended beyond the teenage doo-wop tunes we liked and included sophisticated material such as that of the Mills Brothers. The three young men—Kel Osborn and Paul Williams, and a slender high tenor named Eddie Kendricks—had recently arrived in Detroit from their native Alabama. Though we would have a long and enduring relationship with members of the Primes for the rest of our career, at the time Milton Jenkins was the most important person. He would ultimately be responsible for our early success.

Like his clients, Milton also hailed from Alabama. One of thirteen children—many of whom had died in a tuberculosis epidemic years before—Milton grew up feeling responsible for his family. There was nothing for Milton in Birmingham, Alabama, and after years of streetwise hustling failed to yield satisfactory financial rewards, he decided to try his luck up North.

Upon his arrival in Detroit, Milton became part of the show-business crowd that hung out on Hastings Street, an area which boasted many of the city's hotter nightclubs, hotels, and restaurants. There was something seedy yet glamorous about the area; it was a place where things happened. Here were big spenders and gorgeous women, all living the easy life, or at least a life that seemed a lot easier than working in an auto factory. Milton moved into a residential hotel —actually a four-family house that had been converted into a single-room-occupancy hotel—across from the Flame Show Bar, and was only too happy to meet and rub elbows with the musicians and singers who passed through. Although he lacked artistic talent, he loved show business. As we would later learn, Milton was a man of contrasts.

Much of Milton's early success can be attributed to his enthusi-asm and a real drive to make money—big money. When he met the Primes they were just one of many unknown groups around. Once he saw their show, he was convinced they had star potential. They were young, good-looking, and talented, and that, combined with his busi-ness savvy, could take them all to the top. He convinced them to let him develop them, and soon he was investing every extra cent he made into the Primes' new suits and stylish processed hairstyles, or processes. The Primes moved into Milton's apartment. Though Mil-ton's formal education was limited, he always impressed people; he seemed worldly and easily commanded attention. He was obsessed with appearances, and insisted that everything about him and his act be first class, from his sharply tailored suits to his red 1957 Cadillac, in which he chauffeured the Primes to every gig they played. Years before it would seem feasible to most people, Milton Jenkins saw the music business as his ticket out of the inner city.

We never knew exactly where Milton's investment capital came from—he never had a nine-to-five job, and he never volunteered any information. Of course, to the streetwise, the answer was probably obvious. Because we were so young—Diane and I were fourteen, Flo was fifteen—we didn't really think too much about it. Milton was one of the most interesting people any of us had ever met.

Paul Williams was dating a girl named Betty McGlown, who he thought might be good in the group, and he also knew two other girls who liked to sing. It didn't take much for Paul to sell Milton on the idea of developing a sister group, a briefly popular gimmick. And Flo sold me. I knew this could be my dream come true, and with typical youthful optimism, I believed this might even be the chance of a lifetime.

I rushed home, bursting with excitement. "Mama! Mama! Can I

join this singing group? It's called the Primettes. Please?" I said it all in one quick breath and then looked at my mother pleadingly.

"The Primates?" she asked distractedly. She was concentrating on dinner and not paying much attention.

"No, Prim*ettes*. My friend Flo says the Primes are looking for a sister group, so she asked if I wanted to be in it with her. Please, Mama, please. And the man who is their manager says he will pay for all our outfits and everything. Flo says that he has a lot of money and he drives a big red Cadillac. And he's real nice. Flo says the Primes can really sing good, too. And—"

"What about your after-school chores?"

"Roosevelt and Cat can help out, can't they? Please, Mama, they're big enough now. Flo says—"

"And just who is Flo?"

Now, I thought, Mama will listen. I took a deep breath and repeated everything as calmly as I could. After I told her all about Flo and her family I pleaded, "Please, Mama. Flo says the Primes are gonna be stars someday. Maybe we will, too. I know we've got a chance because my music teacher said—"

She didn't say anything else for a while, but I wasn't worried. Like any child, I could read my mother's face. She was thinking hard, but I sensed that she was pleased about the prospect. Rehearsing and performing in shows would keep me out of trouble and off the streets. I had my fingers crossed as I watched her. After what seemed like an eternity, she agreed. I was ecstatic.

The next day I was floating on a cloud. Flo promised that we'd meet the Primes and Milton Jenkins right after school. I don't remember how we got there, but the next thing I knew we were standing in the lobby of his hotel. Though anyone else would have thought it shabby, I remember it as being very fancy. What was left of the plasterwork inside revealed that at one time the house had been a very nice place; from the outside, it just looked dilapidated. To me, the east side was a place where the people seemed like peacocks, strutting about in flashy clothes, but with cultivated manners that set them apart from everyone else.

Up in Milton's room—a bachelor suite he shared with the Primes —I was one of four nervous young girls. There was me; Flo; Paul Williams' girlfriend, Betty McGlown, a tall, pretty, dark-skinned girl who seemed a little older; and a fourth girl, about my age, with large, luminous brown eyes—my new friend Diane Ross.

The Primes were in the middle of rehearsal. They were a lot more polished than I expected. Their voices harmonized so beautifully, the songs seemed to float through the air on velvet waves. Then I noticed Eddie Kendricks' clear, romantic falsetto, and from that moment on I was madly in love with him. In fact, this attraction was the beginning of a crush that, though unrequited, continues to this day.

When the Primes finished their tune, Milton looked the four of us over with a bemused smile. He seemed to like what he saw. Milton was tall, dark-skinned, and slender. He was always impeccably dressed in sharkskin or mohair suits. Milton's suits were tailor-made, in black or dark colors, and he wore a tie and matching handkerchief. He was always immaculately groomed, soft-spoken, and, from the day we met him, had his arm in a cast and a sling.

We were all pretty quiet; only Betty seemed a bit more relaxed, but that was probably because she was Paul's girlfriend. Flo and Betty looked like real women, while Diane and I, each weighing less than one hundred pounds, were waifs. After Flo replied "yes" for me to all of Milton's questions, I knew I was a Primette.

Then something almost magical happened. Milton asked us if we knew any songs, and Flo jumped right in and started singing "(Night Time Is) The Right Time," a Ray Charles hit. Without having had a minute of rehearsal, without having even discussed what we were going to sing, we all fell into our parts, and we sounded wonderful. It was like a miracle. Milton had the Primes critique our performances. Getting the Primes' nod of approval boosted our confidence. I was impressed and a bit intimidated working with new people who were much older and more experienced, even though at the time Eddie Kendricks wasn't more than eighteen.

Paul, Kel, and Eddie taught us some songs. None of us read music, so we had to learn everything by ear. Paul then decided that we should learn a new song, "The Twist." This also was a natural for Flo. Then Diane took the lead on the Drifters' hit "There Goes My Baby." Each time, we all found our parts and harmonized together beautifully.

Paul was a fabulous dancer, and elements of his style were later evident in all the Temptations' great moves. The steps and hand gestures Paul created were clever, sexy, and unique. Since he had already choreographed the Primes' onstage routines, he started working out similar moves for us. When our fancy new steps were combined with our new vocal arrangement for "Night Time"—Flo singing Charles's "call" parts and Diane providing the Raelettes' "responses," while Betty and I sang "night and day" over and over, we sounded like pros.

Milton was obviously pleased with the results. He had a self-satisfied attitude, as if every time he looked at us he saw a way to make his dreams come true.

Flo, Diane, and I whooped and sang all the way home. We talked about how Milton had promised that he would send us out shopping with one of his lady friends, and about what type of stage outfits we would like to wear. I was so grateful to Flo for keeping her word and getting me in.

As we reached the Projects, we could hear all the different groups singing, but it did not daunt our spirits one bit. We believed the Primettes would make it.

We started our daily rehearsals at Milton's the very next afternoon. Once it was clear that we would all be working together, Milton wanted to meet our parents and reassure them that everything was on the up and up. I waited anxiously in our apartment for Milton to arrive.

Living in the Projects was like living in a small town—everyone knew or wanted to know everyone else's business. When Milton and a couple of the fellows pulled up in that shiny red Cadillac, every window flew open. All the little kids playing in front of my building surrounded them. With their finely tailored suits and beautifully styled hair, Paul and Eddie looked like nobody these kids had ever seen before, at least not in this neighborhood. Some of the braver ones even followed them into the building to see what apartment they were going to visit. They might as well have been royalty.

Milton charmed my mother, and Paul's and Eddie's sincerity was the icing on the cake. The fellows explained their plans to make us a popular, complementary component of the Primes. Their praise of my singing made my mother proud. They agreed we would play only sock hops and local social-club engagements—no nightclubs or bars. Milton stressed that we would have to spend hours rehearsing, and asked my mother for permission for me to come to his hotel with Flo and Diane straight from school. When she agreed, everyone was pleased, but no one more than me.

My mother was relieved that I would have my free time occupied by something constructive. This would keep me off the streets, and she would know where to find me at all times. Before access to birth control or legal abortion, all parents worried that their daughters might end up as unwed teenage mothers. That was probably why all our parents agreed to let us become Primettes. If keeping our minds on singing would keep our eyes off the boys, that was good enough for them. Milton, keeping a promise he made to our parents, put his girlfriend in charge of us, and so we had a chaperone, of sorts. The thought that we might also one day become stars never entered our parents' minds, but it was all we thought about.

Once our daily rehearsals began in earnest, we all got to know each other better. Betty was a no-nonsense girl with a great sense of humor. She was older than we were by just a year or so, and because Flo was about six months older than Diane and me, Betty and Flo paired off. They made it clear to us that they were the bosses. Because Betty lived in a different neighborhood, we didn't see her as often as we saw one another, but we liked her a lot and kept in touch with her over the phone.

Just as there had been a strong, instantaneous affinity between me and Flo, Diane and I got along from the start, too. But somehow our relationship was different. Diane was born in Detroit exactly twenty days after me. Even though there was less than a month's difference in our ages, Diane and I were born under different signs. Diane's birth sign, Aries, is the symbol of the ram, an animal often depicted butting its way to the top of the mountain. Aries people are also considered natural leaders and very independent. She was always very energetic and talkative. I really admired her. In her I found a missing part of myself, a more aggressive side I could never express comfortably. Diane was a wonderful friend. I would be sitting around, doing nothing in particular, and Diane would come over to my house, grab my arm, and say, "Let's go!"

Diane was Fred and Ernestine Ross' second of six children and second daughter. The Rosses had moved to Detroit from Alabama, seeking a better life. Fred Ross worked at the American Brass Company. After he was secure in his job, he and Ernestine started their family. Proudly old-fashioned, he refused to let his wife work outside the home, so to make ends meet he always had a second job, working nights as a mechanic.

When I first visited Diane's house I noticed a major distinction between her family and most of those in our neighborhood: There was a father at home. I had been exposed to many more "traditional" families while I lived with John L. and I.V., but here in the Projects most families were headed by a single—divorced, widowed, or abandoned—mother, and things were never easy.

Diane's family was very close, but in a different way than Flo's.

Unlike many other families then, the Rosses didn't cling to the old idea that the family always came before the individual. Instead, they emphasized the importance of each child's personal achievements, and, education was considered crucial. Diane always had a streak of daring and independence. Though Fred Ross was strict, he encouraged his children to be self-determined and to work toward their goals.

Before long, Diane, Flo, and I were best of friends. Almost every day, I'd look out my window and see Diane, then I'd run outside and we'd do something. We were no longer just passing acquaintances. Later, she'd come running over to my house. As time passed, even Roosevelt and Cat would have best friends in both the Ross and Ballard families. Of course, we were obsessed by music, but we also talked about boys, and school, and all of our dreams.

We never could have guessed just how many of them would come true.

CHAPTER 4

Even though we had been coming to Milton's for a few months, the area never ceased to fascinate us; we could watch the passersby for hours, hoping to catch a glimpse of a famous star going into the Flame. Once we saw Sam Cooke. It was on one such afternoon in late 1959 that we spotted Marvin Tarplin and his guitar.

"Can you play that guitar," I yelled down at him from the window, "or are you just carrying it?"

"I can play it," he said, looking up at us and smiling shyly.

"Well, come on up here, and let us hear you play," one of us replied flippantly. We all knew this kind of behavior—calling down to and inviting up a strange young man—would never be accepted at home. But we weren't at home.

Once we realized what we'd done and Marvin was on his way up, we began to giggle nervously, not certain this was the right thing. He seemed genuinely sweet; he was a tall, lanky, somewhat funny-looking kid. Marvin was always soft-spoken and just too nice. I recognized him from school.

Once Marvin was inside the suite we prevailed upon him to play every single song we requested. By this time we knew a lot of songs, and Marvin seemed familiar with all the latest hits. As he played, we sang along: twelve-bar blues, Hank Ballard tunes, "There Goes My Baby," and "(Night Time Is) The Right Time." The combination of our voices and his acoustic guitar added a whole new dimension to our sound, and without too much discussion, Marvin became the fifth Primette on the spot. He was thrilled.

Before we met Marvin, the Primes arranged our harmonies; for that reason alone, none of us ever had to learn to read music. We did everything by sound. Marvin read music, and so he could teach us any song. Having our own musician made us unique among the other local singing groups, because at the hops, they would have to lip-synch to the hit records, while we sang live. And we were very proud of Marvin. Once he became part of the group, he was as dedicated as we were and was with us every minute.

From the start, Flo took most of the leads, singing in her warm, gospel-tinged style. Her raw spirit was always the soul of the Primettes. It all seemed so easy for her. In the beginning a concerned Milton attended every rehearsal, making sure that we had everything we needed. The Primes continued to teach us songs and everything they knew about staging—how to stand, what to say, how to give and follow cues. Some days, Milton would pick us up at our houses and drive us to rehearsal in his Cadillac. The minute he pulled up, everyone on our block gathered around, wondering, I'm sure, just what we were doing. Though Milton seemed to have more than his share of beautiful, sexy girlfriends, we attributed his success with the ladies to his handsome face and irresistible charm. When it came to us, however, Milton was always a perfect gentleman, sometimes acting as if we were his daughters. "Look at those girls, those are my girls," he would say proudly to anyone around.

Several months later we had our first professional engagement, singing at a gigantic party in a hall for a large local union. Milton's well-dressed lady friend took us shopping for stage outfits. Milton wanted us to look sharp but innocent. We all looked forward to these shopping jaunts. Fortunately, her taste in clothes was not as brassy as we feared it might be, and we all agreed on the collegiate look that Frankie Lymon and the Teenagers had made so popular. We picked out white pleated skirts, white sweaters embossed with big letter Ps, white bobby sox, and white gym shoes.

The people attending were bigwigs, or at least fairly well to do, or so we thought, since none of them came from our neighborhood. Also on the bill with us was a young singer named Freda Payne. The union's membership was primarily black and middle- or upper-middle-class, a group we referred to as the "elites." Perhaps they were better educated, or their skin was lighter, or they had managed to banish any Southern accent or language from their speech. These blacks frowned upon other blacks whose appearance, manner of expression, or attitude diverged from the "white" standards the black middle class sought to emulate. In many ways these people, most of whom sent their children to the "better" schools, such as Cass Technical High School, could be as nasty to the blacks they thought were beneath them as any white bigot, and kids from the Projects were in that group.

They say that you never forget your first time at anything, and that's especially true of performing. I can remember this evening so vividly. Flo sang lead on "Night Time," Diane sang "There Goes My Baby," and I sang the ballads. We also did "The Twist." Everything came so naturally for me, and we all did well. Flo was as earthy and soulful as ever. Diane looked as excited as a young leopard, and Betty was her usual sparkling, confident self. We were great. And from the first sound of applause, I knew that my place was on the stage.

After our big splash, Milton tried to book us on any show willing to take us. We began to be popular around the Detroit area playing sock hops. These were dances organized by local disc jockeys, where they played records and presented young local acts, like us, who didn't yet have an extensive repertoire of original material. We did many of these shows with disc jockeys, including Ernie Durham, and later Bill Williams, Long, Tall, Lean, Lanky Larry Dean, and Robin Seymour. Our act usually consisted of our own renditions of the most popular tunes.

Milton was always there beside us. He took his job of manager very seriously, driving us to the gigs, protecting and guiding us. If we were ever paid for these performances, we never knew it. Besides, the money would have represented only a fraction of what Milton spent on us. Still, as time passed, we became increasingly curious about what we had come to think of as Milton's secret life.

We now felt we had arrived, and our top priority became making our group the best around. After all, weren't we the only group in the Projects with our own guitarist? Weren't we one of the few groups who wore stylish matching stage costumes? Couldn't we be considered some of the prettiest girls singing in the Brewster complex (or any-where in town, for that matter)? And, we were proud to say, we had never had to sing on streetcorners; the Primettes played real dates, right from the beginning.

After my mother purchased a new sewing machine on credit, the four of us decided that we could make more original stage costumes than the ones Milton's girlfriends had been choosing for us, which now included things like shirtwaist dresses. I had learned the basics of sewing in my seventh-grade home economics class at Bishop, and Diane, whose mother had done some dressmaking, also knew how to sew. The few skirts and dresses I made were never completely finished, but they were wearable.

Diane and I went downtown shopping. We chose some wonderful

orange and yellow floral print material and a pattern for a short, sleeveless balloon dress, which went out at the waist like any full skirt, but then tapered at the knee. Diane and I spent many afternoons and evenings together pressing, cutting, marking, and pinning the material. Every day for weeks there would be scissors, cloth, pattern tissues, straight pins, and tape measures all over the floors at her house and mine.

I didn't do as much detailing on my dress as Diane had on hers, and later I had to go back and touch up a few crooked seams. Once on, though, our new dresses looked beautiful. These were our very first stage gowns and we felt very grown-up in them. We had our peau de soie pumps dyed orange to match. At last we looked—we thought —as sophisticated and worldly as we felt. These might have been designer creations from Paris for all we cared.

We were four teenage girls convinced we could become the best girl group Detroit had ever produced. We were obsessed with music. Deep down, we knew we could achieve our goal only through commitment, and though each of us was probably more serious about our careers than most of our singing peers, it was Flo's voice that put us over. Though unsure of herself in so many other ways, Flo knew she could sing, and she knew we could make it. Singing was Flo's ticket out, and so the Primettes became her life. Of course, none of us really knew how we were going to accomplish all this, but the details didn't matter then.

With practice, our stage presence became more exciting; with repetition even the most carefully planned movements, gestures, and lines began to look perfect and spontaneous. Once we had learned these basics and they became automatic, we felt more relaxed, and before long being onstage seemed like second nature.

We were still taking turns singing the lead on songs, and we were all good, but almost everyone who heard us agreed that Flo was the best. Her sound and style were very similar to Aretha Franklin's; she would attack each number with a passion that every audience responded to immediately. We were still singing other peoples' hits, but Flo was able to make any song she sang like her own. Diane's voice was higher, and she had gotten into the habit of singing through her nose, with her shoulders all drawn up. Still, on the right song, like "There Goes My Baby," or with the right part, like in "(Night Time Is) The Right Time," Diane was great. Betty's singing was very good, and we urged her to take more leads, but she never would. Because she was an alto, she thought her voice was too deep. She did, however, give the group a special charisma that audiences really warmed to. And for the most part, I stayed cool, projecting a calm, certain air, while my heart pounded a thousand beats a minute. Of the four of us, Diane changed the most once onstage. Her nervous habits, like biting her nails, disappeared and she seemed confident and at home. She also had a way of constantly moving onstage that caught the eye.

I think it's hard for people who haven't performed to understand how it feels to stand up before a crowd of strangers and really open your heart. It was very special to us, and looking back I can see how each of us contributed to keeping it together. After each show we would tell one another over and over again that we were a smash, and we would build one another up, downplaying our own insecurities and doubts. All that mattered was that we excel as a group. We really didn't see ourselves as four individuals. Perhaps we each knew that as individuals, without the others, we had no chance. As the Primettes, though, we had everything going for us. Or, as Flo would later say, "Honey, we is terrific."

When we weren't together, we were talking on the phone. We each seemed always to be talking with one of the others. All our conversations were about singing and the Primettes—where we were playing next, what we would wear, what we would sing, who might see us there, how we would get there, and so on. We would drive our parents crazy asking if we could go to one of the other girls' homes. Once, to do a show, we even lied to our parents, saying we were spending the night at one of the others' houses. Our being such good girls gave us a brazen confidence; we reasoned that since we had hardly ever lied to our parents before, we probably wouldn't get caught. Even boyfriends were on the back burner now.

We weren't the only group making a name. Several other groups we knew—like the Peppermints, and Otis Williams and the Distants —were getting around. Melvin Franklin and Richard Street were members of the Distants, and, like us, they were regulars on the sock-hop circuit, though we didn't meet them until the night we shared a bill at the Gold Coast, a popular local club. The other highlight of that evening was a fight that broke out on the dance floor. Fistfights were so common in many of the clubs we played, we came to view them as added entertainment.

Melvin came to see our group because he wanted to see Betty. For some reason, Betty didn't show up for this particular gig, but

Melvin stayed to catch our act. His cousin, Richard Street, knew Diane from their days at McMichaels Elementary School. There seemed to be an empathy between Melvin and me. Even then, he was very spiritual. He had one of the deepest, huskiest voices I had ever heard. I was just learning how to tell when a boy had a crush on me, but both he and Richard were very shy, so there was no way I could be sure. Soon Richard became infatuated with Diane. I doubt she even knew it; she seemed to have eyes for everyone but him.

Despite these romantic intrigues, the only subject we could all really open up about was singing. We knew we were on the right track, and we were always telling one another to stick to it, to persevere. Richard had been playing in nightclubs since he was thirteen, and because he seemed so experienced, we all assumed that he was older when in fact he was one of the youngest in our crowd. Knowing Melvin and Richard during this time helped me to see more objectively what we were all going through. We were still young, but performing, even in the best places, brought us into contact with parts of the real world most kids don't see. Most of us had come from the South, but some of us were raised with so little awareness of what that life was about that we might as well have been Detroit natives. Other young singers, like our friends from the Primes and Melvin, had trouble adjusting to life in Detroit.

We knew of prejudice that crossed racial lines, but few of us knew that there could be as much discrimination from within our own race as from outside it. Melvin learned about this other unspoken prejudice the first time he failed an audition for a group because he was "too dark." "I have big eyes," Melvin told me later, "and the group's leader, who was gay, showed no mercy. 'We don't want no black, bug-eyed boy over here with us.' They never gave me the chance to sing."

Without Richard's and his own mother's encouragement, Melvin might have given up. Instead he decided that he would one day be accepted in a great vocal group, and he knew that the only way he'd be accepted by the elites was to practice and practice and practice. And that's exactly what he and Richard did. Because Melvin was even shyer than his cousin, Richard had to coax him into talking to us.

Lately, it seemed that all our relationships were growing out of music, and a network of young singers and musicians was forming among our friends. Marv Tarplin, for example, had known Richard years before either of them knew us. Fate seemed to be bringing us all together, and, in my youthful idealism, I believed we would be in one anothers' lives forever.

* * *

As we got older, we came to view school as a mildly annoying necessity. On the positive side, it was a refuge from the group, which by now was taking up so much time and energy that we each felt an acute need for time alone. As enjoyable as performing was, we took it seriously and the realization of how great our responsibilities were could be overwhelming.

Just a few months after the Primettes were formed, in the spring of 1959, Flo, Diane, and I graduated from the eighth grade. I hadn't really thought much about what high school I would be attending until one of my teachers, Mr. Curley, suggested that I consider going to Commerce, where they taught business skills, instead of Northeastern. My mother had been saving up so I could go to college, and all I knew about choosing a career was that I didn't want to be a nurse; I was too emotional for that.

Diane chose to attend Cass Technical High School, her father's alma mater, where she studied dress design and costume illustration. Cass was considered one of the better high schools in the area, and was the choice of many "elites." Few kids from our neighborhood went there, so we thought of Cass as something of a snob school.

My first day at Commerce brought me the shock of my life: There were hardly any boys there! Almost all of the other girls there were white and very businesslike, and there weren't any kids around from my neighborhood. After getting my schedule, my locker, and my home-room assignment, I told my counselor that I'd made a serious mistake. I was offered the chance to go to Cass, but I wasn't interested. Although I was a good student, I rarely studied. I would never have failed anything, but I didn't want to do the extra schoolwork I knew I'd get if I went to Cass. Northeastern was further from my home, but I knew the kids there and—best of all—there would be boys. Though I dreamed of singing professionally, I knew I had to be prepared to take a regular job. Though Northeastern offered no special curriculum for business studies, I didn't care. I took many music classes, including some with Flo. I would probably go to college anyway, and I wanted very badly to be with my friends from the neighborhood and the Brewster Center, the community recreation facility.

Northeastern was considered a rough school. Though it was located in the Polish neighborhood, more than eighty percent of the students were black. I know it's not as common today, but back then the teachers in the inner-city schools strove to make sure the academic standards were high. Our instructors were exceptional, and the faculty was thoroughly integrated. The whites, most of whom were of Polish descent, made an extra effort to mix with the black kids. There were racial problems and incidents all over Detroit, but I was never aware of any trouble during my years at Northeastern. For that I credit the faculty, who socialized together without any regard to race and so set the tone for the whole school.

As I got older, I came to fully appreciate my hardworking teachers' dedication and how much it influenced me. We had an exceptional music department, headed by Mr. Silver, and each semester I took as many different music classes as I could. Both Flo and I were in the glee club, which we loved. However, once we started hanging around at Milton's, our instructor, Mrs. Breaux, got upset. Not only were we missing rehearsals but she felt that both of us should be studying opera. In fact, for one school program, Flo and I sang Handel's *Messiah*. I will always remember Mrs. Breaux for saying to us, "I don't know why you sing all that rock and roll stuff. It's not going to get you anywhere." Still, without the support and guidance of many of those instructors, I would never have even dreamed, much less achieved my later goals. Even when I took a class that I wasn't particularly suited for—like the time I took Latin, thinking it would help me when I traveled the world—I stuck with it. Though it is a dead language, I did benefit from knowing it later on.

When I wasn't thinking about singing, I was daydreaming about boys. Each of our mothers had decided that we were all too young at fifteen to "receive company." But when did that stop young love? It didn't stop me from having my first grown-up boyfriend, Arnett Webster, who was several years older than me and just out of the service. Before I met Arnett, it never occurred to me to want to bring boys over to my house. With Arnett, I soon realized that while I may have been a virgin, I wasn't just a kid anymore. We would sit, talk, and walk around, holding hands. It was very romantic, and Arnett was always a gentleman. In fact, Flo, Diane, Betty, and I seemed to attract only nice young men who treated us respectfully.

Though I'd taken my first tentative steps into the realm of sexuality, I still wasn't aware of all the changes in my body. That didn't mean, however, that certain fast-moving boys in my neighborhood weren't hip to all this. One of these young men was Jimmy Abner, a handsome tenor who sometimes sang with Melvin and Richard. Our mutual love of music brought us together, but it wasn't long before our romance took precedence over everything else. With Jimmy I learned what kissing was really all about.

Sometimes when we were making out, it was almost impossible to stop. I would discover my top off before I could pull away. It was difficult, but I forced myself to hold back. This went on for weeks, with Jimmy begging me to submit to my "true feelings." I really enjoyed all this heavy petting, as we used to call it, so finally I agreed to go all the way. When I told Jimmy that I would, I could sense his excitement, despite his great efforts to appear cool. Unlike many young girls at the time, I didn't bother pretending that I wanted to wait for marriage or that I was too good or too innocent.

The moment of truth came one night when Jimmy's parents were out of town and we had the house all to ourselves. I was eager but torn between knowing it was wrong to have sex (my mother would have murdered me if she found out) and feverishly wanting to surrender to my desires and not look like a coward in front of Jimmy.

When we got to Jimmy's, the house was dark, and I begged him not to turn on the lights. In the back of my mind, I almost convinced myself that if we did this forbidden thing in the dark, no one could know, or maybe I would not have to accept the fact that it was really happening. Sensing my unease, Jimmy slowly undressed me. There was no awkward fumbling, and before I knew it, Jimmy's strong body was on top of mine. Within seconds we were in the throes of passion. After what seemed like an eternity of foreplay, Jimmy gently spread my legs with one hand, and I could feel him trying to enter me. I screamed for him to stop, and he did, but continued to kiss me passionately. He tried again and again, but I stopped him each time. I forgot about how much I loved him and how long I'd waited for this and how good it felt. It just wasn't right. Where were the shooting stars I'd heard about? There was no magic here. Finally, I made him stop. I tearfully told him that I couldn't go on; it hurt too much. We broke up soon after.

With this embarrassing experience behind me, I felt I'd emerged from innocence. I wanted to share this with someone, but I knew it couldn't be Flo or Diane. Betty seemed the logical choice, since I suspected that because of her relationship with Paul, she probably knew a lot more about all this than I did. Ultimately, I told no one. It was just not my nature—or Diane's or Flo's or Betty's—to discuss such things. Our lives inside and outside of the Primettes were kept separate.

I would always go to Diane's house after I'd finished my chores and homework. My mother had agreed that I could join the Primettes, but she didn't let me off the hook from doing housework. I was the eldest, and a girl to boot, so the bulk of the responsibility for keeping the house in order was mine. My brother didn't have to do house-work because he was a boy, and Cat was still too young really to help.

I always looked forward to seeing Diane. We would go out to see a rock 'n' roll movie, go roller-skating, or just run around the neigh-borhood. Diane was always very intense about things. When she wanted to go, she wanted to go, and I enjoyed being caught up in her enthusiasm. Neither of us could afford to buy all the clothes we wanted—what teenage girl can?—so we shared. We wore the same sizes and liked the current style, wearing V-neck pullover sweaters over different-colored dickies.

One day I found Diane feeling really down. She was unusually quiet, and when I asked her what was bothering her, she said nothing. After I'd plied her with questions, she eventually admitted to me that some kids at Cass were making it hard for her to join one of the sororities, the Hexagons. It was a very "in" club, so their snubbing Diane just made her all the more determined to get in. Typically, she would jump right in to be at the center of attention, and while this usually worked with our crowd, the kids at Cass looked down on Diane because she was from the Projects. In order to get into the sorority, you had to belong to another school club, so Diane set her sights on that. Girls at that age tend to be catty, anyway, and for some reason that I didn't see, Diane was bringing out the worst in these girls. Diane never took a snub lightly, and she set out to change things.

She made an extra effort to participate in all the extracurricular activities, and made the swim team. Winning many local competitions for Cass proved to be a real turning point. She had finally found her niche, and the other students began to notice and appreciate her. I was happy for her, and I could see that she was back to her old, happy self. She was thrilled about being accepted by her fellow students, and anything that she loved—like swimming—consumed her.

Around this time, Flo started dating Jesse Greer, who, like most of the boys in our circle, was a gentleman. He was a handsome, intelligent, soft-spoken boy who also sang. Along with some former basketball buddies, he formed the Peppermints. At the time they met, Flo was attending Northeastern, and Jesse was in his last year at East-ern High. Jesse would share his dreams of stardom with Flo, and she was a good listener; she could be very reserved and quiet. He knew that she had a great voice, too. Flo would sometimes meet Jesse at

Carmen Murphy's House of Beauty after school and stay and watch his group rehearse, then Jesse would walk her home.

Jesse respected Flo, who was then only fifteen. After meeting her family, he became even more resolved in his conviction not to sleep with her, and so he took special care not to get carried away with Flo, he later told me.

After Jesse graduated from high school, he and Flo stopped dating. Flo told me that the reason she and Jesse had drifted apart was that he was "too nice" for her, but I never knew what she meant by that. Jesse was a few years older than Flo, and he seemed much more mature. And while Flo could seem much wiser, and certainly appeared to be older, in many ways she was not as mature as she seemed. Some people took Flo's silence as a mark of her maturity; in fact she was often quiet because she feared being ridiculed. Her family still held on to those country ways and made no pretense of being more sophisticated than they were. While Diane and I were encouraged by our families to work toward our goals, even if this entailed some risk, Flo was constantly reminded to be cautious and not to venture too far.

Though Jesse liked Flo, she would just close up around him; she didn't know what to do. Once they stopped dating, they became the best of friends, more like brother and sister. Sitting on her porch, the two of them would talk about everything, but especially music. By then the Peppermints were well known locally, having played the Flame Show Bar and the Twenty Grand Club. At the time, the only local act working those venues was the Four Tops. With the pressure off, Flo told Jesse all about her life and her feelings, and to him she revealed the fun part of her personality, an openness that she shared with very few and kept hidden from the rest of the world.

CHAPTER 5

Any weekend that we weren't booked for a sock hop would find us attending a 25-cent house party. It was at these gatherings that we began testing our mettle by sipping cheap wine; the boys always kept a supply in the basement of whatever house the party was in. The guys and girls would gather downstairs and get down, drinking and making out.

For the most part, we never gave too much serious thought to anything. But in early 1960 things began to change. For one thing, Milton began to fade from our lives. At first he just missed a rehearsal every now and then, or maybe a show. But as time passed, Milton became harder to get in touch with, and sometimes he just disappeared. We later found out that Milton's arm, which he had injured in a serious car accident, had become gangrenous, and he was hospitalized. Things with the Primes had not been going smoothly, and they drifted away from Milton and broke up. But while their career had gone on ice, after less than a year of hard work, ours was just heating up. We had something great with Marvin, so we took it upon ourselves to run our own rehearsals at Betty's house.

We weren't about to let Milton's disappearance affect us, and we'd built up enough momentum under his aegis to keep us in jobs for the foreseeable future. Still, show business is a rough business, and Milton had protected us. There was no telling what might happen to us out on our own. Milton Jenkins saw potential in kids that sometimes even they didn't see. He gave us direction and taught us about discipline. Milton's departure signaled the beginning of some very rough times.

As the Primettes became established, we began to feel like we were leading a double life. On one hand, we were devoting everything to singing. On the other, Flo, Diane, and I still had two years of high

48

school ahead. We were thrilled when people around town started recognizing us. The Primettes sang at one of Diane's school functions at Cass. She still had not been accepted by the Hexagons. Sometimes I would go with her to one of their parties. I never knew if she had actually been invited, but she took me along with her anyway, for backup, I think.

I have to give her credit for persistence. She was finally invited to join the sorority. This was what she'd been working for, and she would do anything they asked, even if it meant scrubbing a floor with a toothbrush. I knew that she wanted to be a Hexagon more than anything, and once she got in, she acted like she'd pulled a real coup and was justifiably proud. The sorority gave picnics and parties, which were a lot of fun.

Diane enjoyed being away at school. Cass was more like a college campus than a high school, and I suppose that had some appeal for Diane. But whereas I lived for the time after school to spend with the group, Diane didn't seem to mind being away from us.

I always enjoyed school; I found meeting other kids and making new friends exciting. I also liked learning new things, even though I wasn't a bookworm. I got good grades with little effort. Flo, on the other hand, really didn't like school very much. She was smart, but not really interested.

The only time I got to see Flo was at rehearsals. Luckily, Jesse Greer began rehearsing us at the Brewster Center. Jesse had been working for Mrs. Murphy, playing music at her fashion shows. Mrs. Murphy taught cosmetology, modeling, and hairstyling at her House of Beauty. Her school turned out the majority of Detroit's black models and beauticians. When Diane and my cousin Josephine took classes in cosmetology, I became their favorite guinea pig/model, and between the two of them my hair changed from one week to the next —from red to brown with blond streaks, to anything else.

Jesse's knowledge of and interest in music made him seem like a real professional to us. He tried to inspire us, and he encouraged me to take more leads; he also told Diane not to sing through her nose so much. Like many people, including me, Jesse believed that if Flo would sing more, she would really catch on, and that the Primettes could make it. At that time, I thought Flo had the best lead voice, then Diane, then me. Betty wasn't singing that many leads at the time; she really had no aspirations to be a singer and was more or less in the group for fun. But Jesse tried to convince me that I would have a stronger lead voice if I would just project more. He thought that I lacked confidence. Maybe I did. Ultimately, though, we split the leads evenly, with me taking all the ballads.

Jesse taught us the standards and classic ballads and how to sing harmony. The ballads were a real challenge for all of us. Songs like "Canadian Sunset" and "Moonlight in Vermont" were among our favorites. We always loved singing any song that called for complex three- or four-part harmonies. We spent hours at the Brewster Center learning the intricate harmonies of the Mills Brothers and the Four Freshmen. As far as the leads went, though, I could see that a rivalry over the singing was already brewing between Diane and Flo.

We felt almost lost without a manager, but we did the best we could. Around this time, I began to notice in Diane a different kind of aggressiveness. Diane was always one to do it by the book. Having studied fashion at Cass, she was certain that she knew everything, and no matter what someone else did, if it didn't follow the rules, Diane would comment on it. I had started wearing what were considered some pretty wild color combinations—pink with red, electric blue with kelly green. Today this style is in vogue, but back then the style was to wear more subtle colors. I wasn't wearing these colors just to be different—though it did look that way; I honestly thought I looked great. One day, I was wearing all blue and green, and Diane said, "Mary, what are you wearing? You know you can't wear that—those colors don't go together."

"Why not?" I replied. "I think they look fine."

"Well, because you can't. Those colors just don't go together." Then she would look at me like I was crazy. It was hard to be offended by her attitude; it was just the way Diane was.

The culmination of our dreams came when we took first place in the Detroit/Windsor Freedom Festival amateur talent contest in July 1960. The festival, an annual event held just across the river from Detroit in Windsor, Canada, was sponsored by radio stations on both sides of the border. The contest was open to all amateur performers, but to participate we needed our parents' permission. That seemed easy enough to get, but when Diane mentioned going there, her father refused to permit it. Diane's father put his foot down; she was not going to Windsor.

We went ahead with daily rehearsals anyway, convinced that we could get Mr. Ross to change his mind. Each of us approached him individually, and then we all spoke to him together, to plead on Diane's behalf, but Mr. Ross, who was usually fairly easygoing, was firm about this. "Diane," he would say, "what about your schooling? You're putting a lot of time into this singing group."

Actually, we probably weren't putting much more time into it than we had a year or so earlier, when we started. But the closer we got to graduation, the more our parents began to worry that we might be singing instead of going to college. Mr. Ross was trying to reason with her, but Diane would have none of it. She wasn't crying, but she was chewing her nails, and you could tell by the way she looked at her father that nothing was going to stop her from going. We took her father's disapproval very seriously. Sure, we had snuck out with boys and told the occasional white lie. But disobeying a parent was still considered the wrong thing to do. Somehow, Diane worked it all out, and we went to Windsor.

Living in Detroit with Canada just across the river, I had never thought of it as another country. Most of the other young performers who were going there, though, saw it as an international event. It was the most exciting and prestigious amateur competition in the area.

Having spent the previous weeks practicing, we felt ready for the big day. We were surprised at the wide range of acts on the bill. There were not only other doo-wop groups, but belly dancers and ventriloquists, including my high school friend Willie Tyler and his dummy Lester. I particularly remember a gay male dancer named Oscar Huckleby; he looked like the actor Geoffrey Holder.

Finally we were on. All I remember clearly was that we were introduced and went onstage. It was so thrilling to be standing up in front of several thousand people. Once we started singing we had no idea how strong our chances of winning were. We could see that the crowd—which included people of all ages and races—was up and moving and having the time of their lives while we were on. From where we stood, the audience seemed to be in a frenzy. I can't recall all the numbers we performed, but the songs that put us over were our old standby, "(Night Time Is) The Right Time," "The Twist," and "There Goes My Baby." On "Night Time," while Flo sang the deeper blues part, the audience looked amazed; then, when Diane took her high part, the whole place just went crazy.

After the show, we waited for the winners to be announced. I had my fingers crossed, but with all the other talented performers there, I wouldn't have been surprised if someone else had won. When we heard our names called out, we were screaming with joy. This was the highlight of our career thus far; we had really made it. Interestingly, unbeknownst to us, there were scouts in the audience, including some from Motown. Years later, some people would claim that Robert Bateman, one of Berry Gordy's early associates, had seen us there and told Berry about us. But we were never approached by anyone that day.

We were all flying higher than kites, and with our prize money—a whopping $15, the first money we'd ever earned performing—we set out for the carnival to celebrate.

After losing Milton, we each took a share of the responsibility for running the group. As secretary, it was my duty to collect and manage the money. We changed from our stage outfits and set out for the park. Every place we went, people we knew were congratulating us. We happily roamed around spending money on rides and snacks. After we'd each exhausted our personal funds, we decided to split up the prize money.

"Mary, where's the prize money?" Diane asked.

I reached into my pocket, but it was empty. I tried all my other pockets, but still nothing. I prided myself on being honest and responsible, and I knew I had put the money in my pocket. But it was gone. When I told the others that I must have lost it, Diane teased, "Are you sure you haven't been spending it on your rides and stuff, Mary?"

I didn't even try to defend myself. We traced our steps back to all the places we'd been that day, but to no avail. Though Diane's attitude was upsetting, I wasn't so much angry as I was hurt, and I quietly punished myself for being so careless.

Later that night, Marv said, "My friend Richard Morris said for me to tell you that you should come over to Motown."

"Well," I reasoned aloud, "we've got to make a record somewhere. If other groups can do it, I know we can too if we sound as good as we sounded today."

I made that statement with all the confidence in the world. All day long the five of us had been strutting and prancing around, acting very much like the stars we felt we were. It must have been that, having won this contest, we sensed that our days as amateurs were numbered. We had to go pro, and the only way to do that was to cut a record.

"Isn't Motown the record company that cheats its artists?" Flo asked suspiciously. We'd all heard the rumors about the up-and-coming company, and in our naïveté we assumed that all other small record labels were totally honest, and Motown was an aberration. For that reason alone, we initially dismissed the idea of going to Motown. We knew that once we got back home we'd have to make some serious decisions about where the Primettes were headed, but for tonight all we wanted was to revel in our success.

After a couple weeks back in Detroit, we realized that we knew nothing about the record business, and so, after much thought and discussion, we decided to approach Motown after all. It was the newest company and seemed most open to fresh young talent. Before Diane's family had moved to the Projects, they had lived in the same neighborhood as Smokey Robinson, and she knew his cousin, Sylvia. We knew that the Miracles had been working at Motown and had a hit with "Got a Job," an "answer" record to the Silhouettes' smash "Get a Job." Smokey had formed the group with some high school friends—Ronnie White, Peter Moore, and cousins Bobby and Sonny Rogers. Sonny had left the group and his sister Claudette had stepped in. They had been around just a brief time before Berry discovered them. In our eyes, the Miracles were big stars with important connections, so Diane talked to Sylvia, and Sylvia talked to Smokey. He said that we could audition for the Miracles first. If we were good, he might talk to Berry Gordy on our behalf.

We planned to meet the Miracles after school at the Rogerses' house, where they rehearsed in the living room. Many girls found Smokey very attractive, with his light reddish hair, fair skin, and beautiful gray-green eyes. We were dying to make a great impression, so we tried to dress as sharp as we could. We took special pains to warn Marvin to be on time. Our guitarist was our pride and joy, and we wanted to be sure everything would run smoothly. Because Diane knew Smokey, she did most of the talking and made the introductions. I also knew Bobby Rogers. He was a year ahead of me in school, so I didn't know him that well, but I had admired him from afar. He had a reputation for being a ladies' man, and with his beautiful smile, quick wit, and gorgeous processed hair, all the girls thought he was an absolute dreamboat.

It came time for us to show our stuff, and without hesitation Flo launched into the verse of "(Night Time Is) The Right Time," and we all fell into our parts. Next we did "There Goes My Baby," and finished up with "There's Something on Your Mind," one of the songs where I took the lead.

Smokey seemed to like us, and when he promised to introduce us at Motown, we were thrilled. Soon, however, it was evident that Smokey was even more interested in Marvin. Smokey was asking Marvin if he could play this song or that song, or this chord or that chord, and Marvin shyly complied with all of Smokey's requests. At the end, Smokey asked Marvin if he could go on a short trip with the Miracles.

"Well, you have to ask the girls," Marvin replied softly.

We all sort of said yes, thinking that it might be good for Marvin to go with Smokey on this one little trip. Little did we know that we had lost Marvin forever. Marvin's been with Smokey ever since then, and has co-written some of the Miracles' and some of Marvin Gaye's greatest hits.

A short time later, Richard Morris, a young writer and engineer at Hitsville whom Marvin Tarplin had told about us, agreed to see us. The appointment with Berry Gordy was set. We couldn't help thinking about all the rumors we had heard. We knew, though, that we had to make a record; it was our main concern. Our faith in ourselves would surely pull us through.

At this time, the Miracles were company pets. Not only were they recording steadily, but Smokey was writing songs with Berry and beginning to show promise as a producer. Being a small organization, Motown looked to everyone there to contribute in more than one area. The Miracles were young, enthusiastic, and hardworking—everything Berry respected. Also, Berry was Smokey's mentor. We had faith that we could carry the audition on our own, but having Smokey and the Miracles as friends and supporters convinced us we'd be in at Motown in no time.

Our audition for Mr. Gordy was set up for sometime in the late summer of 1960. We all met there after school. I remember the four of us walking toward the building and the impression it made on me. It was, in fact, a small nondescript two-story house that had been converted to a photography studio. But as we approached, the big letters on the front that read HITSVILLE U.S.A. seemed to loom over us. In the window was a poster that read "The Sound of Young America." Flo was her usual confident self, and I remember Betty taking long strides ahead of me. Diane and I just kept quiet, though in our silence we each worked hard at being charming. I just wanted to see and remember every little detail. Once we were there, all our doubts about Motown seemed to fade. This could really be it, and we knew it. No records, no career.

Once in the tiny, bare reception area, I was relieved to see a familiar face. Seated behind the front desk was Janie Bradford, whom we had met during our days with Milton Jenkins. We were surprised to see her there. She greeted us warmly and suggested we wait in the lobby, a small area to the left of her desk.

The time we spent waiting couldn't have been much longer than an hour, but it felt like a year. I must have memorized every inch of that room. There was the plate-glass display window and the only thing to sit on was a long, hard upholstered bench, like the ones you find in a doctor's office. Speaking in a whisper, Flo reiterated that we should not appear too eager, that Motown's reputation was none too good. Flo had a cocky attitude about this whole business; she thought that a company like Motown should consider itself lucky that groups as good as the Primettes would even be willing to record with them. I'd have liked to believe that one myself, but it just wasn't true. We would be the lucky ones. To lighten up the atmosphere, Betty kept on making little jokes, while Diane sat quietly, trying to appear sophisticated and worldly. I was silent except to giggle at a joke or answer with a brief remark. Our attempts at being cool were pretty successful, at least until Barrett Strong walked through the lobby. We knew his song "Money," but didn't recognize him until Janie told us who he was. In an instant we became as skittish as kittens.

We were finally shown into the studio and introduced to Richard Morris, Robert Bateman, talent scout and producer, and Berry Gordy. I was surprised to see that the big man everybody in Detroit was talking about was actually small, about five feet seven inches tall. He wasn't what you'd call handsome, but he exuded a certain confidence that hinted he could take care of himself. Berry was nice enough to us, but he seemed much more serious about things than other people I'd met in the music business. I sensed that his mind was clicking every moment, even when he was talking to us. And although he could make anyone feel at ease, if you were smart you knew that there was something going on behind his smile.

The audition began. Richard basically handled it; Berry would go in and out of the room. I remember thinking how small everything was. Once we were in position, Richard gave us the cue to start singing. Since the Miracles had absconded with Marvin, we had to sing our four songs a cappella: "There Goes My Baby," "Night Time," "The Twist," and "There's Something on Your Mind." Undaunted, we gave this private show our all, pulling out all the stops to make it great.

Though we were concentrating on our performance, we were

each trying to read all their faces. He listened very attentively and seemed most interested in our rendition of "There Goes My Baby," on which Diane sang lead. Not everyone cared for Diane's voice, which was sometimes shrill, but Berry seemed to like it.

At the end, Berry told us that he liked the song and us, but he was not offering us a recording contract. In a very serious tone, he said we should come back after we all had finished school. (The press has mythologized this little incident, making it sound like Berry gave us this advice because he felt that we shouldn't quit school, and that may have been at least partially true. But ultimately the real reason for Berry's initial refusal was business. The last thing Berry wanted at this early stage of his career was the responsibility for four female minors. And this gave Berry a good out, so he didn't have to even consider us again for the next year or so. As it happened, when we eventually did sign, three of us were still in school.)

We respectfully listened to Berry's pronouncement. If we had not been so young or so shy or so intimidated, we would have told him that we were good girls and to give us a chance. But he was an adult and we were just kids. Smiling sweetly, he dismissed us.

CHAPTER 6

We didn't want to leave after the audition. The atmosphere at Hitsville was charged with excitement; everyone there seemed to believe that great things were going to happen. The fact that Berry Gordy did not sign us then only fueled our desire to be part of Motown—officially or otherwise. We were forced to make last-ditch efforts; without a record, our singing careers were as good as over. We simply would not take Berry's no for an answer. The day we auditioned and were refused, we just couldn't bring ourselves to get up and leave.

We returned to the reception area, feeling both numb and all wound up from singing. Janie was talking on the telephone, obviously too busy for us, so we just all sat down on the long bench and watched the parade passing through. The first afternoon there we met Eddie and Brian Holland, two short but very good-looking brothers. Eddie was very outgoing, intelligent, and opinionated. He had a head full of curls, half slicked back with grease to create the illusion that it was processed. Brian seemed very quiet, but he had a mischievous look that made you wonder just how quiet he really was.

We also met Norman Whitfield, a young producer, and two of Motown's biggest stars, Marv Johnson and Mary Wells. This was turning out to be our lucky day after all. We knew that this was where we belonged.

We agreed that it would be in our best interests to go to Hitsville each and every day after school. Even without a manager, we were rehearsing on our own at Betty's. We were convinced that someday Hitsville would have to give in and record us, and we wanted to be ready. Every day we would hitch rides with friends to West Grand Boulevard, and the four of us would meet outside the lobby.

Even while we worked our way up to the better clubs, we were still doing the hops. Because our audience was mostly made up of teenagers, we would rush to change from our "glamorous" stage outfits—or uniforms, as we called them—and put on our bobby sox, saddle shoes, and tight skirts, so that we could hang out with the other kids after the show. It was all so much fun. Still, nothing beat hanging out at Hitsville.

The building on West Grand Boulevard was a home away from home for many young singers and musicians then. The company was still serving hot family-style meals for everyone who happened to be around. Those of us who loved Motown remember fondly these times of special closeness and friendship. Things were still fairly casual then, and we were allowed to watch artists—including Mary Wells, Mabel John, Henry Lumpkin, Barrett Strong, Richard "Popcorn" Wiley, and the Rayber Voices—record. We tried to learn as much as we could, and in those days there were plenty of people to watch; young performers seemed to find their way there in droves. The negative rumors about Motown deterred very few; it was still one of the few places in Detroit a young musician or singer could make a buck or get the chance to really succeed.

We got to know Richard Morris, a tall young recording engineer and musician who had been working with Berry in different capacities for a couple of years. Richard had been the leader of a street gang called the Shakers, but he had cleaned up his act. He'd been friendly with us, and there had been some discussion that we might be used to cut some background vocals, but nothing was really happening for us. One day, after we'd been hanging around Hitsville for a couple of months, I began nagging him in a kidding manner.

"When are we going to make our own record, Richard?" I asked.

Diane piped in, "We need to get in the studio and make a recording for the Primettes." Flo and Betty both gave Richard meaningful glares. We were acting as if it were his fault that we hadn't been assigned a producer or cut a record—and we didn't even have a contract!

"After all," Diane reminded him, "you told Marvin Tarplin that we should come here in the first place. Can't you talk to the big man, or something? We're getting tired of sitting around here doing practically nothing."

Richard just laughed and shook his head. "I'll see what I can do." Richard voiced our grievances to Berry, but in the end Berry told Richard that our ages still "bothered" him and he just couldn't be involved with us now. "Well, man," Richard suggested, "let me work with them on the side when I finish my job here." Berry agreed to that.

Richard later gave us the news along with his assurances that he believed in the Primettes and that someday soon we would be making records. Over the next few months we worked with Richard, ceasing our daily visits to Hitsville. Richard helped us run our rehearsals, and we were confident that we would end up back on West Grand Boulevard eventually. This was just a temporary detour; we were well on our way.

With Richard and his friend Homer Davis in charge, the Primettes' bookings increased. Things were on the upswing again, and Richard was working hard to bring the Primettes to the attention of anyone in the industry who might help us. By this point, we needed his support and were grateful for anything he could do.

Because we rarely had time to change after school before rehearsal, we dressed as nicely as we could each morning. No doubt we were some of the sharpest-dressed girls at our schools. Though we weren't wearing our stage uniforms to class, we dressed so that our clothes blended in terms of color and style. None of us had a lot to spend on clothes, but by borrowing from one another, we did all right. Judging from the reactions of the young men whom we met at school or who made up our audiences before, during, and after rehearsals, our efforts were not in vain.

Working with Richard got us into some of the bigger places, like the Graystone Ballroom or the Twenty Grand, where we played on the same bill with such stars as the Falcons, whose big hit was "You're So Fine," and Wilson Pickett. We were working all over Detroit. Other acts on the bills were usually established recording artists like the Isley Brothers, Eddie Holland (who was still singing), Johnny Mathis, and Joe and Al (the Joe in the team was Johnny Bristol, who later co-wrote "Someday We'll Be Together"). The Primettes were the opening act, and our spot on the bill was obviously less prestigious, but we were sure that would change with time. The constant exposure to more experienced singers helped us polish our own act. There were hundreds of teenage singers like ourselves, dying to get a foot in the door. I recall Martha Reeves and her group, the Del-Phis, making the same rounds for jobs as we did. The competition was so keen that we were thankful to be able to work as often as we did and in such good places.

Richard had a very good rapport with our parents, earning their trust with his sincere manner. He took his responsibility for us very seriously. Richard was not always the easiest person to get along with, but because he worked so hard for us, he was easy to forgive. I began to hang out with him. I wanted to learn about everything that was going on and I felt uncomfortable always having to play the diplomat in group crises. Richard and I would have long talks about things in general, and he treated me like a younger sister.

I was flattered when he told me that I had "intelligence, wit, and softness." I also knew that he liked Betty and had the utmost respect for Flo. His problem was with Diane. Though he admired her and liked her, she did things that tried his patience. Once Richard became upset when I asked why he always got angry with Diane for being sick. After all, I reasoned, when someone's sick, they're sick. But Richard didn't buy that. He thought Diane's excuses were pretty flimsy and that it was just her personality.

He was very good about treating the four of us equally and showing no favoritism. He was also patient, no matter how late I was. Most important, he really believed in us.

But things were never calm for too long. Our problems now seemed to come from inside the group. Diane had stopped being a tomboy and was becoming a real lady. Still, her stubbornness about certain things was almost childlike. Often, when Diane would demand to sing a particular song, for example, Betty would step in and say something to her. Because Betty was a year or so older than Flo and I, she had more leverage with Diane. Even Richard came to depend on Betty to help with Diane.

Richard was no wimp, but once Diane set her mind to do something, no one could stop her. Richard had been around; he knew that some of the places we played weren't the nicest, and that men in the audience could be very aggressive. We were working some tough places—sometimes illegally—and Richard once had his shirt torn off by some guys who tried to get at us while we were onstage in Lansing, Michigan. Richard set down rules about how we were to behave at the shows. We were not to talk with or mingle with any of the audience; our only contact with the crowd was our performance. Aside from concerns about our safety, Richard also knew that an unattainable performer has a special mystique.

Diane regularly defied Richard, and once, at the Graystone Ballroom, she jumped out onto the floor and started dancing with a guy. When Richard tried to stop her, she said some unladylike things to him, pouted, and kept on dancing. Richard was about to grab Diane and drag her off the floor, but instead he called Betty over. Betty just walked out to Diane, talked to her for a few minutes, and Diane came back.

We looked to Betty to act as a big sister on behalf of Flo and me, to nip Diane's little displays in the bud. That worked until Betty began to lose interest in the Primettes; she had less time to dedicate to it and she had less invested in it. While those two facts may have made her less prone to start something with Diane, they also gave her an advantage in dealing with her. If for some reason Betty left, it wouldn't be the end of the world for her. She was still having fun with it, but that's all the Primettes meant to her.

I saw the group as something bigger and more important than any one of us. I was content to play on the team. Diane didn't feel that way about things, and her attitude was obvious to everyone we worked with, especially Richard. "I want to keep everyone even with each other," he once said. "That's why I wrote a song for you and a song for Diane." But Richard's efforts weren't enough to keep things in balance.

Looking back, I shouldn't have been surprised to see that, as our career grew, so did feelings of competitiveness, jealousy, and distrust. It upset me once in a while, but I became an expert at stifling my feelings if I thought expressing them would endanger the group. No doubt part of my reactions stemmed from my dealings with I.V. as a child. While I felt very strongly about what was right and what was wrong, my belief that things would work themselves out and my fear of being responsible for destroying our dreams usually won out. Instead of keeping a scorecard on who was doing what to whom, I focused all my energies on singing.

Like many young performers, I was so wrapped up in the music that I did not see what was happening on the business side. Perhaps we thought so little about that part of our careers because we never made any amount of money worth worrying about. Too late we would discover that we had been featured on a bill advertising a show with such performers as Jackie Wilson. We'd arrive to perform and when the promised star failed to appear, we would suffer the unhappy audience's wrath. As it turned out, the stars had never been contacted. It was simply advertising to draw a crowd.

I later worked after school at a record shop. Now that I was earning money, I spent more on clothes. I loved finally getting to wear nice stockings and spent hours just trying to get the seams to run in a sexy straight line up the back of my skinny legs. Skinny or not, I was determined to show them off to the best advantage.

Diane had a job working at Hudson's department store, so she was buying more clothes, too. To us, as teenage girls, wardrobe was everything. We would spend hours discussing the length of skirts, what colors and what fabrics were fashionable, and what accessories to wear with everything. Flo, Betty, and I consulted one another constantly about these issues and each of us kept abreast of what the others were planning to wear. Characteristically, after we'd all agreed how we'd dress, Diane would turn up at the last minute in something entirely different. With hindsight, one can see that Diane had a plan.

One day late that summer, Betty suddenly announced that she was leaving the Primettes; she was getting married. Since her house had become our favorite rehearsal site, we'd become closer, and we were disappointed and frightened by our "big sister"'s departure. Even though Betty was just a little over a year older, at our age that was a significant difference. I thought she loved the group as much as we did. She'd broken up with Paul Williams and found someone else. I guess having a marriage and a family was more important to her. We did everything we could to convince her to stay with us, but her mind was made up. We stayed in touch, and Flo and I attended her wedding that fall.

The most difficult part for us to accept was the prospect of finding a girl to take her place. The three of us had rehearsed together at times and knew we sounded fine as a trio, but in those days singing groups had a minimum of four members. For the Primettes to go on as a trio was unthinkable. And what would our harmonies sound like on all the songs we'd perfected with four parts? Deep inside, I think we knew we could handle the singing; subconsciously, though, Flo and I realized that, with Betty gone, it would be hard to hold Diane back.

Betty's announcement was quite a jolt for all of us, but nothing compared to what lay ahead. Sometime later that fall, we stopped hearing from Flo. She wouldn't show up for rehearsals, and she would not come to the phone when we called. Diane and I were confused. Finally Mrs. Ballard answered the phone one day and told us that Flo no longer wanted to sing with us. She offered no further explanation. Flo not wanting to sing? We just couldn't believe it. One minute we were a group on the rise—the next minute, it was just me and Diane.

We knew that Mrs. Ballard had never really approved of Flo singing so much. She wanted to see her daughter make something of herself, and a singer was not what she had in mind. Knowing this, we greeted Mrs. Ballard's explanation with some skepticism. It all seemed very unlike Flo. We were both upset, but all we could do was meet each other after school, put in a call to Flo, then spend the rest of the day talking about it. As the days wore on, Diane became upset with Flo for not calling, regardless of what had happened. Flo was our friend, and she knew we depended on her. Why was she acting this way?

We would talk about getting new members, but we knew that the group would not be as dynamic without Flo. Looking back now, I feel that had Diane not seen Flo's energy as one of our main assets, she would have been just as happy to replace her.

We continued to call Flo's house every single day, but she never came to the phone. With the passing weeks our apprehension turned to fear. Something had to be wrong with Flo; something terrible had happened. But if so, why hadn't she told us? We were her best friends. None of it made any sense. How could a group that was making so much headway, that had had such potential, just lose it like that? I was learning some of life's hardest lessons: not to depend on anyone, to accept all of life's surprises, no matter what, and, finally, that nothing is ever permanent. I couldn't accept all this. It wasn't fair.

Weeks passed without word from Flo. We'd call every few days or so and get the usual response—"She doesn't want to talk to you"— and go back to our daydreams. Somehow Diane and I would pull it all back together again, but the longer we went without rehearsing or performing, the further the possibility seemed to slip from our grasp.

Our prayers were answered when Flo finally called. She nonchalantly asked, "How's everything been going?" She sounded distant and very strange when she asked if the three of us could get together the next day. Diane was obviously relieved, but acted as if Flo really had a lot of nerve just to call us like that, so casually, as if nothing had happened. As far as Diane was concerned, Blondie had better come with a good excuse.

We arranged to meet. The appointed time came and went and still no Flo. As the minutes ticked by, I began to get scared. Something was very wrong.

The minute I laid eyes on Flo all my gravest fears were confirmed. She was like another person. There was a faraway look in her eyes that was frightening. Everything about her was different. There was no sign that she was happy to see us, her skin was incredibly pale, and she had circles under eyes so large and dark that she seemed to be wearing a mask. Usually a hip dresser, Flo looked unkempt, and her labored steps made it seem as if she were in a trance.

Everything about Flo seemed to be running in slow motion. She'd start to say something, utter a few words, then falter, as if she had forgotten what she wanted to say. She was never totally comfortable being intimate with anyone, and today she avoided making eye contact with either of us, just staring straight ahead at nothing.

After some small talk, Flo eased her way into telling us what had happened. Her calm recitation of the facts had the mesmerizing quality of a primitive story.

It had all started one night several weeks before at the Graystone Ballroom. It was one of Frantic Ernie Durham's sock hops, which were considered safe entertainment for teens, since no alcohol was served and the admission was only 50 cents. This night, Flo was going to the dance with her brother Billy; Flo wasn't dating that much, and Mrs. Ballard would never let any of her daughters go out alone. Sometime during the evening the two got separated, but even when it began to get late, Flo didn't worry. Most of the kids were leaving, so she just stood near the door, expecting to see Billy any moment.

Someone called out her name, and, thinking it was Billy, Flo ran out to a car waiting in a darkened area beside the ballroom. At first she didn't recognize the fellow, but as he pulled his car closer to the curb, she realized he was someone she'd met, either through one of her brothers or maybe Jesse. The important thing was that she knew him and he could give her a lift home.

Once inside the car, Flo sat quietly. He didn't seem interested in conversation, so Flo hummed along to the radio, thinking how fortunate she was not to have to take a bus alone. Suddenly she noticed that none of the streets was familiar; the driver was on Woodward, but headed in the opposite direction of her home. When she told him he was making a mistake, he just kept on driving without saying a word. It was then that Flo knew something was wrong.

A sickening feeling came over her as he pulled the car to an abrupt stop on a dark, empty street. When Flo asked him why they'd stopped, he told her he was going to have sex with her. Though her initial shock had given way to fear, Flo still tried to act tough, and she bravely demanded that he take her home immediately. But he wasn't listening.

At this point in the story, Flo stopped and couldn't start talking again. Tears welled up in her eyes, and some time passed before she could speak again. Diane and I tried to comfort her, but we were scared too. Nothing like this had ever happened to anyone we knew, at least not to our knowledge. Finally Flo mumbled something nearly unintelligible. The only word I could make out was "knife." I leaned closer to Flo and asked her to repeat it, and as I came nearer to her I knew what people meant when they said fear has a smell. Flo's fear was almost tangible. I could see her suffering, and her eyes reflected a gamut of emotions—fright, embarrassment, distrust. I was shocked to realize some of those feelings were directed at Diane and me.

Finally Flo's words erupted from her. As her tears fell, she told us about how before she knew it, the man had put the knife to her throat and forced her into the backseat. She vainly tried to fight him off, but he wouldn't be stopped. He ripped away her panties and began fondling and kissing her all over. Flo was a virgin; she didn't understand what he was trying to do. She was repulsed and scared for her life. When she pleaded with him to stop because she'd never had sex, he ignored her. All she could say to us was, "He hurt me."

Worse than the rape itself was his attitude. When he had finished with her, he acted as if nothing had happened. He was sure she was just lying—that she knew the score. When he dropped her off at her house, he said, "Why are you so upset? The way you walk around . . ." The next day Flo wouldn't even remember where she was or the ride home. His words, though, would be with her always.

"Why did he do it?" Flo repeated over and over again. "I trusted him. I thought he was my friend. Why did he do it?"

Neither Diane nor I nor anyone in the world could ever answer that. Finally knowing what had happened to our friend left us more confused than ever. The brutality Flo had suffered at the hands of someone she trusted was beyond our comprehension. Before this day, boys had been just cute and fun and sweet. We knew now the world was a darker, uglier place.

All women who are raped suffer, some in different ways than others. In Flo's case the betrayal of trust was the greatest shock. Despite her self-assured attitude, she was an innocent. From this day on, I'd see Flo's basic personality undergo a metamorphosis, from being reticent and shy with a sassy front to being skeptical, cynical, and afraid of everyone and everything. We could never have pictured Flo needing help. Her will had brought the Primettes together, and few people would ever try to mess with her. But all that had changed.

My heart was wrenched at the thought of Flo's suffering. My anger over the fact that someone could do this to my friend faded into a quiet fear as I realized that what happened to Flo could have happened to any one of us, including me. When I saw Flo's pain, I became angry with Mrs. Ballard for keeping Flo from us when she needed her friends so badly. I know that Mrs. Ballard was only protecting Flo, but now I began to think about how little anyone could protect anybody, no matter how hard they tried. After this incident, Mrs. Ballard would try to keep Flo further and further from the rest of the world. Her family's love for Flo would become a guarded fortress, with Flo sequestered inside and everyone outside considered a stranger, an enemy. From this day on, Flo would turn to them, not us, and their advice would color her every move.

Flo never mentioned the rape to us again, except when she had to go to the police station to pick her attacker out of a lineup, and later when she testified against him in court. Flo was one of the very few women who ever get to see their rapists convicted and sent to prison. We all tried to be as supportive as we could, but the ordeal of the trial extracted yet another toll from Flo.

There was no question that Flo needed psychiatric help, but, living in an area where acutely ill kids were lucky to see a family doctor, we didn't think in those terms. Her family's background and attitude toward such things was old-fashioned; Mrs. Ballard believed that a mother's love could cure anything. In the meantime, Flo kept having nightmares. Her self-esteem and self-image had been shattered; she became vulnerable in so many ways. Walking down the street with her, I'd catch her looking over her shoulder or off in the distance, checking out every man who even vaguely resembled the man who had raped her.

During the time we'd lost contact with Flo, she had also stopped going to school. Now she was trying to pick up the pieces, and getting back with the group was her first step back into the world. School came next. She soon became wholeheartedly involved with the Primettes again, and I believe this was therapeutic for her. On the outside, she started acting like the old Flo we knew. In our ignorance, we assumed that this meant everything would be all right. But her new belief that no one—not even friends—could be trusted would haunt her for the rest of her life.

Diane and I never discussed it again, not even between ourselves. I chalk that up to our youth. But even today most people still don't know how to respond to rape. What Flo experienced was just a variation of what we now call date rape. Men read different messages in women's mannerisms, dress, words. A rapist's favorite explanation is that the victim "really wanted it," even if she screamed and tried to fight. In Flo's case, her body and her attitude sent a message that told this guy what he did was okay.

The man who raped Flo killed part of her that night. My friend was never the same.

CHAPTER 7

Both Diane and I told Jesse that we wished he and Flo were still going together. Flo's moodiness was beginning to worry us, and since Jesse was the only person outside the group or her family whom she told about the rape, we thought that if they were back together, Flo would be happy again. Meanwhile, whatever doubts Mrs. Ballard had about Flo's being in the group intensified. She thought it was a waste of time, and I now wonder if she would have let Flo go on at all if it weren't for Jesse. After the rape, Jesse had to promise Mrs. Ballard he would walk her home and make sure she got in early after our rehearsals at Brewster Center.

Jesse was probably the only other person who truly knew Flo well, and the change in her after the rape bothered him as much as it did us. "Flo changed after her attack," he once said. "She was a different person. She used to be a little mischievous, and had that haughty air. She was really happy. After that, there was no laughter, no fun left in her."

We were relieved to have Flo back and be a group again, but the weeks in limbo had destroyed our momentum. And we still hadn't replaced Betty. We had lost so much precious time; making a record took on new urgency. We got back to playing all the local places we could, including the Twenty Grand Club, *the* nightspot. Frantic Ernie Durham and the other sock-hop jocks were still hiring us, too. We loved it but began to feel we had sort of outgrown it, too.

Flo's disappearance hadn't dampened Richard Morris' enthusiasm for working with us, and so, that fall, his plan for us went into action. He arranged for us to begin recording for Robert West at the Flick and Contour studios. At the time, Flick and Contour were pretty hot. The group the Contours, for example, took their name from the label, and among the artists recording with West then were the Falcons.

68

Unlike Milton, Richard could not afford to support the Primettes financially. We made the best of our homemade costumes and followed our own instincts about hairstyles, makeup, and the fine points of staging. Still, Robert West liked us enough to record us. We were thrilled when he told us a new label would be created just for us—LuPine. Why that name was chosen, I'm not sure. Richard had two songs for us: "Tears of Sorrow," for which Richard had recorded the music tracks at Hitsville, and which Diane would sing lead on; and a rock ballad, "Pretty Baby," for me. Once we learned the songs, we started rehearsing day and night.

The morning of the session, Richard, Flo, Diane, a male singer named Alonzo, and two other female singers, Barbara Randolph and Betty Kendrick, met and took the same bus down Woodward Avenue to the Flick studios. Richard brought along Betty and Barbara because he was worried that without Betty McGlown, our vocals wouldn't sound full enough. Richard was so furious with me for being late that he told Flo she could sing lead on "my" song, "Pretty Baby," and she would have if I hadn't gotten to the studio within minutes of the others. Punctuality was never one of my strong points.

The "studio" was actually the drab little basement of a small house on Forest Street. It was a hot day, but each of us wore our nicest cotton blouses and skirts with stockings—and matching shoes and bags, of course. When we walked in Wilson Pickett was there rehearsing with the Falcons. He looked and acted pretty much the same as he does now; he was what we considered a real street guy. He had just been chosen to assume Joe Stubbs' (the Four Tops' Levi's brother) place as the group's lead singer. Wilson was only one of many up-and-coming young stars we crossed paths with in the early years.

Richard had assembled a great backing band for us that included Falcons keyboardist Willie Schofield, Charlie Gabrielle on sax and flute, a guitarist named Eugene Crew, bassist Charlie O., drummer Benny Benjamin, and Marvin Tarplin, the onetime Primette.

Alonzo was a dark-skinned guy with shiny processed hair and a high falsetto. He may have been one of Richard's other clients. Richard was no doubt trying to economize, and so, before our session, we all sang backup on Alonzo's record, and on Eddie Floyd's. Next we did the backup for our first recording, "Tears of Sorrow," and Diane sang lead. We all liked "Tears" but were convinced that "Pretty Baby" would be the hit. Both songs were typical of the girl-group records out then—self-pitying lyrics about the boy who got away. Because our voices aren't really separated as clearly as they would be on later records, you can really hear Flo on the backgrounds, her strong, soulful voice overpowering everything—even Diane's lead on "Tears." (Years later, HDH would have Flo stand as far as seventeen feet from the microphone, while I stood right in front of it; that's how strong her voice was.)

Even our first recording session had to have problems. Diane and Barbara were arguing. Barbara thought we should all follow Richard's instructions to the letter, while Diane wanted to sing it her way; she didn't want to follow the melody line as closely as Richard wanted her to. Flo and I had become almost immune to Diane's little outbursts, but you could see that people who didn't know her well took these things to heart. Flo and I were too excited to pay much attention. After the session Willie Schofield gave us a ride back to the Flick and Contour offices, and a secretary there made us a big lunch. We ate our sandwiches and happily daydreamed aloud about our new "hit."

"Girl, do you think they'll play it on the radio soon?" Flo asked no one in particular.

"Blondie, they'll be playing 'Pretty Baby' all over the country soon," Betty Kendrick replied.

"I sure hope so," Flo said quietly.

"I know 'Pretty Baby' will be a big hit. I can just feel it!" As always, I was the most optimistic one, and why not? It was about time things started going our way.

That was the last time we ever saw Barbara and Betty again. Both later married; Barbara is a minister, and still singing in Detroit.

For some reason, Richard wasn't happy with "Pretty Baby," though he never let on about it to us. As far as we were concerned, it was enough just to hear our voices. In the end, however, what any of us thought didn't make one bit of difference. A few weeks after the session, with our first records pressed and ready to ship, Robert West's distributor, B&H—an independent black distributor in Detroit—was targeted for a payola investigation. Without anyone's guilt or innocence proven, our record was as good as gone. The news hit us like a bolt of lightning. The records were eventually released—about twenty years later, in Japan, and some found their way to Great Britain.

Our morale was slipping, and the revived feelings of unity the recording inspired were crushed by dissension. The one thing Richard could do for us now was help us find Betty McGlown's replacement. Not having a fourth member was threatening our bookings.

I was still very close to John L. and I.V. Pippin. I had never forgotten the love and warmth they'd given me, and after I moved to the Projects, I continued to visit them and keep up my childhood friendship with Jackie Burkes.

Jackie was singing in a group in southwest Detroit, but I was so confident that the Primettes were on to something that I tried to woo her to join us. Once, when it seemed that Flo was never coming back, I'd given Jackie a big sell about the Primettes and even introduced her to Diane over the phone. From the beginning she and Diane didn't get along, and Jackie could never understand why.

One day that fall, I took Diane over to John L. and I.V.'s house, where Jackie was going to audition for us. After we'd run through a few songs, I said, "Diane, see how nice our blend is?"

Diane made it obvious that she was anything but impressed; Jackie was confused and disheartened. "Maybe she doesn't want me," she said.

"Don't pay any attention to her," I replied. "She's funny like that. When you get to know her, it'll be fine."

"Mary," Jackie insisted, "this chick just doesn't like me."

We sang a couple more songs, like Gladys Knight and the Pips' "Letter Full of Tears," and we were having fun, but there was a definite lack of warmth between my two good friends. Finally Jackie told me to forget it. She could see how things would be with Diane and she wasn't interested. I tried to convince her otherwise, but after getting the cold shoulder from Diane, Jackie would have been crazy to pursue it. We were desperate for another girl, but I knew deep in my heart that Jackie had made the right decision.

Word was still out that the Primettes needed a fourth member. Like me, Flo had studied music all through school. One of her teachers, knowing that Flo's group needed another singer, remembered that Barbara Martin sang with Richard Street. Since Flo knew Richard, the teacher told Flo about Barbara, then Flo told Richard Morris. None of us knew Barbara personally, but we all knew she was the tall, pretty girl who danced like a dream every weekend at the Graystone Ballroom. We didn't even know if she could sing all that well, but we were hoping.

For some reason, I was the only Primette with Richard when we met Barbara. We could hear right away that Barbara was not a great singer, but she had a wonderful attitude about the Primettes that was very appealing. When we all got together a few days later, we all got along very well.

Flo and Barbara seemed to have an instant rapport, and we all got along beautifully. No matter how anyone acted toward Barbara, she could just win them over. Diane's ego was still smarting from Betty's reprimands, and so Barbara's open personality was a great help. The tension in the group caused by Diane's conflict with Betty disappeared. We'd suffered so many disappointments in such a short time —we'd only been together now a couple months short of two years— we really appreciated having Barbara around. Barbara joining marked a turning point in the group relationships. Feeling like a whole group again, the four of us couldn't have been happier. We assumed our cheerful dispositions and kept building one another up: We were great, we were stars, we were the Primettes. I was just happy that we were back on the track. I crossed my fingers and prayed that Barbara would have the commitment to stick with us. The prospect of another change was unthinkable.

The situation with LuPine was out of our hands. Years later, I would learn that B&H's problems with the payola investigators were the product of racism; only black distributors had been harassed. I was still too young to fully comprehend the significance of this.

Only days after we'd discovered Barbara, our gigs petered out, and we didn't hear from Richard for a few days. We gave it little thought until Flo told us that Richard had been arrested for a parole violation. Not again, we thought. We'd heard of the triple whammy, but our bad luck was running in fives and sixes. We questioned Flo, but she knew no more about it than we did. What were we going to do now? we wondered aloud to one another. We knew the answer: Go back to Berry Gordy and Motown. The only question was, would they want us?

Berry Gordy hailed from a prominent, middle-class Detroit family. His parents, Berry and Bertha, had moved up from the South in 1922, but, unlike most blacks who came North during that era, Berry Gordy, Sr.—or Pops, as we all called him—was an experienced businessman, having run and managed his family's farm after his father's death. In an environment where whites controlled most black people's property, Pops had saved his family's assets by learning all he could about business and law. He believed in hard work, discipline, and education, and, after several tough years in Detroit, eventually established his own businesses, including a printing shop. The eight Gordy children —Esther, Gwen, Anna, Loucye, Robert, Fuller, George, and Berry— would find varying degrees of success in life. None of the others would realize a dream as grand as Berry's.

Ironically, as a young man, Berry seemed to show the least promise of all the Gordy offspring. By the mid-fifties, at age twenty-seven, Berry had been a prize-fighter, serviceman, jazz record-store owner, auto assembly-line worker, and husband. He had children to support and no desire to join his brothers working in the family business. Berry had worked hard, but so far had failed to find either his niche or the kind of money he wanted. While living in his sister Loucye's house following his separation from his first wife, Thelma, Berry was writing songs.

The Flame Show Bar was the Apollo Theater of Detroit, and every major black performer played there at least once. For black entertainers, the Flame Show Bar was as prestigious as the Latin Quarter, New York's Copacabana, or the Hollywood Palladium. Many of the old-time performers who played there had started in vaudeville and burlesque. A few black artists then were fortunate enough to work both circuits, but they were the exception. In the fifties, though, Sam Cooke, Sarah Vaughan, Della Reese, Brook Benton, B. B. King, and Bill Williams were regulars at the Flame, and Berry's sisters Anna and Gwen, who ran the photography concession there, introduced their brother to anyone who would listen to his songs.

Knowing Berry as I do, I'm not surprised that he made headway as quickly as he did. He was confident and determined. There were lots of young entrepreneurs like Berry around in the fifties, and we were fortunate to meet and work with some of them. Milton, Jesse, Richard—they all had the same idea. In those days, some of these men were looked upon as hustlers and, to some degree, I guess they were. The music business, though, was unlike any other hustle. Smooth talk went only so far; sooner or later you had to deliver the goods. Berry started looking at other business people and companies, analyzing the way they worked with the same discriminating eye for detail and judgment he applied to songwriting.

From the start, Berry was guided by the bottom line. While other young writers toiled in solitude, Berry sought out collaborators. He had exceptional instincts about melodies and knew what was commercial, and while he wasn't especially good at writing lyrics, he knew what kind of lyrics made for hits.

One of the first people Berry teamed up with was Billy Davis, an aspiring young musician who was dating his sister Gwen. Davis introduced Berry to the Reverend C. L. Franklin. Each of the reverend's daughters—Aretha, Erma, and Carolyn—was known around Detroit as a great singer, but Berry and Billy were interested only in Erma.

The Reverend Franklin told Berry that he should work with Aretha, but Berry didn't care for Aretha's singing style. Erma sang on some of the demonstration records, or demos, Billy and Berry made for publishing companies and record labels, in the hope that one of the songs might be recorded by an established act. Because demos aren't finished records and generally are never heard by the public, they can be very basic, maybe just someone singing to minimal accompaniment. There's no telling what Berry, Billy, and Erma's early demos sounded like, but Berry and Billy (who wrote under the name Tyran Carlo) spent a great deal of time crafting them. Often Berry had just scraped together enough money to cover the studio costs and the musicians' fees, so every detail had to be carefully planned beforehand and the demo cut in as little time as possible.

Berry was getting around and making contact with other young writers, singers, and musicians. Gradually, Loucye's basement became a hangout where songs were written and rehearsed. Any friend of a friend with the slightest bit of talent was welcome.

"It seems unusual," Janie Bradford recalls, "but at that particular time in Detroit there were no outlets like there are today. Berry was into what he was doing and wanted to bring in whoever he could to help him build it." At this point, Berry still hadn't defined what "it" was, but he was headed in the right direction.

In 1957 Berry Gordy met two young men who changed his life. Berry either was introduced to Jackie Wilson during one of the latter's engagements at the Flame, or knew him from their days as Golden Gloves boxers. At the time, Wilson was one of the hottest and sexiest singers around. Women were wild about him, and one look at any film of him shows why. Wilson had been solo for about a year, and was already known to fans, having replaced Clyde McPhatter four years earlier in Billy Ward and His Dominoes, but he still hadn't scored a hit. Berry, Billy, and Gwen started writing for Wilson, and Billy and Berry's "Reet Petite" was Jackie Wilson's first big pop success.

Janie Bradford was a fourteen-year-old poet when she met Berry shortly after the success of "Reet Petite." Though Berry was making a name for himself, Janie was naturally more impressed by the singer. She and Berry's first conversation ended with Janie telling Berry she could outwrite him any day, and Berry promising to take her up on her challenge. She gave him her phone number and then forgot all about it.

A few months later, Berry and a friend turned up on Janie's doorstep. When he had to remind her who he was, she was embarrassed and invited them in. She showed Berry her collection of poems, and she and Berry began working on songs together.

Berry and his collaborators kept Wilson in hits for almost two years, with "Lonely Teardrops," "To Be Loved," "I'll Be Satisfied," and "That's Why (I Love You So)," one of my favorites. Wilson's album *Lonely Teardrops*, which included two of Janie's compositions, went gold, and Berry's place in the music business seemed secure.

One summer afternoon Berry met the Miracles—then known as the Matadors—when they came to audition for Jackie Wilson's manager. Because of their four-boy, one-girl lineup, the manager thought they were too much like the Platters, so he passed. Berry got to talking with lead singer Smokey and soon learned that Smokey also wrote poems and song lyrics. Smokey would later admit that most of what he had written at that point wasn't even that good, but Berry saw something in his work worth developing. As he had done with Janie and would do later with others, Berry told Smokey his ideas on what made great lyrics. They had to be written in the first person, usually in the present tense, and they had to have some kind of clever gimmick in the use of the words.

Things seemed to be going Berry's way until Jackie Wilson's manager decided to move his offices from Chicago to New York. This, coupled with Berry's realization of just how little of a hit record's profits went to the writers, convinced him that he needed more control. He'd already started producing his demos and a few acts' records because that was the only way he could faithfully translate to vinyl the sounds he heard in his head. Still, no matter how good a song was, the odds were against it being a hit, unless a star recorded it. And Berry had no idea when or if he would ever hook up with someone as hot as Wilson again. Erma Franklin had dropped out of the music business, and the Miracles hadn't yet found the right song.

Along came Eddie Holland, a young singer Berry had met at the Graystone Ballroom, and who he thought sounded just like Jackie Wilson. In 1958 Berry released Eddie Holland's "You," his brother Brian's "Shock," and the Miracles' "Got a Job." He also met Raynoma Liles, who would become his second wife, business partner, and collaborator.

Soon Berry, Ray, and anyone else around them was working on songs. Thomas "Beans" Bowles, who would play a major role at Motown in years to come, recalled working with Berry back then. "Berry invited me over to his and Ray's two-room apartment. I was surprised they had a piano in a little place like that. They were rehearsing some stuff, and Joe Hunter was there, too. Ray wanted me to be in on the music thing."

Robert Bateman, a singer and talent scout, was acting as engineer. Like everybody around then, Bateman wore more than a couple hats, and was also a member of the Rayber Voices, a background vocals group that included Ray, Brian Holland, and others.

Late in 1958 Berry began recording Marv Johnson, another singing songwriter. Marv recalls, "I went around to Berry's house and took some of my material. One of the songs was 'Come to Me.' That was a song I had written, but I got a lot of help from him and his wife as far as producing was concerned, with chord changes and things. The song originally was mine, but by the time it came out, the writing credits were shared with Berry Gordy."

Marv Johnson's "Come to Me" was Berry's first big hit in early 1959, but because Berry had leased it to a major record company his take wasn't as large as it could have been. That summer the Miracles' "Bad Girl" did well, but Johnson was Berry's hottest act, and "You Got What It Takes" and "I'm Coming Home" followed in 1960. In the meantime, two other men had joined the Gordy venture, Lamont Dozier and Mickey Stevenson.

On the advice of his protégé, Smokey Robinson, Berry started his own label, management firm, and studios. He'd already moved the operation into a two-story house that had been a photographer's studio on West Grand Boulevard, and now he set to work converting it into a recording facility and offices, with living space on the second floor for him, Ray, and her kids. It became a second home to all the writers. No one thought of it as a job; they just loved being there. There weren't yet deadlines to meet and orders to follow. Things just seemed to happen.

One evening, Richard Morris was listening to Barrett Strong, a young singer. "Barrett was trying to start his career," Richard recalls. "He hadn't made a record yet. I was in the control room putting some machines together, but I also had the monitor open so that I could hear because I always did enjoy Barrett.

"Berry came down and—I'll show you what kind of mind he had. 'So,' he said, 'what is that Barrett is playing?' Let's go down and listen to it.'

"So we went down to the studio and Berry starts nodding his head.

'Hey, man,' he says to Barrett, 'can you change that up just a little bit?' So Barrett started changing it up—just a little bit—and came up with a new rhythm. Berry said, 'That's great. Richard, go put this on tape,' which I did.

"The next morning Berry called Janie Bradford down for the lyrics. She had written something but it wasn't what he had in mind. 'See,' he said, 'I wanted something like I need a new pair of shoes. Well, give me a title of something that everybody wants.' "

"Janie replied, 'Money, that's what I want.' And there was Berry's first big hit."

And "Money" was an apt title. Berry's cohorts loved their work, but very few got paid, and those who did made maybe eight dollars a week. Coming from the ghetto these kids were hip that money was what they wanted—like all of us, they longed for the freedom they thought money would buy.

Gradually people on the local scene began to regard Berry as the man with the golden touch. Over the next decade, some of our generation's best writers, musicians, and performers would find their way to Berry. But not just anybody got in and not everybody stayed. From the start Berry surrounded himself with only the best and the brightest. Janie Bradford had her sights set on becoming an attorney; Eddie Holland was studying to become a certified public accountant. You had to have brains, energy, ambition, and a degree of class to pass muster with Berry.

By the time we returned in the winter of 1960, Motown was firmly established and running very much like a family. Loyalty, honesty, and obedience were demanded and often gladly given. In the days before people got paid, Smokey brought in Miss Lily, a woman who had cooked for him most of his life, to cook up hot meals. These big "family" meals were the closest thing to board meetings we had in those days. Projects were discussed, assignments given, gossip exchanged.

Not surprisingly, Berry's parents also became part of Hitsville. All of the Gordys seemed to have been born with the gift of gab, and I'm pretty sure they all inherited it from Mrs. Gordy. And Pops was a favorite. No one was immune to the Gordy charm, least of all the Primettes. Pops was a sweet gentleman fond of making wolfish remarks to attractive young girls. Flo was his favorite, and we'd tease her about Pops' flirting.

The making of Motown was not unlike the building of the pyra-
mids. Countless people—some known and others long since forgotten
—toiled literally night and day. Of course, most of us were teenagers
still living at home, so we didn't make the same demands independent
adults would. And Berry inspired and excited us. Berry himself was
something of an outcast, still not being taken seriously outside the
music business. Berry saw the bigger picture, grasped the importance
of details, and often found ways of getting things done other people
either couldn't or wouldn't tackle.

When Berry realized that he couldn't write great songs by himself,
he used other people. As Motown expanded, he would take this approach one step further, seeking not only the best person for a job,
but the best that person could offer. Berry was a perceptive judge of
character and a quick study of almost anything. He knew how to get
people to do his bidding. He knew their talents and weaknesses. After
years of observing him, I believe he often knew more about us than
we knew about ourselves.

CHAPTER 8

When we got back to Hitsville everyone there seemed overjoyed to see us. We had been away only about four months, but the way our friends there carried on, it might have been years. Before we could fully explain our absence to anyone, we spotted Berry coming out of the control room on his way down to Studio A. He hugged each of us, we introduced him to Barbara, and then he told us to come into the studio with him.

Stepping down into that basement studio was like entering a whole new world. The musicians there who knew us gave us little waves and nods of acknowledgment. After that day, we could usually be found either sitting in the lobby or scrunched up together on the stairs to the studio, peering through the smoke at the musicians and singers working below.

Mary Wells was soon to become Motown's first premiere female artist. Although her first big hit was still a year away, she was cutting tracks regularly with Motown and was also a songwriter; Berry decided to sign her after she sang one of her own songs for him. Doing background vocals for her was one of our first assignments. We sang with her on a number of tunes, and though I can't remember all of them —especially since Motown's artists sometimes recorded many times the number of songs that were released—I believe they included "He Holds His Own," "Honey Boy" (which the Supremes later recorded), and "You Lost the Sweetest Boy."

Mary's voice had a sweet, sexy quality I admired. None of the songs we cut with her became hits, but I thought she had a certain star quality, and tried to learn from watching her. She was only eighteen, about a year or so older than we were, yet she was definitely more sophisticated.

"Can't that girl sing? Whoo!" Flo said as we left a Wells session.

"Honey," Barbara replied, "Mary Wells sounds real good."

As we'd sit on our favorite bench in the lobby, we'd catch people walking through. Many of the fellows, especially Brian Holland, would stop and remark on how beautiful we each were or tease us. Humorous come-ons would be matched line for line by Barbara, while Flo and I would laugh it off. Diane would play coy. Other girls who were friends of ours, like Janie, would comment on our clothes or make small talk. The Motown scene was completely new to Barbara and she tried acting nonchalant, but one look at her when a celebrity passed by or when she got to see a session in progress and you could see she was starstruck.

Out of curiosity, I once asked Janie what she thought of us, and was not entirely surprised when she said that she thought we were rather naïve. I knew Janie could be brutally honest, so I braced myself. But when she said that we were good, though "nothing to knock your socks off," I was stunned. Maybe she was right. She had no ulterior motive, and I generally valued what she had to say, but this was something else. My faith in the Primettes was unshakable, and after that I never asked anyone outside the group for advice about anything. What would they know, anyway? We'd stuck it out for almost two whole years and we were going to make it. What other people thought didn't matter anymore.

After a few weeks of being everyone's favorite prodigal daughters, the fuss over our return died down, and before long we were wondering when we'd finally get to make our own record. Fame wasn't our goal and money wasn't yet that important; we just wanted to make music. Despite our youthful impatience, we knew better than to pester Berry about this. We'd learned our lesson and weren't going to blow it again. It was enough that we made sure to catch Berry's attention whenever we saw him. I was sure he'd get around to us someday.

In late 1960 Mrs. Ballard used the insurance and Social Security money she received following her husband's death to buy a new detached house on the west side of town. Even though the new home was larger than the row house in the Projects, it was always filled with family. Because Flo was now technically living outside the Northeastern district, she enrolled in Northwestern High School. We were all in our junior year of high school, still wondering what the future might hold. As far as our parents knew, all of us were going to college, but we weren't so sure. We had school and the normal teenage responsibilities and headaches. I was still working at the record store, making next to no money but bringing home copies of all the latest records. I'd hole up in my room, doing my nails or setting my hair, and play my current favorite hit over and over again. "Girl," my mother would say as I played "Will You Love Me Tomorrow" by the Shirelles for the hundredth time, "you're going to play those grooves smooth." I'd just laugh. My little sister Cat would sometimes join me in dancing to the songs. My brother, like most young boys, was seldom around and hardly useful when he was. I adored them both.

Even with all the activities—school, chores, dates, rehearsals, sock hops, and the daily pilgrimage to Hitsville—I never felt tired or pressured. I'd go to West Grand Boulevard every day, never knowing what to expect but praying for a miracle. No one ever said anything about us hanging around. We were always ladylike and fashionably dressed. We spent so much time sitting on that bench that I'm amazed we didn't leave fanny prints in it. Everyone knew our names, but soon we were known collectively as "the girls."

One day Smokey popped into the lobby on his way to a session with Mary Wells. While we were all chatting, he suddenly got the idea to use us on Mary's record. We were so thrilled at the chance to record we almost thought we would die. Then Smokey told us that handclaps were all he had in mind.

By early 1961, more and more acts were migrating to Hitsville. Soon we were joined at Hitsville by our old affiliates, the Primes. A lot of things had happened since we'd last seen one another, and now Eddie Kendricks and Paul Williams, with Eldridge Bryant, and Otis Williams and Melvin Franklin of the Distants, were the Temptations. Over the years, the Tempts' lineup would change, with old friends like Richard Street joining later on.

Otis Williams and Melvin Franklin had first gotten together while both were attending Northwestern High. As Melvin recalls, he first knew Otis only by sight. When Otis first approached Melvin, Melvin ran like hell away from him, thinking he was a gang member intent on beating him up and taking his lunch money. Shortly after that, Melvin returned home one day to find Otis on his doorstep, waiting to ask Melvin's mother if Melvin could join his group, the Distants.

"In truth, I was really scared of Otis because he had a process and looked like a tough customer," Melvin recalls. "I would never have thought that he and I would be cut from the same cloth."

Melvin became a Distant and finagled a place in the group for his cousin, Richard Street. This version of the Distants broke up. Otis,

Melvin, and El Bryant, another Distant, got together with Eddie Kendricks, but Eddie refused to join unless they took his friend, Paul Williams, too. At this point in the group's history, it's unclear whether or not Richard was still an official member, but everyone recalls him being around. Somehow, though, the chemistry between Richard and Eddie just wasn't right, and Richard stopped hanging around with them altogether. Richard wouldn't finally join the Tempts until 1971, when Paul Williams quit.

Melvin's mother belonged to a ladies' club with Anna and Gwen Gordy. When Mrs. Franklin mentioned that her son was singing with a group, the Gordy sisters suggested that they audition for their brother. So Otis Williams and the Distants sang their repertoire for Berry, a cappella. Berry was very impressed with the group, but he didn't like their name. He wasn't ready to sign them right away, either, but the guys started hanging around Hitsville anyway.

Newly signed to Motown were the Contours. They would have only a few hits, and have been sadly overlooked in the Motown story, but they were good friends of ours and lots of fun, especially during the tours.

Billy Gordon, Billy Hoggs, Joe Billingslea, Sylvester Potts, and Hubert Johnson started out in 1959 as the Blenders. They would walk up and down Twelfth Street singing in bars for beers, just trying to perfect their harmonies. The first record company they approached was Flick and Contour studios. Wes Higgins wanted one of their songs, "Come On and Be Mine," but didn't want them. Next stop: Hitsville. Berry liked the three songs they sang; Raynoma liked the songs and the guys. But Berry didn't like the guys. They struck him as being too hardcore R&B, which wasn't Berry's taste.

Unbeknownst to the other group members, Hubert Johnson was Jackie Wilson's cousin. Hubert took them all to Jackie's home in Detroit, where Wilson kept them waiting for an hour and a half before he'd see them. Later, Wilson told them that he was just testing their patience to see how badly they really wanted to sing. After they explained their problem, Jackie called up his friend Berry Gordy and arranged another appointment for them later that day.

"We went right back to Motown," Joe remembered, "and sang the same three songs *again*, and signed the contracts."

Another future Motown star was also there by now. Martha Reeves was working as Mickey Stevenson's secretary in the A&R department. We knew Martha because she and her group, the Del-Phis, also rehearsed at the House of Beauty. The group had a different original lineup, but when we met them, it was Gloria Jean Williams, Annette Sterling, and Rosalind Ashford. After Martha told her boss Mickey about her group, they got into Motown as background singers. Because they had recorded with and were technically under contract to another label, they recorded as the Vels.

Gloria eventually left the group, and Berry decided to sign them, but first they needed a new name. Martha took "Van" from Van Dyke Street, and "Della," for the popular singer Della Reese, and came up with "the Vandellas." They backed Marvin Gaye on several of his early hits, including "Pride and Joy," "Stubborn Kind of Fellow," "Hitch Hike," and "Can I Get a Witness," and often toured with him. Like most of us girls at Motown, Martha had a crush on the handsome, soft-spoken young Marvin.

In December we got our first shot in the studio. Freddy Gorman —who'd been our mailman in the Projects—had written "I Want a Guy." We didn't care about what kind of song it was; we could make a hit out of anything, we thought. We spent days with Freddy, trying to perfect the harmonies, which was usually the hardest thing about learning a new song. We got to the studio early the day of the session. Berry was very excited for us; he thought "I Want a Guy" was a good song for the Primettes to record. He took us aside, offered some words of encouragement, and promised to come down later and see how we were doing.

The song was written to sound coy and girlish, so it needed a high lead vocal, and Diane did it. The recording went off without a hitch. Berry showed up later and suggested some changes to the musicians and discussed altering the tempo with Freddy; he also added and deleted a few words. Everyone agreed with everything Berry said.

Having finished the first track so quickly, we decided to go ahead and record the flip side, figuring that the sooner both sides were finished, the sooner the release. Diane also took the lead on "Never Again," a slower song in the style of the Chantels' "Maybe." When the four of us were all done, Freddy hugged each of us and praised us for our good work. He took us out for a bite to eat and then drove us home.

After "I Want a Guy" was finally released, Freddy complained to us in private that Berry had heard the song before we recorded it, changed a few words, and then took credit for co-writing it. Freddy's resentment was short-lived, though; we all knew we were lucky just to be able to make records, and the incident was forgotten.

One of our favorite people there was Smokey. He was also one of the busiest, but he was always sweet. "How are you young ladies doing?" he'd casually inquire on his way from an office to a studio and then back again, nonchalantly delivering news we hoped would change our lives: "I've got a song I want to use you on," or "This I just wrote would be perfect for you girls," he'd say just before disappearing again. Each time Smokey mentioned recording we'd eagerly pipe up, "Use us!" "We're ready!"

We weren't even signed to Motown yet; still, Berry assigned us to Smokey. We were all pleased that the first song we got to record with Smokey was a Miracles tune, "Who's Loving You." Because it was a ballad, I assumed I would be singing the lead, as I always had. I stood in the studio that day, expecting Smokey to hand the lead sheet to me. When he gave it to Diane instead, my heart sank. There was nothing I could say, and in the excitement of recording, I forgot my disappointment and turned my attention to singing the best I could on what I hoped would be our first hit record.

We were earnest and professional, but, being young girls, we started off the session laughing, with Flo and me teasing Barbara about her new boyfriend. We knew the song so well that we thought recording would be a breeze, but Smokey was a perfectionist, and he would stop us repeatedly because one of us was always too loud— usually Barbara. The technology then didn't make it easy for producers to do punch-ins—rerecordings of just the few seconds of a take that needed to be corrected—so a perfect recording had to be literally perfect from the first second to the last.

We had come to the session straight from school, and the studio —which we called the sweat shop—was so hot we just weren't concentrating. Diane was in one of the two vocalists' booths and the three of us were all crowded into the other. When we reached the part where Diane sings the words "My life, my love," and we had to repeat them, Barbara sang loud and flat. It was such a sad song, but the three of us stood in our booth cracking up. Of course Diane didn't see this happen, and we hoped that the goof wouldn't be so obvious on the playback. Today I laugh when I play that track from *Meet the Supremes*; it doesn't even sound that bad. We were certain "Who's Loving You" would be a hit. Diane's voice had lost some of its nasal tone and was developing a more confident, brassy sound.

One day in early January 1961, Berry called us into his office and offered to sign us. We were ecstatic. "But," he added, "you girls need

That's me at the age of three in Chicago. I was all dressed up to move to Detroit to live with my aunt and uncle, and I wasn't about to let go of my doll, or my Oreo cookie! (*Mary Wilson Collection*)

My brother Roosevelt, my sister Cat, and me in 1955. (*Mary Wilson Collection*)

Our first manager, Milton Jenkins,
before he started wearing his sharkskin suits.
(*Mary Wilson Collection*)

The Primes were our brother group
when we were starting out.
They named us the Primettes.
(*Mary Wilson Collection*)

The original Primettes in 1959, before the Motown Artist Development Department got a hold of us. Left to right: Betty Travis, me, Flo, and Diane. My little cousin Cynthia wanted to be part of the act too! (*Mary Wilson Collection*)

Before there were the Supremes, we were the Primettes. These were the dresses that Diane and I made with the help of my Aunt Moneva. Clockwise from the top: Diane, Flo, me, and Barbara Diane Martin, 1961. (*Mary Wilson Collection*)

My graduation photo from Northeastern High School, January 1962.
My goal: to one day write a book.
(*Mary Wilson Collection*)

Left: Florence and I always wanted to see our names up in lights, but on our summer 1964 tour, it looked like this was as close as we would come. Later that year "Where Did Our Love Go" became our first number-one hit. (*Mary Wilson Collection*) Below: Annette of the Vandellas and Flo sharing a room on the 1962 Motown tour. (*Rosalind Ashford*)

Above: Mary Wells and Diane on the first Motown tour in 1962. (*Rosalind Ashford*) Right: When Florence laughed, everyone around her laughed too. This was taken on the 1962 Motown tour. (*Rosalind Ashford*)

One of the Motown family's benefits for Beans Bowles, after the car accident on the 1962 Motown Revue tour. Beans is the tall one standing behind "Little" Stevie Wonder. (*Mary Wilson Collection*)

The "no-hit" Supremes at the Apollo Theater, New York City, 1962. (*Mary Wilson Collection*)

This was our first photo session as a trio.
(*Mark Bego Collection*)

On the bus: Diane sleeping next to one of the guys on Dick Clark's Caravan of Stars, 1964. (*Mary Wilson Collection*)

Below: Flo, Diane, and I get our first taste of fish and chips in London. (*Mary Wilson Collection*)

Left: The first time we went to England. We heard about "A Foggy Day in London Town," so we brought our umbrellas. (*Mary Wilson Collection*)

Below: Our first trip to London, 1964. Berry decided we needed chaperones, so he brought the whole Motown staff. Left to right: Butch Edwards, Diane, me, Barney Ales, Flo, Esther Edwards, and Berry. Ales was the man who made the Supremes a "pop" act on the record charts. (*Beans Bowles*)

While in Paris, Flo and I couldn't resist seeing *all* of the historical sights. (*Mary Wilson Collection*)

In London. (*Carl Feuerbacher Collection*)

The Motown Revue in England, 1965. Left to right: the Temptations, Stevie Wonder, Smokey Robinson and the Miracles, the Supremes, and Martha Reeves and the Vandellas. (*Mary Wilson Collection*)

On our 1965 tour to London to tape the *Ready, Steady, Go* show. I'm holding Florence's fox fur, and Diane's holding Smokey Robinson. (*Mary Wilson Collection*)

Flo, Diane, and I on one of our first television appearances, *The Bill Kennedy Show* in Detroit, 1965. (*Mary Wilson Collection*)

Below left: The Supremes on the TV show *What's My Line* in 1965. (*Allan Poe Collection*) Below right: Thing's go better with Coke! Diane, Flo and I singing a rewritten version of "Baby Love" as a Coca-Cola jingle. (*Mary Wilson Collection*)

One of our early publicity shots. It wasn't long before our wigs became as famous as we were! (*Michael Ochs Archives*)

Many people thought that Florence should be the center of attention in the Supremes. Here she is proudly in the spotlight. (*Mary Wilson Collection*)

Florence and I checking out the crowd from the window of our limousine, while our chaperones weren't looking: "Girl, did you see that guy?" (*Mary Wilson Collection*)

Diane being interviewed in our hotel suite. By now, Flo and I were on our way to being seen and not heard. (*Mary Wilson Collection*)

This was one of our most famous publicity shots.
(*James Kriegsmann/Mary Wilson Archives*)

a different name. Primettes won't do." He told us to come up with suggestions. We didn't really want to change our name at all; we really liked Primettes. But Berry had already set the date for the contract signing, so we had about a week to come up with something new. The Primes didn't exist anymore, so we had no obligation to keep the "sister" tag. We thought of all the group names we liked—modern, smooth-sounding names like the Platters, the Shirelles, and the Chantels. The name we chose had to convey something about us—class, beauty, quality. We came up with countless suggestions, but none was perfect.

Flo was in charge of keeping a list of the names we'd collected. We were each pretty vocal about our favorite choices, but Flo kept her opinions to herself, dutifully writing down our ideas. The contracts were drawn up, so we had to decide about this soon. One day Flo read off her list: "The Darleens, the Sweet Ps, the Melodees, the Royaltones, the Jewelettes, the Supremes." None of them really impressed any of us, but Flo seemed to like one. After a minute she said, "I like this one—the Supremes."

We weren't exactly crazy about the name; I had my heart set on something that ended in "ettes." But we were anxious to sign the recording contracts, so even though we didn't all like the name, we were now the Supremes.

On January 15, the four of us, my mother, Flo's mother, Diane's mother, and Barbara's mother met with Berry, his sister Esther Edwards, and someone else from Motown to sign the contracts. None of us thought about hiring our own legal counsel. Our parents trusted that Berry and Motown would do only what was best for us. Berry reassured our mothers that Motown would not only work on our behalf, but manage all of our earnings as well. Everyone seemed happy with the arrangements.

Then, suddenly, Mrs. Martin announced that she had changed her mind, that Barbara could not be in the Supremes. We were very upset with Mrs. Martin because she had promised us earlier that she would sign for Barbara and now she was reneging. Furthermore, her attitude was somewhat condescending; she implied that her daughter was too good to be a singer.

After a few minutes, everything was smoothed out, and Barbara's mother signed. But even if she hadn't, we would have carried on without her. Even though we'd been together barely two years—a very short time compared to how long other groups were around before they got deals (i.e., recording contracts)—it felt like an eternity to us. We would not give up.

As I now look back, my first recording contract was fourteen pages of double-spaced type outlining my obligations to Motown as a "singer and/or musician" for the next year. Somewhere in all that legalese were some revealing terms: no advance, no salary, and permission for Motown to recoup any monies they'd advanced to us or spent on our behalf from the royalties we would be entitled to. The purpose of this was to reduce Motown's loss if our records didn't sell. Despite the fact that we formed and named our group, in the event one of us chose not to continue with the Supremes, her replacement would be chosen by Motown. Similarly, if someone was to be fired from the group, only Motown could do it. We no longer had any say. Ironically, however, the space in the contract where the name of the group should have been placed was left blank.

Furthermore, for records sold in the United States (and not returned) I was to be paid 3 percent of 90 percent of the suggested retail price for each record, less all taxes and packaging costs. What was especially interesting about that was the 3 percent royalty applied only when I cut solo records. I did not know the terms of the other girls' contracts, but my contract said that theirs were substantially the same as mine. Based on my figures, this meant that as a solo artist I would get approximately 2 cents for every 75-cent single sold. So, if I or any of the other Supremes had recorded a million-seller as a solo, that person's net would be around $20,000 *before* other expenses were deducted.

However, this was not the whole story after all. Ten pages further on in my contract is where the real deal was. There it states that the recordings we made as a *group* (which was the only way we ever recorded) were subject to a different royalty formula. Instead of each of us receiving the 3 percent royalty rate, we had to divide that 3 percent royalty four ways. So the real royalty rate for each of us was three-fourths of one percent (or .0075); thus, my earnings per 75-cent single would drop from two cents (the solo royalty formula) to about half of a penny. At this point a million-seller would earn about $5,000. Again, without knowing the exact amount for which Motown sold our records, these figures are based on the assumption, conservative I am sure, that the price for a single 45 rpm in the 1960s was 75 cents. This also assumes that Motown sold our records to distributors for one-half that price and then deducted another 20 percent for taxes, packaging, arrangements, copying and accompaniment, and all other related costs for each recording session, regardless of whether or not the particular record was released. I might add that, at the time of this writing, only very recently has Motown released some of the many unreleased records we cut back then.

Over the next several years the terms of my contract changed somewhat, but ever so slightly. In the next contract I signed, in 1965, I was also given $12.50 for every master (which the contract defined as a 2-sided single record) we recorded and a new royalty rate of 8 percent of 90 percent; but this royalty formula was based on the wholesale price and not the suggested retail price of the record, as was the case in my first contract. So, during the very height of our career, we basically worked under the same terms as in the early days.

Looking back, people might wonder how Motown got away with this sort of thing or why so many artists just seemed to have accepted it. In truth, few of us knew anything at all about the business, and fewer still knew to have legal counsel for any business dealings or contracts. There was also the problem of how Motown was structured. Today most performers have an attorney-at-law, a booking agent, a manager, an accountant, a financial adviser, and many other professionals attending to their business. This forms an intricate and indispensable system of checks and balances, since each professional protects the performer's interests in his particular area.

Motown, however, did everything. Motown was your booking agent, your manager, your accountant, your financial adviser, and everything else. The corporation also made it difficult for outside people to ascertain the accuracy of its earnings reports, since, according to contract, there were two auditing periods per year, but an artist was allowed only one audit per year. In other words, even the most astute artist could only know the details of his finances for half a year. Without seeing the second period's figures, there was no way to know exactly what was going on, how much money you had earned, how much was being spent on you and deducted from your account, or how much you were entitled to. To this day, I still don't know exactly how many millions of copies any of our records sold, although I still receive royalties.

Our new official status as Motown recording artists made us more popular than ever at the sock hops and we were booked all over the area. Accustomed to always having someone like Milton or Richard around to handle the logistics of traveling, we were in for a rude awakening. Marv Johnson and Mary Wells not only had their own cars, but drivers as well; unbeknownst to Berry, we were hitching rides from friends and other artists to and from shows. We wouldn't dream of mentioning this problem to Berry for fear he'd think we were unprofessional or unable to handle the demands of a career. After Flo's rape, we had all become more leery about going out at night, and as the bookings outside Detroit proper increased, we faced having to decline offers.

Only a few weeks after our signing, we were sitting in the lobby discussing how we were going to get to a date on the other side of town. We were upset at the prospect of canceling. Little did we know that an angel was listening.

John O'Den was a big man who worked out daily and was into bodybuilding and fitness. He was fair-complexioned, had a deep, gruff voice, and on first sight appeared menacing. When we first met him, he was in his late thirties. Despite his appearance, he was very gentle, always smiling, and happy to help anyone who needed him.

John had met Berry when they were both boxers, and they also worked in the same auto plant in the late fifties. John was one of several old friends Berry brought into the Motown organization. John was Berry's personal valet and bodyguard; he also drove for Mary Wells. Even though Berry had a wife, John was responsible for his personal care.

"Disappointed about something? Y'all looking real sad " He was sympathetic, but teasing us, too.

"It's not funny," I mumbled, trying to hold back tears. "How are we going to get to the hops without a car of our own?"

"Well, how have you girls been getting around? I hear the Supremes are busy little girls. Mr. Gordy and Mrs. Edwards think you'll be moneymakers—just wait."

"We don't have time to wait," Diane interjected.

"We sure don't," Flo added. "We need a way to get to and from all these shows we're booked for."

"I'll be happy to drive you after work, and I'll wait around for you till it's over, too."

At this, Barbara jumped up and hugged John, as we followed, smiling with glee.

True to his word, John took us to the hop, and on the way home treated us to burgers and fries. We felt comfortable with him immediately, and he soon became our daily companion, driving us every-where, covering little expenses out of his own pocket. There were many people around Motown like John. I remember Bobby Smith of the Spinners also driving us around. Some of these people weren't even on the payroll, yet they would help out whenever they could.

As we were coming in one day, we heard Berry ask the receptionist, "Where are the girls?"

Elbowing each other to beat a path to Berry's side, we cried, "Here we are!" We were now Berry's shadows; wherever he went, we followed. Our mentor had finally taken us under his wing.

CHAPTER 9

The year 1961 was starting off as a great one for the Supremes, and within a few months it would prove to be a banner year for Motown. The Miracles' third Tamla release, "Shop Around," had gone to #1 on the R&B chart and #2 pop. This phenomenal showing was Berry's biggest crossover success so far and set a standard he would try to match with every release that followed. Smokey worked so hard with everyone, writing, producing, arranging—it's no wonder that in 1962 Berry made Smokey a vice president of the Motown Corporation, a position he holds today.

It was exciting to see all the different groups and artists who came aboard. Mary Wells finally hit with "Bye Bye Baby" (which she had written) and "I Don't Want to Take a Chance," and in December the Marvelettes' "Please Mr. Postman" became Motown's first pop number-one hit. The Miracles also released "Ain't It, Baby" and "Mighty Good Lovin'," which, while not as big hits as "Shop Around," kept their name in the public eye.

While acts were coming to Hitsville, Berry was assembling Motown's support staff; the producers, writers, musicians, and business people whose work behind the scenes was as important to the company's success as the biggest star.

The Motown musicians are legendary. How Berry acquired the services of the finest players in Detroit when it was common knowledge among them that Motown paid well below union scale was a mystery to me. When I learned that Mickey Stevenson was the scout who lured them in and that Thomas "Beans" Bowles was functioning as his backup, it all fell into place.

Beans Bowles knew the Gordys from his days as the sax player in the band at the Flame Show Bar. Like most local musicians, Beans had trouble supporting his family on his wages. In discussing Berry's plans for Motown with him, Beans was struck by Berry's enthusiasm

90

and apparent willingness to do things that would really help his employees. Promising promotions and bonuses, Berry's sister Esther Edwards convinced Beans to join Motown. Most of the local musicians knew him, and when they would drop by Hitsville and ask what was happening, Beans would go into the spiel: "This is a young company that is still growing. It is the only company in America that you've got a chance to grow with . . ." and so on. And Beans believed it.

In 1960 Beans had toured with Marv Johnson, then Berry's hottest property. Functioning as Johnson's musical director, road manager, driver, and accompanist, Beans was doing the jobs of several people, which was impressive enough. But when he returned to Detroit and gave Esther a stack of meticulously neat and correct financial records, she and Berry snatched him up right away. Musicians were all over the place, but a musician with business and organizational skills was something they weren't going to see again for a while, if ever.

It fell to Esther to lure Beans into the fold. He was reluctant at first; he saw himself first and foremost as a musician. But after spending years on the road—which was a lot more uncertain and dangerous for blacks then—and never knowing where the next job was coming from, Beans decided to go with Berry. There was also the sense that something unique and wonderful was happening at Hitsville. For one thing, Berry promised Beans a company car. But more impressive were some of Berry's other ideas: plans to buy food, cars, and other items in bulk and form a cooperative plan for all Motown employees, were quite lofty and appealed to even the most cynical. Of course, these plans were never realized, and what ultimately won Beans over was the promise of a large starting salary.

Mickey Stevenson was another young writer/musician kicking around Detroit waiting for a break. Mickey was handsome and always very nice-looking. Years later, he married Kim Weston. "I used to work with Mickey's mother, Kitty Stevenson," Beans said. "I watched him grow up. He would come to my office and say he couldn't get anybody to listen to his songs. I said, 'All you have to do is stay on that porch [meaning the one at Hitsville], and when Berry comes out, just walk beside him and talk with him, because he is fast.'

"Mickey worried Berry to death, and that's how he got in—at least that's how I got rid of him," Beans recalled.

I remember sitting on that same porch and seeing Beans for the first time. Beans was a hip dresser in the fifties jazz style—dress slacks, turtleneck sweater, and a sports coat were standard attire. He was extremely tall—over six feet four—and very fair and handsome, with twinkling eyes. He was charming and well-spoken, and he always impressed people as an honest, wise man. Beans also had a charming smile. His confident, refined demeanor and aptitude for business would prove great assets to the company, especially out on the road.

Mickey started working for Berry in early 1961, and eventually he was put in charge of supervising everyone at Motown. Mickey made schedules, set up sessions, and enforced deadlines.

"I think Mickey started to recruit, and then they all started coming up," says Beans. "Earl Van Dyke got guitarist Robert White from Harvey and Gwen Fuqua's Anna Records. He also had Joe Tex at one time, but I don't think he stayed. Joe Messina, who was Italian, but who no one really considered white. There was Jack Ashford on percussion, and other guitarists as the years went by. Earl Van Dyke added Eddie Willis, Johnny Wah-Wah Watson, and eventually some other white boys got in there. Of course, bassist James Jamerson came in, too. Mickey would go to different places and hear their sound. Then they found out I was part of it. Mickey was working on them, and then he would refer them to me, and I'd corroborate everything he'd told them about working here."

Between the two of them, Beans and Mickey were turning 2648 West Grand Boulevard into more than just a big house. Though there were several bandleaders before him—including Joe Hunter, who brought in Hank Cosby, among others—Earl Van Dyke, a keyboardist, was the undisputed architect of the Motown sound. Jazz pianist Barry Harris was the leader of the young local musicians who would come together as Earl Van Dyke's Funk Brothers band. Many of them were, like me, alumni of Northeastern High. Almost all of these early players were well trained and had years of experience, mostly with playing jazz. Before they'd come to Motown, they'd each backed countless established stars. They knew their stuff. I've often thought that their mutual respect for one another kept the competition among them to a minimum. You never saw anybody trying to upstage anybody else. They were just there to do the best job they could.

Among my favorite musicians was Benny "Papa Zita" Benjamin, one of the greatest drummers ever. Everyone believed he was a musical genius. He didn't read music as well as some of the other players, so to get started he'd say, "Just give me the feeling, man." Sometimes he would be so into his drums he would miss a change, but whoever was producing would leave it on the recording because it still sounded great.

I was too young at first to really know what went on down in the Hitsville basement, so it's hard to say exactly what Papa Zita's thing was. I recall him being a chronic complainer; he never came in to work without something being wrong. He was late for sessions because his uncle died—over forty times. One incident I remember vividly occurred after he'd undergone an operation to have glass removed from his face. He had been thrown into the windshield in a car accident. Apparently, some of the glass was left in, and for months afterward he would come in and show everyone another piece he'd taken out himself. His poor face was a mess. Years later I'd learn that many of Papa Zita's little quirks were the product of drink, but everyone loved him all the same.

Another musician who will always have a special place in my heart is the bass player James Jamerson. He was young, good-looking, and one of the funniest men at Motown. He wrote all the fabulous bass lines that are the pulse of the Motown hits. I can just picture him, playing the bass, smoking a cigar, and grinning. No matter what was happening or how tired we all would get working for hours in that steaming studio, James still managed to throw out a funny line and get producers, engineers, singers, and the entire band laughing. James' wisecracks were the cause of many retakes. We'd all try to keep it in, but sooner or later someone would let loose, and we'd have to start all over again.

At the beginning, Berry still wasn't offering anybody much more than carfare to work with him. When union scale was approximately $47 to $60 per session for three hours' work, Berry was paying musicians $5 per side, and a side could take a whole day to record. An exception to that rule were the strings players whom a young Motown arranger named Paul Riser worked with; they were from the Detroit Symphony Orchestra. Though at first these classically trained musicians resisted some of the producers' ideas because they weren't "correct," once the records became hits, the symphony musicians were always proud to have been on them.

None of the early producers wrote out his arrangements—sometimes not even the basics of the melody. Because the musicians created and improvised from simple lead sheets, it was they who actually made the music. I've heard that lead sheets would be brought in for saxophone players with instructions that they play notes that weren't even on the horn. Nor was B.G., as we began calling Berry, known to write down musical notation on paper. Like many of us, Berry lacked formal musical training; I believe he played piano by ear. I must say that I've never met or heard of another man who did as much musically with so little. He'd walk into a session, hum a line or two of a tune, and say, "Play this. This is what I want to hear. Can you do this?" The musicians would take it from there. Then Berry would add, "Make me a riff back here," and so on.

Generally speaking, the musicians knew more about music, in the technical sense, than anyone else at Hitsville. When the producers and songwriters came into the studio with a new idea for a song, they had only what they heard in their heads, and maybe they could hum it or play a couple of bars. Not knowing that much about music, one of them might hum a part for, say, piano, that someone who really knew about music would have written for horns, or someone might ask for a rhythmic change or guitar riff that was technically impossible to play. Had a musician who knew of these limitations tried to write the same song, he probably would not even have considered these ideas. But as limited and rough as some of the early ideas were, the musicians rose to the challenge and tried to get the music they could play to fit the producer's or writer's original conception as closely as possible. This process entailed a lot of give and take, and in that exchange, possibilities not only doubled, but probably quadrupled. The products—the songs—speak for themselves.

Arrangements were the key to the Motown sound, for the arrangers provided the bridge between what the producers wanted to hear and what the musicians could play. Most of the early ones were done by Joe Hunter, who wrote them out and painstakingly structured each part. Organist Willie Shorter arranged all of the Miracles' earliest stuff. In the beginning, you could often find young Smokey watching Willie to learn how it was done.

The original recording facilities were limited, to say the very least. The basement studio's control booth was separated from the rest of the room by a plate glass window and elevated two steps higher than the rest of the room. Motown's famous echo chamber was actually the toilet behind the control room. Anyone who needed the toilet had to either run all the way to the top floor and use the facilities there or wait. Many takes were lost when someone knocked on the door, not knowing that the "chamber" was occupied. The vocalists' booths were no larger than telephone booths. And the band was often so close to the singers that it was ridiculous, but the excitement was infectious.

Working in such close quarters may have been cramped, but it was conducive to a better rapport between the singers and the players. Really making music, as opposed to making sounds, demands an emotional exchange among everyone involved. When the band got into a groove it inspired the singers, and vice versa. There was a real chemistry there, and I think the best Motown records—Mary Wells's "My Guy," Marvin Gaye's "I Heard It Through the Grapevine," the Four Tops' "Baby I Need Your Loving," and our "When the Lovelight Starts Shining Through His Eyes," which featured the Four Tops and Holland, Dozier, and Holland on backing vocals—have a spontaneous intensity to them. Today's records are often made by musicians and producers who are abetted by a plethora of technological gimmicks and tricks; to my ears, the sound is sterile and flat.

Though Berry and the Motown producers and writers did experiment with different methods of writing and producing, they were not, as is generally assumed today, looking for a specific sound. Berry had known as far back as his days with Erma Franklin that he wanted a smooth, clean, classy R&B-cum-pop style. One of the reasons Berry liked writing for Jackie Wilson was that Jackie could—and did—sing almost any style. Berry wasn't rejecting the earlier, rougher R&B style so much as he—and everyone at Motown—was formulating what could be more accurately described as the next step in R&B. What "experimenting" was done with individual groups was more a matter of fitting an act to the right material and right producer to achieve a sound that would appeal to all listeners. Still, virtually all the hits that came out of Motown—whether they were by the Supremes or the Contours—fell within the stylistic parameters Berry had set years before.

Handclaps, heavy drum accents, and repeated choruses and melodic hooks made Motown's sound unforgettable, even to people who didn't especially care to remember it. Every producer had his own trademark, and some of the best Motown songs have several kinds of hooks in each song, in the lyrics, background vocals, chorus, rhythm sections, and melody. People everywhere—all over the world—identified with that sound. There are as many interpretations and definitions of the Motown sound as there are people who love it.

Part of the credit for the sharp attack of the instruments on any Motown record goes to dumb luck. The acoustics in the first studio were so tacky, they amplified the sound of any instrument naturally. The room emitted a big, booming sound that Berry at first believed would mar the records. Instead, like so many other things in Berry's life, it had the opposite effect and worked to his advantage. This inadvertent recording ambience was so haphazard that it can't be duplicated today with millions of dollars of sophisticated equipment.

Of course none of this would have mattered at all if it weren't for the great songs. As a songwriter, Berry's great strength was that he didn't set out to write poetry, or make a statement, or pen a classic; he just wanted to tell a story. Berry's approach is summed up in this quote:

"Try and make it appear it's happening right now so people can associate with it. Not 'My girl broke up with me' but 'My girl's breaking up with me.' "

Quality Control, the division that screened every single track for release, was tough to please; their standards were high. Someone from Quality Control might tell a writer to his face that his song was "garbage" or great. There was nothing in between. Grading a song for the lyrics, title, arrangement, lead and backing vocals, style, and sound became standard procedure.

Many songwriters were upset whenever Berry started rearranging a tune or rewriting a line, especially since he would then take a co-writing credit, no matter how little he may have contributed. As it was, all Motown writers' songs was published by Berry's Jobete Music, so he was already getting a sizable cut of a song's royalties even when he didn't have credit on it. But Berry's input also turned many mediocre or borderline efforts into first-rate hits.

Another erroneous impression about Motown is that several acts recorded the same song, then the different versions "competed" for release. In fact, we recorded songs that other groups had hits with for our albums simply because Jobete—and Berry—earned the royalties on a record, no matter who sang it. The Supremes recorded the Vandellas' "Come and Get These Memories," and the Tops' "I Can't Help Myself" and "Shake Me, Wake Me (When It's Over)." These recordings were not considered for release as singles, they were just filler.

Artists were usually the first—and probably the only—ones to hear a writer's grumblings when he or she thought Berry had taken more than his share of credit. Lots of independent record companies were a lot less particular about these things; today they're all out of business. In its final form, any great Motown record was a product of equal parts artistic expression and quality control. Berry took this idea as far as it would go; soon, artists would be subject to another kind of quality control.

*   *   *

In July 1961 "Buttered Popcorn" became our second release on Tamla. It was another sweltering summer, and of course the studio was hotter than hell. Each of us wore lightweight clothing, but by the end of the session we looked like we'd all been dunked. Capturing that carefree sound took a lot of hard work!

Flo sang lead on "Buttered Popcorn," a song written by Berry and Motown's vice president of sales, Barney Ales, and she really jammed with it as only she could. Everything about the record—the background vocals, the lyrics, the music—was upbeat and sassy. The song had a great dance riff, and I think "Popcorn" was the most raucous thing we ever released. The musicians were pleased with the session, and we all left the studio believing we had a hit.

Though Barney Ales wanted to give this record a big push, for reasons unknown to us it never got any real support from the company. The B side was "Who's Loving You," the lovely ballad we had recorded earlier with Smokey. Naturally we were proud of our first two singles. At last we felt we had the credibility we needed. Later I learned that Berry didn't care for "Buttered Popcorn"; though most people who heard Flo's voice loved it, Berry didn't think it had the commercial sound he was looking for.

It was such a thrill to go to the sock hops and sing our own songs, songs no one else had ever recorded before. This is where we learned to lip-synch, though very often we would be really singing along with our record with our microphones off. Standing up and singing songs that belong only to you is the most satisfying and exhilarating feeling on earth. We were legitimate. Finally.

About a month after we released "Buttered Popcorn" in the summer of 1961, the Marvelettes recorded their biggest hit, "Please Mr. Postman." The record was one of the few early Motown releases to be written by one of the singers (there were a couple of exceptions: Mary Wells's "Bye Bye Baby," and Smokey's tunes, of course). Seventeen-year-old Georgeanna Dobbins wrote it overnight after Motown talent scout Robert Bateman had suggested that her group, then known as the Marvels, work up some original material. It was Berry who changed the group's name to the Marvelettes. Of the original group —Georgeanna, Gladys Horton, Katherine Anderson, Wanda Young, and Juanita Cowart—only Wanda had graduated from high school when "Please Mr. Postman" hit.

The first time we saw them was a Saturday afternoon, and they were entering a studio as Mary Wells was leaving. They were new around and absolutely thrilled to see a big star like Mary. The office was buzzing about the fact that the Marvelettes had written their song themselves, so we were anxious to find out more about them.

We were awful, at first, whispering to one another about the fact that the Marvelettes not only looked square but were from Inkster, Michigan, in the sticks. Coming from the inner city, we considered ourselves far more sophisticated. The Marvelettes were always very down to earth; sometimes they even seemed unsure of themselves.

The Marvelettes had been rehearsing in the basement and Robert Bateman was walking around looking real proud. We were a bit jealous of this new girl group. There was a feeling of family at Motown, but they were still encroaching on our territory. After all, we had been the first girl group to join Motown. The four of us, however, were curious, so we introduced ourselves. Flo never stood on ceremony. She was always ready with compliments and encouragement for other singers, so when she overheard the Marvelettes practicing, she offered to help.

"I heard you girls practicing," Flo said to Gladys. "Why don't you ad lib a little bit more?"

"That's a good idea," Gladys replied. "What do you have in mind?"

"Like say, 'Plea-ea-ea-ea-ease Mr. Postman.' Or add some 'Oh yeah's."

"Great! Come downstairs and show me that part again. I think it will really work."

"Sure," said Flo as they all trooped down the stairs together.

Flo returned after a while, smiling. "Gladys can really sing," she said. "She is nervous because another girl named Georgeanna Dobbins wrote that song and was supposed to be singing the lead on it, but she dropped out at the last minute."

Flo was always willing to help someone, and she and Gladys soon became fast friends. (For the "Mr. Postman" session the drummer was none other than Marvin Gaye. The song's memorable backbeat wasn't written into it; Marvin had just started playing, and all the other musicians fell in.)

Like many other groups at Motown, the Marvelettes were recording for Berry before they even had a contract. Of course, the record was a smash, and Berry wanted to put them out on the road as soon as possible. But there were problems. Not only were the girls still in school, but Gladys was an orphan and a ward of the court. It was necessary for Motown to appoint a legal guardian for her, and Esther Edwards's husband, a Michigan state legislator, George Edwards, was called upon.

Esther Edwards recalls how obtaining this guardianship was almost impossible. "I had to talk to Jim Lincoln, judge of the probate court, who I knew because we both worked in Democratic politics. He was not enthusiastic about it; you know, nobody wanted their kids to be in show business. I explained the situation and told him I would be the chaperone with them while they were on the road for that three weeks. I also promised I would make the girls study. I handed him a copy of 'Please Mr. Postman.'

"Bright and early the next morning he called and said, 'Esther, let me tell you one thing. When I showed my kids the Marvelettes' records, they screamed and ran out of the house. I couldn't believe it! They ran all over the neighborhood telling the kids and everybody that their father was the guardian of the Marvelettes. I get more respect for that than for being a judge or their father.' "

The Marvelettes' first tour included a week in New York City at the Apollo Theater, a week in Philadelphia, and then on to Washington, D.C., for a week at the Howard Theater. True to her word, Mrs. Edwards saw to it that they rose early each morning and took in all the historical sights, even the U.S. Mint. She had promised not only that the girls would keep up their schoolwork while on the road, but that they would deliver oral reports on all the places they'd been once they got back to school.

"We thought traveling would be fun," Gladys said, "but all we had time to do was the show, go to bed early, and then get up early to visit all the sightseeing spots. You know, Mrs. Edwards was real hard on us."

We'd started traveling to shows outside the Detroit area on the weekends. Our first big show was in Cincinnati, followed by another in Pittsburgh. John usually drove us to the gigs in his trusty VW van, but because this was a longer trip John's wife, Lily Mae, was coming along with us, and Berry lent us his Cadillac. We were scared, nervous, thrilled, and happy to be playing real theaters, where we could sing live, which we hadn't been doing much of since losing Marvin Tarplin. Also, we weren't doing the cover tunes anymore. For these shows, the promoter in each town supplied us with a band, and each act on the bill sang just a few songs. Our repertoire included "Buttered

Popcorn," "Who's Loving You," "He's Seventeen," and "I Want a Guy," all records Barbara sang on, but for which she never received royalties.

Our first show was on a bill with Gladys Knight and the Pips. They were simply fabulous. We watched their performance from backstage and were so in awe of them. By then Gladys had been singing professionally for over a decade; the group's command of the audience made it seem easy. We wondered if we would ever be that good.

We were terrible! Without Marv, and singing with an unfamiliar band, we were lost. Barbara sang lead on "He's Seventeen," and from the downbeat, she was singing in one key and the band was playing in another. This was the first time Barbara had sung this song live, and she was terrified. We knew something was wrong from the first second, but this being the first time we'd ever sung live with a strange band, we didn't know what to do to correct this mistake. We were up there for what felt like an eternity. When it was over, the four of us ran off the stage in tears.

Gladys and the Pips were so kind to us, telling us not to worry, it could happen to anyone, and we would do better next show. Their encouragement helped us a lot, and we tried to put it behind us. For some reason, though, Diane just couldn't leave it alone, and was still complaining about the incident as we drove to Pittsburgh, where we would spend the night with her relatives. Barbara apologized to us, but there wasn't much any of us could do about it now except vow that nothing like it would ever happen again.

The next show was uneventful, and as we left Pittsburgh, Barbara begged John to let her drive Berry's car. John had been teaching all of us how to drive, but we took the wheel only when we were out on a highway, never in a busy town. At first he wisely told Barbara no, but she kept bugging him, so at the next light, he let her take the wheel. Of course, none of us had any business driving any car, let alone Berry's, and we all knew it.

When John parked, he'd turned the wheel at such an angle that the second Barbara pulled away, she rammed into a car on our left. We were in trouble. John's wife was the only female with a driver's license, so she agreed that she would take the blame for what happened.

The car was barely scratched, but because we were from out of town Barbara and John had to appear in court a few days later. Barbara was supposed to be Mrs. O'Den, but it slipped her mind. When the judge called out, "Mrs. O'Den, please step forward," Barbara just sat on the bench like a bump. The judge called her name a couple more times, and John kept nudging her in the ribs. She finally came to her senses and rose. It was all cleared up, and we were all certain that our secret was safe.

Once we were home, though, it wasn't long before the truth got back to Berry. We never knew who spilled the beans, but no one—except John—was above suspicion.

One evening Berry summoned us into his office, one at a time. I don't remember whom Berry questioned first, but he made it impossible for anyone coming out of his office to say anything to the others, so we had no way of knowing what Berry knew or who had said what. I was literally shaking as I entered the room. Speaking gently, Berry asked me all kinds of questions about what happened to his Caddy. The office seemed to be closing in on me until I felt like a prisoner in a cell. After a few minutes of this interrogation, I surmised that Berry might know the truth, but I'd promised to back up my friends, and that's what I did.

"Mary, who was driving the car when the accident happened?"

"John's wife—"

Before I'd even finished, Berry said, "I know who was driving the car, so you might as well tell me the truth! The one thing I hate," he continued in a firm voice, "is a liar, and for that reason, *you* are no longer in the group."

I couldn't take it. It was hard enough for me to lie to anyone, but to have it lead to this! I started crying.

"Yes, I lied to you, because we agreed to tell this lie. My loyalty is to my group. My girls are the most important thing in the world to me. And I'd lie to save them again, if I had to, because we can always get another manager. I may never get another group like this."

With that, I ran out of the office and into the darkened street. My eyes were almost swollen closed as I walked up and down West Grand Boulevard in confusion. At my age, what was I going to do—be a secretary? I regretted lying to Berry. My head was spinning and my eyes ached, but I continued pacing the block. Who had cracked? Why hadn't everybody stuck together?

Finally I was summoned back to the office. Flo, Diane, and Barbara were already there, and everyone had pretty much calmed down. Berry was sitting behind his desk, leaning back in his big, overstuffed executive's chair. For the longest time, he just stared at us the way a parent looks at a child who has learned his lesson.

"You girls shouldn't have lied to me," Berry said quietly. "I will not tolerate that kind of dishonesty, and you ought to know you will always be found out in the end, so what's the use? And Mary, don't worry—you're back in the group."

It's strange, but at that moment I was proud of myself, even though I had done something against my principles. I had stood up to someone who was bigger and stronger than me. Years later, I would have to stand up to Berry again, but he wouldn't confront me personally; he'd have the company do it for him.

This episode marked a real turning point in our relationship with Motown, for it proved that even though we didn't have a hit, we were still worth hanging on to. We were doing more hops and shows, and we were still *the* live local act, but we were anxious to get beyond that.

Though we were spending as much time as possible at Hitsville, we still liked hanging out with our friends. We weren't really stars yet, but we weren't exactly your typical teenagers anymore either. Being around our friends provided an escape from the responsibility and pressure, and we could be normal kids.

We were still running with a pretty wild crowd that included Tall George, Berry Fletcher, Silky, Willie Peeples, and Richard Street. They were mostly friends of mine, but Diane would hang around with us, and before long our friend Silky developed a crush on her. She wanted nothing to do with him, but instead of letting it drop, Silky decided to pursue her. Like many sixteen-year-old boys, he thought that by being obnoxious he would win her heart.

We were at one of those crazy parties when Silky yelled across the room to Diane, "Hey, come here, girl!"

"What do you want?" Diane replied indifferently.

"Come on, girl," Silky mock-pleaded as he grabbed her arm. "Do you want to fool around?"

"Oh, leave me alone!"

With that, Silky gave Diane what we called a body slam, which was actually a dance move. He grabbed her by the arms and pulled her up against him forcefully. Everyone roared with laughter. I was shocked but couldn't help but be amused by the look on Diane's face.

"What did you do, Silky," Tall George yelled, "get too close?"

Diane was furious. "Leave me alone!"

"Let her alone, Silky," I said, trying to sound as serious as I could without cracking up. I knew Diane was really angry, and I didn't want her blaming me and Flo for this predicament.

"Mary, I am going home," Diane said.

"Now see what you've done?" I said to Silky, giving him what I hoped was a meaningful look. Diane didn't like not being in control of a situation, and seeing her like this was amusing. Obviously she saw no humor whatsoever in the situation and was leaving. I helped her gather her things and followed her out. I wanted to stay because my new boyfriend Willie Peeples was there, but he came out right behind us.

"Do you girls want me to give you a ride?"

"No, thank you," Diane huffed as she began walking away rapidly.

"Oh, come on, Diane," I pleaded. I wanted to spend time with Willie, and Diane knew it, but because Diane and I were the only ones from our neighborhood at this party, we were pretty much obliged to travel together.

Willie had a white Dodge, which I thought of as our lovemobile. I knew he would want to drop Diane off first and then he and I would cruise around for a while before parking somewhere and spending a couple of hours in the backseat.

"If you don't let me drive you," he warned, "I'll follow you anyway."

With that, Diane finally gave in.

I could never convince her that Silky wouldn't bother her again, and she refused to go with me to any more of that crowd's parties.

Around this time, my family had the good fortune to move into one of the row houses, like the one Flo's family had lived in before her father died. Though still technically part of the Projects, the row houses were single-family dwellings, and moving into one of them was a step up.

All through school, I dated several guys, but didn't have a real boyfriend again until I met Ronnie Hammers. With him, my emotions were more intense than ever. I was madly in love.

Ronnie and I were true high-school sweethearts. Being older, he was set to graduate a year ahead of me. To my young, romantic mind, the only sure way to protect our precious love was to announce our engagement. I think what made him agree to it was that whatever we did after we became engaged would be overlooked, since we'd be practically married anyway. And we did "whatever" right away. Wisely, our parents kept their reservations about it to themselves. They must have known that our wedding plans wouldn't come to fruition and that forbidding the engagement would make us more serious than we really were.

We were nearing the end of our high-school years and beginning to feel very grown-up. We were all changing. I had the feeling that things had changed with Diane, too. Perhaps it was Richard Street, or someone else, but I could sense in Diane a different attitude toward boys. They weren't just cute anymore. Her tomboyishness had completely vanished, giving way to a more feminine style of competing. Suddenly, for no apparent reason, Diane would make some statement, comparing her figure and mine. Since Flo and Barbara were both referred to as "stacked," Diane could find little to remark on there. But when it came to me, it was another story. We were both skinny, and then thin was most definitely not in. Still, Diane found plenty to say about everything from my legs to my hairstyle, which I changed every other week.

Even at that young age, I could see that Diane was trying to build up her own self-confidence. Her haughtiness was just a front; deep down, she believed that she wasn't as pretty as the other girls. She craved attention, and in her attempts to get it, she could seem almost ruthless. Sometimes she would throw a childish tantrum, then moments later pretend it was all a big joke, that she was just being silly. Her bluntness could be disconcerting and feelings were hurt, but we saw Diane's actions as the product of thoughtlessness, not malice. If Diane ever criticized one of us in public, none of us would call her on it. It was more important to us then to be ladies than to settle some score. Besides, we knew where she was coming from. Diane was our friend, and we accepted her. At one time or another, each of us lost our patience with her, but compared to our main goal—the success of the Supremes—everything else was secondary. Forcing a confrontation with Diane didn't seem to be worth risking the group. Nothing did.

Most of the time it was easy to ignore Diane's behavior, but things took a different turn when she decided that she could borrow my boyfriend as easily as she borrowed my clothes. Diane was one to covet anything that belonged to anyone else, and, as we got older, those things could include men. Diane liked a challenge—whether it was to get into a sorority, make a team, or get a guy—and she never walked away, no matter how what the odds or who would get hurt. Toward the end of high school, Diane would complain about other girls not liking her, and we would all sympathize. But over the years, I began to wonder which problem came first: Did other girls treat her badly and force her to prove herself, or was her willingness to compete against them so obvious that they couldn't help but dislike her? In those pre–women's lib days, lots of girls thought fighting over men was what being a real woman was all about. Other women who weren't your friends were the competition; men were the prey and the prize.

Around this time Diane and Smokey's interest in each other was well known. We had cut a few records with him and we would see him around Hitsville. Everyone knew he was married to Bobby Rogers's cousin, Claudette, so I was surprised when one day Diane said, "Guess what? I went out with Smokey!"

"You did what?" Flo and I replied. She had been flirting with Smokey openly for some time, but we never suspected it would come to this. They were very discreet, never going out too much in public. Diane would tell us where Smokey had taken her to dinner, or whenever he had sent her flowers.

After Ronnie and I had announced our engagement, Diane began dropping hints that she wanted Ronnie for herself. Fluttering her eyelashes at him, she tried to charm him. If we were all out together, she would act as if he were her boyfriend. Ronnie and I would be dancing, and she would cut in. Not being very sophisticated, Ronnie didn't know what was going on. "Why is she always talking to me?" he'd ask. But all I could do was shrug my shoulders. I could never have said what I thought without looking bad, and, more than anything, I wanted Ronnie to see me as a nice girl, a mature young lady. When Diane made disparaging remarks about my thin legs or flat behind in front of Ronnie, I'd be torn between rage and fear that any rocking of the boat might destroy the group. Of course the Supremes were important, but standing up for myself was even more so. I was just too young to know how.

One afternoon, we were on a bus when we heard "This Magic Moment" being sung a cappella from the very last row. Five boys, who seemed younger than us, were straining to emulate the Drifters' sound. I smiled to myself, knowing we were on our way to make our own record, and I wondered if someday, somewhere, other young girls whom we would never meet would be singing along to our records and trying to capture our sound.

CHAPTER 10

We had been officially signed to Motown for almost a year and a half now, and from where we stood it seemed everyone except the Supremes was forging ahead. Mary Wells' "The One Who Really Loves You," the Marvelettes' "Beechwood 4-5789" and "Playboy," the Contours' "Do You Love Me," and the Miracles' "I'll Try Something New" had been climbing the charts, while we had barely scraped into the Hot 100 with "Your Heart Belongs to Me"—and that had been the high point. In the fall we would release a light tango-tinged girl-group song, "Let Me Go the Right Way," but after it took four months to perch at #90, we were beginning to worry. Even the diehard optimists around Motown, who had thought everything we'd released would hit, were beginning to wonder.

By now, almost all of the artists who would make Motown great were on the roster. Of them all, I will always remember Marvin Gaye. He was one of the truly gifted.

They say behind every great man is a great woman. Berry Gordy had several women behind him, and among the first were his sisters Gwen and Anna. The pair can also be credited with having a hand in launching Marvin's career. Marvin arrived in Detroit with his mentor, Harvey Fuqua, after they both departed the Moonglows, a Washington, D.C., vocal group whose best-known hits were "Sincerely" and "Ten Commandments of Love." Harvey had been the group's lead singer, but in Detroit he was working as an independent producer with a couple of small labels, including his own Tri Phi and Harvey. In late 1960, he had married Berry's sister Gwen, and when their Anna Records folded, many of their artists came with Harvey over to Motown. Marvin seemed to flow in with that transition. Early on, he recorded a few unsuccessful singles—"Let Your Conscience Be Your Guide," "Sandman," and "Soldier's Plea"—and was still trying to find his niche.

"Who's the cute guy wearing the beret?" I asked the first time I spotted Marvin Gaye in the studio in 1961.

"Oh, he's a drummer. Used to be in the Moonglows," one of the musicians replied.

"Sure is cute. What's his name?"

"Don't know. Friend of Harvey's."

Overhearing this, Barbara stage-whispered, "Come on, he's got to have a name."

Somehow Marvin sensed that we were talking about him, and we saw him blush. It was rare to see that genuine shyness in a man, and it endeared him to us all the more. We giggled behind our hands about it, but from that moment, Marvin was very special to us. As I learned more about him, I attributed his lovely manners to the fact that he was a preacher's son.

Marvin was known around Motown for wearing kookie hats— tam-o'-shanters, berets, and jaunty fedoras, each perched slightly to the side of his head. His unusual appearance was probably his way of hiding his shyness; ironically, it only attracted more attention. We knew him from seeing him around in the studio, but we only got to know him well when he would sing just to us.

By coincidence, we all wore pedal pushers to the studio one day. Nothing was going on in the lobby or out on the porch, so we sauntered down to the studio, not knowing what to expect. The studio was very dim, and sitting in the middle, as if on a deserted, spotlit stage, was Marvin softly playing the piano. He surely heard us as we came in, but he didn't miss a note.

"You girls look real nice today," he said. Other guys would have said it one way, but Marvin spoke in a hushed tone that was very respectful and polite.

"Oh, these old things?" Feminine wiles!

"If I knew you'd be here, Marvin, I would have gotten dressed up."

"It was too warm to wear anything else."

In Marvin's presence, we became as shy and reticent as he was. Then everything began to fall into place like the most carefully blocked scene from a movie. We each took our places around the piano, arranging ourselves in what we thought were our most seductive poses. Maybe one of us would make eye contact with him, and that would be the most romantic thing in the world.

Times like this were so precious. Even though there were four of us, we each felt like we were in some beautiful dream with him. Other guys were cute or sharp; Marvin was beautiful. Other guys teased and joked around; Marvin was always considerate and solicitous.

"What do you girls want to hear next?" he would ask quietly, looking up at each of us in turn.

" 'Mona Lisa,' " Flo would say.

" 'Come to Me,' " Barbara always yelled.

" 'Tears on My Pillow.' " I loved hearing Marvin sing in that high register.

"Try something different," Diane suggested.

"We just love your LP with all the love songs," Diane said, referring to *The Soulful Moods of Marvin Gaye*, his first album.

"You all like it?" he would ask as if he couldn't believe anyone would.

Later, on our way home, we would daydream aloud about him. "How old do you think he is?" I mused.

"Nineteen or twenty," Flo guessed.

"Girl, can you just imagine him singing to you while he held you in his arms, in between kisses?" Barbara would say this while clasping her hands to her breast and rolling her eyes heavenward. Now this might seem a little silly, but we were all very serious. Being with Marvin was like having every girlhood dream come true. He was a prince, and there was just no one like him anywhere.

"He can't have a girlfriend. We would know about it, wouldn't we?" I reasoned.

"Not necessarily." Flo wasn't so sure.

"It doesn't matter," Barbara proclaimed, "I say Marvin Gaye is one of the best-looking men around here and I sure wish he was *my* boyfriend." At this time, Barbara was dating Willie Richardson, her future husband, but you could tell she wasn't kidding about Marvin.

Our attraction to Marvin was not really a sexual one. The minute we laid eyes on him we knew that we loved him in that pure, sweet way few people ever get a chance to love anymore. It was enough just to be around Mr. Gaye. Everyone seemed to enjoy being in his company. We were still in our early teens, and Marvin was twenty-three or so; no doubt he saw us as silly teenage girls, and our attraction to him must have been comically obvious to him and anyone else. But he never treated us as if we were silly, and so we continued to hang on his every word. In the next year or so, as Marvin's star rose with "Stubborn Kind of Fellow," "Hitch Hike," "Pride and Joy," and "Can I Get a Witness," I knew no one deserved it more.

*   *   *

The biggest event of this most eventful year came early in October. We had arranged to rehearse at my house, and Flo and I were there, working with our friend Diane Watson, who was a great dancer. She was helping us put together some new routines, and we were practicing when Barbara called—she was pregnant! After I recovered from the initial shock, Flo and I started talking about Diane replacing Barbara. We still felt we needed four voices, and she seemed the most obvious candidate at the moment.

When Diane Ross showed up, we gave her Barbara's news, and we talked about it a bit, then all sat down to wait for Barbara. I was beginning to see how hard it was to keep a group together. It was one thing to be schoolgirls, with your lives pretty well defined, but now it seemed like everyone we knew was getting married or going off to college or work.

Finally I said, "We've got a new girl here; she can teach us to dance."

Diane didn't say anything for a minute. Flo was on the couch, drinking a soda, and Diane Watson just stood in silence.

We dropped the subject again and sat around waiting for Barbara, but she never showed up.

"I'll tell you what," Diane said, as she jumped out of her chair, "Barbara's out! If the three of us can't make it, then we won't make it. I'll see you later." Then she left.

The year 1961 slipped through my fingers before I had much of a chance to grasp all its lessons. I was so caught up in everything—every day seemed like a new adventure. I knew that I loved this lifestyle. Barbara Martin had married in December, but she planned to continue with us for a while, even though she was pregnant. Flo and I didn't want to see her go. Though her husband supported her in her decision to continue her career, we wondered just how long this would last.

At Christmas, none of us could afford gifts for anyone but our closest relatives, but we didn't care. The four of us spent our time together thanking God for all our blessings and thinking about what the future held in store. We always shared our daydreams, but now it was clear: we had to be stars. Part of this was all girlish musing, but suddenly it seemed that anything could happen.

There was much to look forward to, but nothing was as important to me as graduating from high school. During my time at Northeastern, I studied English with Mr. Boone, a very good teacher known for being tough. My first encounter with him wasn't entirely pleasant. Before he even had me in one of his classes, he pulled me aside in the hall one day to inform me that my thinking I was a "star" cut no mustard with him. I was a bit frightened of him and confused as to why he would even bother me. Sure enough, I did get his class, and the first time, he did fail me. But when I took his class again, I grew to know him better and he seemed to take a special interest in me.

I was a basically happy-go-lucky kid, and I never thought too much about my early childhood, at least not consciously. For our final exam in Mr. Boone's modern literature class, in the first days of January 1962, we had to write an essay. I don't remember exactly what the question was—it dealt with psychology—but whatever it was prompted me to write a short autobiography in which I revealed to my teacher thoughts I never knew I had, and, reading it years later, I would find answers to many questions.

Psychology is the study of the mind. An individual who cares about himself may become a psychologist. This may seem strange, but if a person senses that he has a psychological problem, he can analyze himself and possibly overcome his problem. There are many ways in which people become mentally ill. Mentally ill persons may be what we call crazy, *but there are some situations where a person has just a small problem and is disturbed, which causes a maladjusted personality. I am was [for some reason, I left both words] such a person." My problem began when I was a very young girl.*

Of my confusing early childhood with I.V. and my real mother, I wrote:

Situations such as this cause people to react in different ways. I have developed a protective shell, which whenever I feel I may face a conflict, I draw into. Why? Is it because I subconsciously feel I might be snatched again? For a little girl, this problem can become so great that anything might happen.

. . . I try to cover up my deficiency by developing a pleasing personality. Actually, underneath this, I am still a young and

frightened girl. I also try to better my physical appearance, so that, even though I might be dumb, I will be pretty, and this might cause people to look over my deficiencies.

I recognized my problem but I still can't overcome this constant veil of fear. . . . If many of the parents would realize that children have feelings and that they need love sometimes, this problem might be destroyed.

A few days later, Mr. Boone told me privately that he had read my paper before his church congregation. He told me that I was exceptionally perceptive and suggested that I consider becoming a writer. From that day on, I have kept a diary, in which I have recorded my thoughts and feelings.

My mother was still clinging to the dream that I would stop singing and start earning a decent living as a secretary or go to college. All I wanted was to wear that cap and gown and hold my diploma in my hands. I had promised Mom that I would finish school, no matter what happened with the Supremes.

I was also looking forward to taking my diploma with me when I visited my relatives in Mississippi that summer. I especially wanted my father to see it. A few years before, my father had married one of the daughters of Big Daddy, my maternal grandmother's husband. and they had a child, my half-sister Robin. When I'd seen him in the summer of 1961 we had spent more time together, and I got to know his new family. Just before I'd arrived that year my father suffered a severe stroke. He was very weak, and I knew that he would never be the same again. Still, like all children, I suppose, I could not accept that my father, whom I'd come to know so late and grown to love so deeply, would die. He was so proud of my accomplishments, and the one thing he said to me over and over again was, "I just want to live to see at least one of my children graduate from high school. Promise me you'll graduate. I will send you money for your dress or anything else you need. But, baby, I just want you to get a diploma. It will take you a long way in life." I promised him I would be back the next year, diploma in hand.

My father died one week before the graduation ceremonies. It comforted me to think that at least he knew that I kept my promise, and I have since wondered if my father didn't hold onto life, as some terminally ill people have been known to do, until he was certain that I would be all right. His passing didn't come as a complete surprise, and though I was very sad, I was determined to go to Mississippi to bury him.

It was during my trip down South to arrange my father's funeral that I first encountered blatant prejudice. On previous visits down South, I'd never noticed too much difference between the way my family there was treated by the whites and the way I'd been treated in Detroit. When I was very little, tagging along with my older cousins Josephine and Christine, we all talked to and joked with the white kids outside the movie theater. Of course, we were separated from the white kids inside, but we never thought much about it. You grow up being taught certain attitudes and, not knowing any differently, you may never think about it. At that age, you don't see the evil behind such seemingly innocuous practices, and you are in no position to do anything about them. When I arrived in Greenville, however, I was a different person: confident, self-assured, and proud. I'd been around, and, as a result of my experiences, I had a sense of self few blacks in my father's community could imagine.

When I walked into one of Greenville's major department stores with my cousin Josephine in tow, I don't know what kind of reception I expected, but it certainly wasn't the condescending rudeness I got from a white redneck salesman. As the eldest child, it was my duty to select the clothes my father would be buried in. I had already purchased the shirt, tie, and white gloves. When I asked to see socks, the salesman showed me a cheap, shoddy pair.

As he casually flung them on the counter, he said, "Oh, these will be okay." I could hear in his tone of voice the unspoken words "for a colored."

"No, they won't! My father just died, and these are for him. I can afford the best and that's exactly what I want." I was stunned; I had never in my life been made to feel different or inferior because I was black, and in my grief and shock I was far more aggressive than I might have been. The salesman was taken aback, but he complied without another word. As soon as she could, Josephine hustled me out of the store and tried to calm me down. As we made our way back to Grandmama's house, I was crying and screaming, "It is ridiculous to be treated this way! Our money is just as good as anybody else's! These people have got their nerve!"

What I didn't know then was that down South I was the one with the nerve. I felt as though I had suddenly matured in ways I couldn't describe. I was anxious to go home, and Flo, Diane, and Barbara were happy to see me. They'd continued going to Motown each day, but all plans were on hold until my return.

We were at our usual stations in the lobby when we first saw Stevie Wonder.

"Flo, who is that boy Ronnie White is helping up the stairs?" I asked one day as we were lounging around the lobby.

"Looks like the kid is blind," she whispered.

"Oh," someone else said, "that must be be the little blind boy Ronnie was telling Berry about. He's nine or ten years old and really gifted in music."

Stevie's mother and brother led the him into B.G.'s office, and the four of them emerged minutes later. As Berry's shadows, the four of us fell in behind and followed them into the studio. The little blind boy—Steveland Morris, soon to be rechristened Stevie Wonder—played piano and every other instrument the boss requested.

"What else can you play, Stevie?" Berry would ask after Stevie had demonstrated his ability on one instrument. Stevie would jump up, find his way to something else, and start playing that—keyboards, horns, percussion. Nothing seemed beyond him. I especially remember him playing a harmonica he'd brought with him. Of course, we were all dumbstruck with amazement. At the time, the Supremes were still the youngest artists on the roster. To see someone as young as Stevie was something else.

"This Stevie is truly a young genius," Berry muttered. (In a recent interview, Berry says that he wasn't impressed with Stevie, but I was there. We were *all* impressed, to say the least!)

Stevie Wonder was immediately accepted into the Motown family, and he came to the studio all the time. Learning every inch of the place, he eventually got to the point where he didn't need help getting from room to room, and before long he was pulling his practical jokes. Everyone loved him, and that was a good thing, because he was full of mischief. Stevie seemed to always know who was standing near him, and one of his favorite pastimes was to run up and pinch young ladies on their bottoms. He would also tell one of us exactly what we were wearing—what color it was, and how it was styled. Some of us would act amazed, or at least feign amazement; of course, he was in cahoots with somebody. We all loved him.

Early in the spring of 1962, Barbara left the group. Her baby was due in July, and she was really showing. Having a child is a huge responsibility, and I was sure she made the right decision. We would miss her, but we kept in touch and attended her baby shower. Flo, Diane, and I decided it was just too hard keeping a fourth member. The Supremes would be a trio from now on.

Our career seemed to have stalled. Not much was happening for us, so when one of the Marvelettes turned up pregnant that summer, Flo was asked to replace her for a tour. Flo went to Hitsville and rehearsed with the other three girls every day. Their steps were pretty simple and their harmonies weren't all that complex, so it was easy for Flo. After all, compared to the Marvelettes, the Supremes were old pros, having been at it for over three years now. Their short tour followed the usual itinerary—Philadelphia, D.C., and some one-nighters scattered between.

During this tour, Flo and Gladys Horton became closer than ever. Years later Gladys told me about their talks. Gladys would explain to Flo why she felt that, after living in a series of foster homes, Motown really was her home. Flo felt comfortable with Gladys and told her things she would never tell anyone. They shared a room, and Flo told her about everything, including the rape.

The tour was rough; sometimes they'd do eight shows a day. No matter how tired they were, though, they'd lie awake in bed and talk until sleep overcame them.

"I wish I could be more outgoing," Flo said. "Do you think I act too stuck up or anything?"

Gladys replied no, then Flo continued.

"Well, the reason I act this way is because it takes me a long time to get used to guys because of what happened to me."

Gladys understood.

Flo could be friends with some guys, though, and one of her friends was William Knight of the Pips. Mrs. Ardeena Johnson, the girls' chaperone on this trip, caught the pair talking backstage and reprimanded Flo, saying "You can't get too serious . . ."

While Flo was out with the Marvelettes, the Supremes were on hold. Now if anyone around the studio were talking about "the girls," they were talking about the Marvelettes, not us. Diane and I were alone together, again. We became disillusioned and decided to run away from home.

I don't know exactly what went through our heads. Maybe we got nostalgic for the days when we'd just returned to Motown and were treated like we were really something special. Those days were over, and we were beginning to be known as the "no-hit" Supremes. My cousin Josephine had married a man named James Jenkins the summer before. The wedding had taken place at the Pippins' home on Bassett Street, and my family, Jackie Burkes, and the other three Supremes attended. The Jenkinses had since moved to the West Side of Chicago, so that was our destination. We packed our best clothes and took a Greyhound bus to Illinois.

Our parents knew we were going, so we weren't exactly running away from home, but we were running away from Motown and everything else. We were young ladies now, fresh out of school and ready for life. Besides, we needed to get away. We knew where we would stay, and we set out to have a good time. We loved the Chicago nightlife, and we even started dating a couple of the Dells.

Things were going pretty well, but Diane was getting on my nerves. We had to share my cousin's living room, and all she had was a couch, so one of us had to sleep on the floor. During the whole two weeks Diane was there, she never once offered to switch places with me, so I slept on the floor. She went home, but I stayed on for another month. Finally, I got homesick too, and returned to Detroit.

We resumed our old, familiar places in the lobby. Not only did we not get the kind of reception we'd received after our first extended absence, but we could see that Hitsville was crawling with new acts dying to get in.

Around this time, Diane decided to try and get a real job at Hitsville. On slow days, when there were no sessions and nothing for us to do, we got bored. Also, it was now obvious that Diane had a crush on Berry. "I'm going to get him," she'd say. I always liked Berry, but it was hard to picture him as a boyfriend. I thought nothing of it. Diane did land a job as Berry's secretary, but it was more—and less— than a real position. Her duties included keeping us posted on our assignments and bookings and cleaning Berry's desk. Many people around Hitsville thought the job was a joke, and Diane got her share of teasing about it. But she just ignored everyone else and did her work.

Through the years I've come to accept certain tenets of astrology, and I certainly saw them at work in the Supremes. Flo, a Cancerian; Diane, an Aries; and me, a Pisces—three completely different, insecure people. What each of us saw in the other two were the parts of herself she lacked or couldn't assert or tried to deny: Flo's earthiness, my nice-guy demeanor, and Diane's aggressive charm. We accidentally discovered that three separate, incomplete young girls combined to create one great woman. That was the Supremes.

CHAPTER 11

In the fall of 1962 Motown began sending its artists out on extended tours across the country. Touring the South in those days, we learned more about people and the world than most of our parents ever wanted us to know. For many of us, being in the South allowed us to experience firsthand the hatred and bigotry that had driven many of our parents North years before.

At the same time, these tours were the most exciting thing ever. Not only did we have lots of fun, but we established friendships—and in some cases, love affairs—that have endured. We were thrilled to go on the tour, especially since the Supremes were just about the only act—except for Stevie—included that hadn't yet had a big hit.

That summer Esther Edwards and Beans Bowles organized a tour that would last from mid-October to Christmas 1962, and include the Regal in Chicago, the Howard in Washington, D.C., and the famed Apollo in New York. These theaters were part of the chitlin' circuit, a loosely organized group of venues that catered to the black audience in major cities. In those days, every black performer dreamed of playing the Apollo, and we were no exception.

Mrs. Morrison, a heavy-set woman who resembled singer Ethel Waters, was the chaperone for all the girls on the tour. She was the first of many official escorts who would travel with us in the early days. Esther Edwards had been the first woman to accompany us on the road, and after her strict, overbearing attitude, Mrs. Morrison seemed like an angel. Still, she lectured us.

"Now, girls, this is an opportunity for you that shouldn't be marred by an overeagerness to become intimate with the boys on this trip," she began. And then went on and on to tell us about the perils of impetuous affairs and the effect the consequences might have on our families, our futures, and—especially—our careers.

"Yes, ma'am," we all answered dutifully.

No matter how strict or easygoing our chaperones, each took every available opportunity to lecture us. The only chaperone who didn't lecture was Diane's mom, Mrs. Ross. She was my favorite of all the chaperones, because her expectations were realistic, and she was the most lenient.

The tour lineup consisted of the Contours, the Tempts, the Marvelettes, the Velvelettes (now best remembered for "Needle in a Haystack" and "He Was Really Sayin' Somethin'"), Stevie Wonder, Marvin Gaye, Mary Wells, the Miracles, and the Supremes. Thrown in for good measure was Singing Sammy Ward, a blues singer, and a comic; in this case it was Winehead Willie, my cousin by marriage, who also functioned as master of ceremonies. He can be heard introducing the acts on the first live recording from the Apollo. Willie and I are the only entertainers in the family, and we were excited to be sharing a bill.

Choker Campbell organized the band, all first-rate Detroit musicians who had been working sessions and club dates. Most of these players made more money playing on recordings than touring, and often in the middle of the tour or after a few stops, one of them would go back to Detroit to work, then meet up with us later on. For this reason, Choker sensibly contracted more than one player on the important instruments, such as drums, guitar, bass, and keyboards.

As was Motown's way back then, all agreements were oral. Neither the bandleaders nor the musicians ever signed papers. Though many people working for Motown complained—justifiably—about the money, I never heard a word from the musicians or leaders.

"No," Choker said once, "I never had a problem with Berry. Everybody was very happy. That makes me feel so good. Happiness, togetherness—that's a beautiful thing. Fifteen, maybe sixteen musicians—if they're happy, they're going to play happy." And Choker was right.

There were so many great musicians on the early tours. I remember sax players Tate Houston, Miller Brisker, Norris Patterson, Joe Collins, Willie Smith, who was also an arranger, and Choker; trumpeters Herbert Williams, Little John Wilson, and Tommy "Shaky" Perkson. The rhythm section included Benny Benjamin and "Swing" Lee, guitarists Marvin Tarplin, Cornelius Grant, keyboardists Teddy Harris and Joe Hunter, and of course, James Jamerson on bass. Trombonist James "Chips" Outcault could make his instrument sound like a person talking, which would have us all screaming with laughter.

Working with a sound of that magnitude behind you makes you feel that music really is bigger than life. The vibrations flowed up from the stage floor and through my whole body, dispelling any nerves or fear. I just couldn't wait to go on.

It was quite a mix of people on that first tour: proper, refined chaperones; young, eager kids; the old show-biz pros like the musicians, who couldn't be fazed by anything. We would all be living together in close quarters for up to four months. Forty-five of us squeezed into that rattling old bus, while others traveled in three cars and a couple of station wagons.

On the day of departure, everyone was in high spirits. It was as if we were all going off to Monte Carlo, or some other exotic place. Even those of us who were habitually late were punctual. A few days earlier, Berry made it clear that he wouldn't tolerate tardiness and that those who tested his rule would be left behind.

There were stacks and stacks of luggage—everything from old battered suitcases tied together with string to cardboard boxes. The Supremes had their fair share of pieces—probably more—and we got upset when some of the others complained that we were bringing along more than we needed. Clutching our cosmetic cases, which were filled to the brim with night cream, powder, mascara, eye shadow, eye-liner pencils, and every other conceivable necessity, we tried to ignore their gripes.

Minutes before we boarded the bus, Berry called all the guys in and warned them that he'd better not hear of any messing around on the road. The fellows promised to behave—if the girls wouldn't bother them! And then Berry said to the girls, "I want you girls to leave the fellows on this trip alone. Especially the Contours—they're nothing but trouble. Just leave them all alone."

With the last-minute instructions taken care of, we were all eager to hit the road. A head count was taken, and Beans Bowles checked to see that all the roadies and assistants were accounted for. That done, we all posed in front of the beat-up old bus with MOTOR CITY TOUR painted on the sides. Our smiles were genuine and filled with optimism, despite the wreck looming behind us. Had we been older and wiser, most of us would have wisely refused to board such a decrepit contraption. But fear never crossed our minds, and no one voiced concern about the vehicle's reliability. As we headed out of Detroit, I was sure I was embarking on the greatest adventure of my life.

As the bus chugged along, we all got situated. Once we got comfortable, we started chattering excitedly:

"What's our first stop?"

"Who cares as long as it's outside of this city?"

"Do we go on before you all do?"

"Depends. Who has the biggest hit record?"

"How come Smokey and them get to ride in their own private car?"

"They paid for it, didn't they?"

"Girl, do you think we'll ever have our own car?"

"Can you all sing good enough to get a hit that will buy you a car?"

"Can your mama?"

We were finally on our way.

Passions ran high and it had little to do with who got to sing lead or which group had top billing. We were only onstage a few hours a night; the real thrill was in the traveling and what was happening on the bus.

Despite Berry's last-minute admonishments, people were pairing off before we'd crossed the Michigan state line: Bobby Rogers of the Miracles and Wanda Young of the Marvelettes; Gladys Horton and Hubert Johnson of the Contours. Off the bus I saw Diane eyeing Smokey. Eddie Kendricks was my choice, and I took every opportunity to be alone with him. Frankly, Berry could have saved his breath. We were too young and too excited to care about consequences. For most of us, this was the first big trip away from home, and we were going to have a good time.

While most of the performers sat up in the front of the bus talking and singing, the musicians sat in the back, which they had designated as their private domain. They had what seemed like endless card games, and the gambling, joking, and storytelling went on through the night, but nobody minded. It was as if we could absorb the wisdom of the road, even in our sleep. Since they were older and a lot more savvy about touring and the South, we took comfort in having them around. Nothing seemed to bother these veterans, and their dry sense of humor about things could put otherwise upsetting situations into perspective.

Our first big stop was the Howard Theater in Washington, D.C., followed by seventeen one-nighters. Every few days we would stop at a cheap motel to bathe and wash some clothes. We seldom got to sleep one to a bed, but compared to sleeping sitting up on the hard bus seats, being able to lie on any mattress was heaven. Living in cramped quarters, eating irregularly, going days without the most basic comforts—this was baptism by fire, but none of us complained. With every bump in the road, bad meal, or sleepless night, we knew we were one step closer to being real professional performers, and we cherished every moment.

As we pulled into Savannah, Georgia, we were surprised to see the Staples Singers going into a motel. A number of the other artists with us had worked with them before, so we all jumped off the bus and were introduced to Pops Staples and his daughters Mavis, Cleo, Yvonne, and his son Pervis. Though the Staples weren't as well known as they would be after signing to the Stax label in the late sixties, their gospel style had been popular with blacks since the forties.

"Oh, I love your music," I told Mavis.

"Well, thanks. What is your group called?"

"The Supremes," I answered proudly.

"Well, if you girls sing as good as you look, you will really go places," she said, smiling.

"Thank you!" I was so thrilled. After that they talked with us a while, giving us encouragement and tips on how to deal with life on the road.

As we continued through the South, we ran into bigotry head on. These were the years when blacks were openly challenging the white supremacists, and with civil-rights legislation right around the corner, some racists seemed more determined than ever to keep what they considered "uppity niggers" in their place. Of course, I was no stranger to racism, but somehow I'd come to think that a troupe of artists like ourselves might escape confrontations.

I learned quite differently in Macon, Georgia, when a big barrel-bellied white sheriff stopped our bus. He introduced himself, then said, "I am the peace officer in this here town, and if you folks have any trouble, you just let me know. I'll take care of you."

As it happened, we'd just come from a local service station where the workers had refused to do some work on our bus. "Y'all go right on back down to that same fillin' station," he said. "I'll make sure they do the repairs y'all need."

We turned around and headed back. As we pulled in, we could hear the attendants loudly "muttering" about "them damn niggers."

Even if they had never said a word, we would have known what they thought from the looks of disgust and hatred on their faces. They stood around, just shuffling their feet and refusing to help us until the sheriff arrived.

"Hey, service that bus!" he yelled. "Don't y'all know a new integration law has passed?"

The attendants reluctantly gave in and did some minor repairs and filled the tank. A satisfied sheriff boarded our bus just as we were about to leave. At this point, we were all convinced that we'd found a champion.

"As y'all can see, the local folks down here are not adjusting too rapidly to the new laws and the change in customs. But never you mind. If you run into any problems, you just let me know. In this county, you are under my jurisdiction, and I will not fall short of my duty to uphold the law just because y'all are black and I'm white."

Once he learned our destination, he told us that the theater we were going to play had a "colored"-folks night where blacks were allowed to sit downstairs and the whites were relegated to the balcony. Since this was the opposite of the usual blacks-in-the-balcony arrangement down South, this was considered pretty progressive.

"Take the intermission time to let the people get settled before you start. Because if niggers and white folks get to fighting, I'll put the lights on so bright, it'll all be over. Do you hear me? The dance will be over." Then he added, "I don't want them blacks and whites together anyway."

At first we were shocked, but we were impressed that he put the law before his own personal prejudices, and not the other way around, as so many people did.

A few days later, as we headed out of town, we had many a laugh imitating the sheriff. He was the perfect prototype of the Southern lawman. Unfortunately, however, we didn't have too many more encounters with bigots that we would be able to laugh about. People like the sheriff were few and far between down there. Our biggest problems were always with restaurants. The bus driver would stop and check out the atmosphere, but most times he'd be told, "Yeah, sure y'all can eat here. Tell 'em to come around to the back."

Hearing this, we would all scream indignantly, "We're *not* going around to the back!"

Once, after being told to come in through the back door, Bobby Rogers of the Miracles jumped off the bus and told the owner, who was standing out in the parking lot, that he wanted to enter the place like everybody else—through the front door. "Hey," he informed the owner, "I'm Bobby Rogers of the Miracles!"

Unimpressed, the owner replied, "If you want to eat, you're going to use the back."

By this time, some of the other guys started shouting insults at the owner. A few had gotten off the bus and were practically up in the guy's face.

"Don't you know there's been a law passed against this kind of stuff?"

"Who do you think you are, anyway, honky?"

"I don't want to eat in your funky old restaurant—"

"You need your ass kicked by us niggers. That will show you—"

"Well," the owner said after a few minutes of this, "I'm gonna get my pistol and . . ."

With that he ran inside, and the fellows ran for the bus. The man was serious, and we expected shots to be fired any second. We tore out and after a few minutes all breathed a sigh of relief. As usual, though, the musicians found something to laugh about.

"What did that man say, Bobby?" a voice from the back of the bus teased. " 'You're going to need a Miracle to get your behind out of this'?"

Although our itinerary followed the chitlin' circuit and we performed in the larger black theaters, we also played other gigs, some in open-air arenas and smaller clubs. In Birmingham, Alabama, we were scheduled to perform at a ballpark—picture the bandstand set up over the pitcher's mound and you get the idea of how small-time and tacky it was. What made this particular show special was that it was the first time in the community that an integrated audience got to see a show.

I saw more blacks and whites mingling and certainly more integrated couples than I'd ever seen in Detroit. During the show I heard there had been some trouble in the crowd and that the police had shot someone, but that may have been only a rumor. The show itself went along quite smoothly.

James Jamerson passed a guard backstage and asked if he could use the rest room. As James was coming out, another guard was called, and he said to James, "Hey, nigger, what are you doing here?" James was understandably upset; after all, the promoter should have seen to it that there were accommodations. We seemed to have been put in the middle of a conflict between the townspeople and the promoter, but nothing was said. No one wanted trouble. We just wanted the show to be over so that we could get out.

We were pleased that the shows were a success and the crowd begged for encores, but it had been a long, tense day, and we had to go. We were slowly boarding the bus when we heard several sharp, loud cracks.

"Someone's throwing rocks," one of the Vandellas said as we all looked around to see where they were coming from.

"Them's bullets!" Choker shouted, and at that we ran for the bus. In her panic to board the bus, Mary Wells had fallen down on the bus steps and refused to get up, barring the entrance to the rest of us. Everyone tried to push her out of the way, but she was so big it was impossible.

"Get out of the way, girl!" we all shouted, but she just screamed back, "I am not getting up!"

Finally she moved, and we all got on board as fast as we could. Once the bus was loaded, we flew out of Birmingham. Only after we'd traveled quite a distance did the driver stop to examine the bus. Sure enough, there were bullet holes in some of the windows. None of us —not even the musicians—could find anything to laugh about this time.

The big problem with touring the South was that even when you weren't being shot at or called "nigger," you could never forget where you were. Bigots who were too smart to get violent used intimidation and insults to put you in your place.

One day we stopped at a motel in Miami Beach, where we were scheduled to play that evening. Beans Bowles went into the front office to book our rooms. Suddenly, from out of nowhere, there appeared fifteen police cruisers with dogs. They didn't make a move toward us; they just sat outside and watched us.

At first the owner didn't want any blacks staying at his motel, but once Beans explained our situation to him, he became a total businessman. "I'm not supposed to rent you any rooms," he said, "but this is my motel and I need the money. Come on and check in."

This motel wasn't the Ritz, but it was clean and comfortable. After days on the road, just being able to bathe and rest a few hours before the rehearsal and show was a luxury. It was also a relief to know that we would get a good night's sleep after the show.

But things could never be that simple down South. When we returned after the show, the same cruisers and dogs were waiting.

"You would think we're Martin Luther King on a freedom march," Choker remarked.

Beans decided that enough was enough and approached the police. As road manager, he was responsible for our safety and well-being. Always articulate and personable, Beans was invaluable in this kind of situation. He told the police who we were, what we were doing, and so on. After he'd finished talking with them, they took their dogs and left.

The other interesting thing about people in general is that they have two different standards: one for common blacks and another for entertainers and other famous blacks. I saw this clearly demonstrated once in South Carolina. We pulled up in front of a motel called the Heart of the South, and the whole time we were unloading our stuff and checking in, two rednecks stood outside making offensive remarks, which they made sure we could hear very clearly. It was hard to believe that they wanted to provoke a fight, especially since there were so many strong young men in our group, and one of them was old enough to be a grandfather, but they kept it up, ending their little tirade with this gem:

"By gosh, that's a shame. We gotta get rid of that President Kennedy 'cause he ain't doin' the right thing letting them niggers go and do whatever they want."

Of course, we were all insulted, but we regarded them as just a couple of backwoods fools and ignored them. As I entered the hotel, I saw Choker sitting on his horn case with his back to the two fools, cracking up. I could see that he didn't want them to see that he was laughing, and I can't blame him. But one look at Choker and I almost started laughing myself. After we'd checked in, Choker was still sitting there, wiping tears of laughter from his eyes. Here they were acting like they were so superior, yet talking like idiots. We couldn't help but laugh at them.

As soon as we were settled, we jumped into our swimsuits and headed for the pool. The minute we dived in, the white people started climbing out. They sat on the lounge chairs and stared at us for a while, but when they saw what good divers and swimmers some of us were, they eased themselves back in. A few minutes later, they started getting out again. It took us a while to figure out what was going on. Unbeknownst to us the local radio stations had been playing all of our records over the past few weeks. Once word had spread that they were sharing the pool with the Miracles, Little Stevie Wonder, the Marvelettes, and so-and-so, they ran to get paper and pens for our autographs and asked how they could get tickets for the show.

Our tours made breakthroughs and helped weaken racial barriers. When it came to the music, segregation didn't mean a thing in some of those towns, and if it did, black and white fans would ignore the local customs to attend the shows. To see crowds that were integrated —sometimes for the first time in a community—made me realize that Motown truly was the sound of young America.

As we should have expected, the tour bus finally broke down, in South Carolina. It was hot as hell inside the bus, so we all piled out, only to discover that we were standing next to a jailhouse.

"Hey, who are you guys?" came a voice out of nowhere.

It was obvious from the sound of their voices that most of the inmates were black. All we could see were black hands clutching at the iron window bars, and before long, they all started pleading with us to help them. We girls hung back, afraid to get too close, but the Miracles and the Tempts went up and shook hands with the prisoners through the bars. Once the men understood who we were and what we were doing, they opened up to the guys. The prisoners told their stories, and some of them broke down crying, asking us to talk to someone for them. It was so sad.

"Isn't there something we can do for these fellows?" I asked one of the musicians.

"Are you kidding?" he replied. "We'd better get this bus fixed and get out of here before they throw us in there, too. They don't care about no innocence or guilt down here. That's how they treat niggers in the South. Besides, to hear them tell it, all jailbirds are innocent."

The ugly realities of the South were becoming more evident to me the further we got past the Mason-Dixon line. By the time the bus was repaired and we were on our way, there was little talk and no laughter.

We were in the Carolinas, relaxing after a series of well-received shows, when we decided that we really deserved a big party. We were leaving the next day for Florida, but we stayed up partying all night, and then took off with just a couple hours' rest.

Usually Beans and his driver, Eddie McFarland, left either before or after us. Generally, they stayed behind a few hours to finish up business. This particular morning, Beans and Eddie left a few hours after us, in the Contours' station wagon.

When we arrived at the hotel hours later, there was a message saying Esther Edwards was on her way down by plane and that there had been an accident. We had no way of finding out what had happened to Beans and Eddie; all we could do was to wait.

Before we'd finished breakfast, Mrs. Edwards arrived. She called us all together in one of the rooms. We were anxious to find out what had happened, but before she would tell us, Mrs. Edwards asked us about the night before. Once she was satisfied with our answers she told us that Eddie had fallen asleep at the wheel and crashed into a semi. Beans had been in the back of the car, practicing on his flute. In the collision, the instrument had punctured his armpit and emerged through the back of his neck. Both of his legs were broken and doctors feared he would never walk again. Beans was alive. Eddie had been decapitated and had died.

We were stunned and saddened. Everyone was crying, but Mrs. Edwards kept her head. She got Choker to help her organize things and give her an update on all the business dealings. Somehow everything was settled, and the tour proceeded as planned.

I went back to my room speechless. That night, when the announcer called out "the Supremes," and we pranced onstage, flashing our biggest, sweetest smiles, the oldest cliché in show business ran through my mind: The show must go on.

Our last stop on this tour was New York's Apollo Theater. The manager there was Honi Coles, the ex-partner of Motown choreographer Cholly Atkins. We had been well received by all the crowds so far, but we'd heard that the Apollo was a tough venue. For one thing, if the crowd didn't like you, Coles would come onstage with a long hook and physically drag you off the stage. We won the crowd over from the first minute, though, and came off the stage thrilled to death—we had played the Apollo.

CHAPTER 12

Diane always had enormous energy. She would flit up and down the aisle of the bus, teasing people and mussing their hair. Sometimes she'd sit quietly for hours, in deep concentration or listening intently to what was being said. But usually she had a mischievous playfulness that she thought was very cute but that most people—especially under the stress of touring—found annoying.

"You do so wear dirty underwear!" Diane, laughing, said to Marvin Tarplin.

Marvin took it as a joke, but Gladys Horton jumped to his defense.

"No, he doesn't!" Gladys screamed.

"I'm not talking to you!" Diane hissed.

Diane and Gladys seemed to be fighting all the time, most often over something silly. Gladys was a country girl and, like Flo, she could be very outspoken. She and Flo understood each other, partially because they both believed that you should speak out whenever you saw a wrong being committed, whether it was your business or not. This trait earned the two of them the occasional wrath of Motown management, but they didn't care. It was obvious they both enjoyed being the defenders of the underdog.

After any set-to with Diane, Gladys would come to the seat I shared with Flo and ask, "Why does Diane act like that?"

I'd shrug it off. "Don't pay any attention to her."

"That's just Diane," Flo would add philosophically. It was clear, though, that few people shared our forgiving attitude, and things could really heat up.

We were playing a show in Philadelphia and had just finished "Let Me Go the Right Way." The song ended abruptly, so the audience didn't start applauding right away. In the silence, I heard Gladys' voice from the wings: "Oh, her dress looks like a nightgown!" I didn't think anything of it. We were wearing long white dresses and there was some competition among the acts regarding stage costumes. The Supremes were always a little more sophisticated, so I just wrote the comment off to jealousy. It didn't mean anything. The three of us bowed and exited the stage.

Diane ran around to the other side, and she was steaming. "Flo, did you hear what she said? She said our dresses look like nightgowns!"

When Diane confronted Gladys, Gladys set her straight. "Diane, I didn't say *their* dresses—I said *your* dress!"

Diane was extremely thin before it was fashionable, and some people thought that our gowns looked nicer on fuller figures. But that wasn't what this was really about. Because Diane was known to have a very high opinion of herself and a low tolerance for criticism, no matter how well intended, some people liked to let her know that they didn't think she was so hot.

The spat continued, with Diane sending a girl who worked at the theater around to Glady's room to deliver a message: "Diane is going to kick your behind after the show."

Later that evening, as we were leaving the theater, Gladys was helping a little blind boy named Lee across the street. She was headed for the station wagon we all shared on this tour, and Diane was sitting behind the wheel. The minute Diane saw Gladys, she pulled out, hit the gas, and stopped just a few feet short of Gladys and Lee. Gladys left Lee standing in the street and ran over to the car screaming, "Go on and hit me!"

Diane gave Gladys the finger, rolled up her window, and sped off. Mrs. Ross, who was in the car, was shocked and reprimanded Diane for her behavior, but Diane didn't seem to be listening.

The next day Diane surprised all of us when she announced that she was going to Gladys' room to apologize. Diane told Gladys, "I called Berry last night and told him about our argument. He said I should apologize because you didn't approach me and you weren't talking to me individually, and I shouldn't get so upset."

Gladys felt very bad after that. This was Berry's way of getting to you psychologically. When he wasn't around, he wanted Diane to learn not to get caught up in petty fights. That was all well and good, but Diane had access to Berry none of us had, and the effect of her doing everything he said—and doing it just because he said to—was a little disconcerting. He was so paternal toward us because he believed that artists should never be allowed to think for themselves. It wasn't that he thought they were particularly stupid; he just thought they should stick to making music.

Over the years, Diane's spats with Mary Wells, Gladys, Dee Dee Sharp, Brenda Holloway, and especially Martha Reeves were company knowledge. If you ever asked Diane why she got into fights, she'd say, "They're picking on me." But that wasn't always the case. Once when Mary Wells suggested helpfully that Diane wear a girdle onstage, Diane flew off and started insulting her.

A few weeks into any tour, everyone got tense. Riding for days in that funky old bus, crowding more than a dozen girls into a tiny dressing room meant for one—it could all get to you. But no matter who was fighting with whom, each of us was loyal to our group. All the girls in the girl groups seemed to stick together that way. I noticed that it was different with the guys; they could be friends with whomever they wanted, and their "fights" were usually playful and full of teasing. With the girls, however, it could get downright vicious.

In addition, there seemed to be a lot of resentment toward the Supremes. Though we still hadn't had a hit, we did get special treatment—Diane's direct line to Berry being just one example—and other groups resented this. Flo, Diane, and I could be friends with other performers, but when it came to business, there was always the feeling that the Supremes were, in some way, different.

The next big event after we'd come home from the first tour was the Motown Christmas party. The Marvelettes were riding the crest of "Please Mr. Postman"'s success, and the Supremes were someplace much further down the totem pole, regardless of any "special treatment" people thought we were getting. We all received gifts. Artists who had sold lots of records got very expensive things; the Marvelettes were each given ⅓-carat diamond rings, which we thought were so extravagant. The rest of us got tiny transistor radios and tape recorders, but no one went away empty-handed.

Everyone in attendance was sharply dressed, and you couldn't tell the secretaries from the stars. Detroiters are flashy dressers to begin with, and people in the music community were even flashier than the rest. All the men wore suits; mohair was the thing then, and there was every color from beige to black. They also wore very expensive, classy ties. The women wore little jewelry except chic custommade pieces, and everyone wore hats. Hardly anyone wore beads or sequins. And, of course, all the girls wore pointed-toe shoes to match their dresses. None of us was making that much money, but almost every cent we did make went on our backs.

These were some of our happiest days. The fame and fortune to come would never replace the caring and true affection we felt for one another in the early years. Of course, we couldn't know that then, and so we were jealous of the attention being lavished on the Marvelettes. Feeling this way seemed out of character for me, but I couldn't help it. The fact that I liked each of the Marvelettes as an individual didn't change the fact that we were all in competition for the same things.

Besides the Marvelettes, the Vandellas were one of our favorite groups. Even as a young girl, Martha Reeves was one of the most soulful singers I'd ever heard. Over the next year, they had hits with "Come and Get These Memories," "Heat Wave," and "Quicksand," and were near the top of the Motown roster. Things happened faster for Martha and her group than they did for us, and this only fueled the rivalry between Martha and Diane. Both had drive and charisma, and neither would ever back down.

Flo and I would get caught in the middle, and though we both liked all the Vandellas—Martha, Rosalind Ashford, and Annette Sterling—our relationship with Martha was strained by her feuds with Diane. Flo and I would always admit—privately—who was right in a spat, and it wasn't always Diane. But she was in our group, and solidarity was crucial, right or wrong.

One time, we were on the bus and Gladys was talking to Hubert Johnson, her seat partner and would-be suitor. "You think you're the cutest one in the group."

"No, I don't," Hubert replied, obviously embarrassed.

Gladys then turned to Billy Hoggs, Hubert's fellow Contour, and said, "Oh, I think you have the prettiest gray eyes, Billy." She smiled, knowing she was driving Hubert wild. He looked over at her and said nothing, but you could see the hurt in his face. This was like watching a soap opera, and Hubert's love might have gone unrequited had it not been for Diane agreeing to speak on his behalf.

"Gladys," Diane said during one of their truces, "Why don't you give Hubert a chance? Hubert wanted to be my boyfriend, but I just didn't want to go out with him. I don't know why—"

"Really?" Gladys was shocked by Diane's revelation and surprised that she was trying to help her.

"Yes," Diane continued. "He's a swell guy. I used to like him a lot—"

"Diane, are you telling the truth?" Gladys was understandably suspicious.

"Yes. I used to like Hubert a while ago, and we didn't hit it off, and I really wanted to. . . . Hey, he's such a nice guy. You should be glad that he chose you."

You could have knocked Gladys over with a feather! Of all the people on the tour, Diane was the last she would have pictured playing Cupid. This was a facet of Diane's personality seldom seen, but Hubert knew exactly what he was doing. Diane's powers of persuasion were strong even then, and she pleaded his case to Gladys beautifully.

We were all sitting in our dressing room after a show, anxious to get out of our costumes and makeup and go out for dinner. Diane was still working on Gladys, and I removed my makeup a little more slowly, trying to hear every word. Whatever Diane said definitely worked, for Gladys and Hubert were soon an item.

Wherever we were, the three of us spent most of our spare moments practicing as quietly as we could, or talking about boys.

"Girl, that Bobby Rogers is good-looking!" Flo would say.

"Well, why don't you and he get together?"

"Mary, I think he likes somebody else."

It was sad that she was still so frightened of men. Flo was always more comfortable around other girls, where she could relax and laugh. We would all be backstage, coping with preshow nerves, running down our songs, or mending a stage costume, and always talking girl talk. There would be Mary Wells, Martha and the Vandellas, the Marvelettes, Claudette Robinson, and us, all squashed together in a tiny room. Flo would tease and joke around with everyone, good-heartedly offering pointers and suggestions about makeup and hair to the other girls.

We saw this side of her, but people who didn't often commented that she was hard to get close to, moody. And when she was uncomfortable, I suppose she was. We were all so involved with the shows and the tour that we paid little attention to things like that.

In between the four or five shows we did each day on these tours, we all looked forward to meeting at the local soul-food place and having a dinner of gravy-smothered steak, greens, and cornbread. For young kids far from home, the phrase "like Mother used to make" took on a whole new meaning. We especially liked the Uptown Theater in Philadelphia, because right outside the stage door was the house of a woman who made the best dinners I'd ever eaten north of the Mason-Dixon line. No restaurant license was displayed, and she never had to advertise. Word of mouth from veterans of the road kept the place packed. Eight people would crowd around a table meant for four, and some of the older musicians who didn't want to wait for a table would eat standing up.

Mealtime was the best time of the day. We could relax for a change and think about something else besides the shows. Flo would eat with Gladys, Rosalind, Annette, or any of the other girls. The guys would start up a card game, and we would fix our nails, touch up our makeup, or attend to our hair. We would turn on the nearest radio to keep abreast of the latest hits. If a Motown hit came on, we'd all stop talking, listen, then cheer at the end. There was such optimism in those days. We knew that our turn was coming, soon.

These were good times, and we never seriously considered doing anything else, but as we got older we started to realize that money would become a more important consideration than it had been. The allowance we received for travel was little more than spending change, and I remember looking to the back of bus and hearing the heated betting, and wishing I had learned to play poker.

One day we got a real surprise. We were sitting on the bus, getting ready to take off, when Berry came aboard and shouted, "I've come to take you suckers' money!"

"Man, where did you come from?" Choker howled before he doubled over with laughter.

"Hey, everybody, Mr. Gordy's here!" one of the girls yelled.

"How are you all doing?" Berry asked. We all said "Fine," but Berry wasn't really listening as he made his way to the back.

Choker was gleefully rubbing his hands together. They all stopped talking and the game was on. All the regulars sat in for the first few hands, but the number of players thinned out as the stakes rose.

After several hours it was down to just Berry and Choker. As he often did, Berry was chewing on his tongue as he concentrated. I always found it amusing that a number of the younger producers around the company, including Smokey Robinson and Brian Holland, adopted Berry's mannerisms; they would chew their tongues, too.

By the time we reached our destination, Berry was ready to catch the next plane back to Detroit. He'd lost $6,000 to Choker, and though I know Berry didn't necessarily mind losing, I'm sure he hadn't expected to lose that much. But Berry was a risk taker, and he taught us all not to fear taking a chance.

Whenever we were on tour, we would do our set, then we'd change into our street clothes so we could watch the rest of the show. Every night we'd watch to see if the Contours got a bigger response than the Tempts, or if the crowd favored Martha and the Vandellas over the Marvelettes. The lineup was determined by whoever had the biggest hit record out (they would go toward the end), and the order was arranged so that one act would leave the stage hot for the next one. When you hit the stage, you really had to go for blood, because everyone on the tour was so good. The polish and poise Motown acts were famous for came not only from practice but from watching other acts. I especially enjoyed watching Marvin Gaye and Stevie. They were always great.

Little Stevie Wonder never failed to get a crowd going. Though he was the youngest in the group, he had one of the best senses of humor and we loved him.

Motown went to great pains to protect Stevie and provide him with the best care when he was away from home. Because of the legal restrictions and labor laws regarding minors, Stevie had to finish his performance by a certain hour. This was a curfew, and the hour varied from state to state, as did our show times, so we would always have to juggle the lineup to accommodate Stevie. He also had to travel with a tutor. Like all young kids, Stevie would do anything to get out of doing his schoolwork, and during one trip he would feign sleep whenever he heard his tutor approach. His teacher was a kind, studious young man who took his responsibility for Stevie's education very seriously. Nonetheless, he could never bring himself to awaken this poor exhausted child, and Stevie got away with murder.

One night in Chicago, we were all standing around backstage watching the show from the wings. Stevie had just finished his set and Mary Wells was waiting to go on. Because of the curfew, Stevie had done an abbreviated set and then quickly left the stage. Each act had its own conductor; Mary had bass player Joe Swift, and Stevie had Clarence Paul. Stevie had just finished "Fingertips—Pt. 2" and left the stage. When the crowd demanded an encore, Clarence—an old show-biz veteran—pushed Stevie back onstage. It was a choreographed ploy designed to make the audience think that Stevie didn't know where he was. Joe Swift had already taken over the conductor's spot, and when Stevie started the reprise of "Fingertips," Joe was shouting, "What key, Little Stevie, what key?" Many people don't know that Motown regularly recorded our live shows, and has in the vaults countless unreleased live video and audio tapes, most of which I've never seen. Stevie's number was one of the few that was released, and in August 1963, it became his first number-one hit.

Like the musicians, the performers sometimes snuck away from Hitsville to do a little session work on the side, which was strictly forbidden. One day, Joe Hunter pulled me aside and said, "I can give you a hundred dollars to come with me to Chicago."

"Say no more!" Compared to the lousy five or ten bucks we got for every song we recorded, a hundred dollars was a fortune. I went to Chicago with James Jamerson, Hank Crosby, and anyone else Joe wanted to take along. Like many of the other bandleaders, Joe was very generous about sharing his freelance work with others. Also with us were the Andantes, Motown's in-house background vocal group— Jackie Hicks, Marlene Barrow, and Louvain Demps. These three appear on about three quarters of all Motown's releases, including those by the Four Tops, the Temptations, Marvin Gaye, and even the Supremes.

This was a session for Jerry Butler that Curtis Mayfield was producing for Vee Jay. We recorded a song called "A Teenie Weenie Bit of Your Love." I also worked on blues legend John Lee Hooker's "Boom, Boom, Boom."

Back in Detroit, we were always out of town on smaller tours, with just one or two other acts. The Motown groups would share the bill with other performers, such as Ike and Tina Turner, Dionne Warwick, Flip Wilson, Jackie Wilson, and Richard Pryor. When we were playing the Howard, there was another girl group, Patti LaBelle and the Blue-Belles, and everyone remarked that one of their members, Cindy Birdsong, looked a lot like Flo.

Instead of using a professional driver for these trips, the company relied on people who had approached them for jobs. Many of these people were aspiring artists or people who just liked hanging around. Among the upcoming artists who drove for us were the Spinners and the Dells.

The Supremes never missed any opportunity to practice our craft. Once while we were singing "Canadian Sunset," the Marvelettes were awestruck by our harmonies.

"I wish we could do that," Gladys said.

"Well, we've been at it a long time," Flo replied, trying to reassure Gladys.

We were riding in John O'Den's van to Virginia, and Diane was talking constantly. Before long, she almost had Gladys in tears, going on and on about the fact the Supremes still hadn't gotten a hit, and she was blaming Billie Jean Brown, who was in charge of screening all the recordings for Berry. Though Janie Bradford was still the queen of the lobby and there were many more secretaries around, Billie Jean was the one Berry seemed to have the most trust in. Billie Jean had attended Cass and was now the head of Quality Control. Some of the guys around Hitsville complained about how hard it could be to persuade Billie Jean to give their tapes to Berry.

"Gladys," Diane said, "we have all this great stuff, and Billie Jean will not let Berry hear it. She doesn't like me."

Gladys seemed shocked and sympathetic to our plight.

"We never did anything to her," Diane went on. "When Fridays come and they're playing all the records for Berry to review, she sticks our good stuff in the back, and Berry doesn't even listen to it."

Mrs. Edwards was our chaperone on this trip, and I'm sure Diane was saying all this as much for her benefit as for Gladys'. Mrs. Edwards said nothing.

"Don't worry, Diane," Gladys said, trying to reassure her. "You all will get a hit record. It just takes time, you know."

We knew.

CHAPTER 13

By late 1963, we were getting tired of waiting. Many of the other Motown acts were doing great: the Miracles had "You've Really Got a Hold on Me," the Vandellas had "Heat Wave," and Marvin Gaye had "Hitch Hike." Though we were still the "no-hit" Supremes, we were working very hard doing numerous one-nighters and minitours. Coming to this point had been a long, happy struggle, and it seemed to be getting more difficult each year. We were working at a whirlwind pace, with our schedules for dates and recording sessions often in conflict.

Another thing that frustrated us was the amount of attention other groups were receiving. In the beginning, it sometimes seemed that the public didn't understand us. The songs we'd been recording were sweet and usually soft, and we found ourselves put in a "charm" bag. We complained to one another and to our friends, but we knew we were lucky to be with Hitsville, and we made the best of it. Being out of school, we were doing more out-of-town dates, and learning more and more about the world.

Once at the Royal in Baltimore we followed a very popular show called the Jewel Box Revue. It was a gay revue, something that I'd never even heard of then, and the show, complete with men in drag, attracted a largely homosexual audience. Perhaps because there were so few shows of this type anywhere, the crowd was extremely well integrated for the Howard, and they seemed to enjoy our show, too.

We were boarding the bus after the last show when a very masculine-looking lesbian ran up to the vehicle and started screaming for Martha Reeves. This woman had been following and bothering Martha the whole week we were there, and Martha was embarrassed and uncomfortable about it. Martha was sitting on the bus when the woman started screaming, "Martha, I love you," and pressing her face against the window. She was crying, and Martha was humiliated beyond words. Being young and wild ourselves, we all thought it was a big joke, and we teased Martha, but deep inside none of us really knew what to think of it either. Traveling around the country, there was no end to what you could see.

We played some pretty rough places. I remember a time in Cleveland when we did a show with Flip Wilson. Flip's material was as blue as Redd Foxx's, and Berry asked him to tone it down around us. What really concerned us was that the Supremes weren't generally considered as "soulful" as some of the others, and once we heard acts like Patti LaBelle and the Blue-Belles, whose style seemed more dramatic and histrionic, we knew we were in for a rough time. We didn't really look very soulful, either. We weren't yet wearing sequined chiffon gowns, but while the other girl groups were in cute, matching outfits that seemed designed to play up their sweetness and innocence, we were wearing the most sophisticated dresses we could find, short dresses with full, solid taffeta skirts covered by floral-printed nylon, usually in some pastel color. We also had one long black sheath; that was our first really elegant gown. The Supremes seemed to be everything a funky crowd would not like, but as we became more experienced we noticed that once we stepped onstage, everyone quieted down. They could see that we were different, and we rarely had a hard time.

Even though we were out of high school, we were still underage, so we never traveled without a chaperone. Up until 1965 or so, when we turned twenty-one, we'd always be accompanied on the road by an older woman. Of course, each had her own ideas and attitudes, but one thing they all shared was a love for lecturing us. "Now, girls . . ." was the standard opening phrase, and what followed could be answered only with polite "Yes, ma'am"s. Several, like Diane's mother, Mrs. Ross, were wonderful to have around, but there were others who were entertaining for reasons they would never have guessed. One woman, Mrs. Ardeena Johnson, was a friend of Moms Gordy and, except for Esther Edwards, was by far the strictest. Mrs. Johnson prided herself on being an educated woman, and she spoke and acted like an aristocrat. What was so funny about her was that, despite the hoity-toity façade, she loved to drink and was sure that no one knew her little secret.

The cardinal rule of chaperoning was never to leave your charges unguarded, and, as a result, we had some interesting substitutes. Once, when Mrs. Ross ran out for a bite to eat, she left us backstage at the Howard Theater under the watchful eye of Jackie Wilson. People who knew Jackie would equate this with leaving a kid in charge of a candy store, but Mrs. Ross had made him promise to keep us out of trouble. The minute she left, Jackie let us out, and we were down the hall, flirting with the Dells.

This was all great fun, but we needed a hit, and Berry Gordy was becoming obsessed with making us stars. The word went out to everyone at Hitsville: "Get a hit on the Supremes." We had worked with a couple of other producers, including Berry, but most of our records were done under Smokey Robinson's aegis. Still nothing. Berry decided in mid-1963 that there should be a "marriage" between the Supremes and writer/producers Brian Holland, Lamont Dozier, and Eddie Holland, or HDH. Although early indications weren't promising, by year's end this would prove to be a match made in heaven.

Brian Holland, Eddie Holland, and Lamont Dozier joined up with Berry the same way so many others did in the early days. Eddie was a sixteen-year-old aspiring singer when he met Berry at the Graystone Ballroom in the late fifties. Unlike many of the early Hitsville crowd, Eddie's love of music wasn't everything for him—he wanted money.

Eddie's younger brother Brian also had musical talent. "At an early age, Brian was much better at music than I," Eddie recalled. "I knew my brother was interested in music, so I told Berry about him. Berry asked me how old Brian was, and I told him Brian was about sixteen. Berry thought that he was too young, but I convinced him to listen to him."

By this time, Eddie had joined Berry and some of his collaborators in trying to create hits. Eddie recalls that at first Berry wasn't crazy about Brian; he thought he was a little fresh. Eventually, though, Brian was working with Berry's group, and writing with Janie Bradford.

Lamont Dozier had been singing around Detroit since the age of fifteen. He also met Berry in the late fifties and, like both Holland brothers, briefly pursued a recording career, under the name Lamont Anthony. Freddy Gorman (our producer and ex-mailman), Lamont, and Brian wrote together until about 1961, when Freddy dropped out. By then, it was clear that Eddie's singing career wasn't taking off, and he told his brother that he thought he had a feel for writing.

"Why don't you let me write the lyrics?" Eddie asked Brian. "If you and Lamont do the melody and I do the lyrics, you could move at a faster pace, and we could get more songs done quicker and deal with more people, and finally make a lot of money." Brian said okay, but Lamont hedged at first. Eventually, the three worked out a system: Lamont created the melodies, Eddie took care of the lyrics and working with the singers, and Brian was in charge of production and working with the musicians. Of course, there was some overlap—Lamont, for example, also knew a lot about production—and the chemistry was only perfected over time, but eventually the HDH style would be Motown's calling card.

After Diane's relationship with Smokey ended, she set her sights on another married man—Brian Holland. He was a real gentleman and he liked Diane a great deal. They would work late in the studio, and Brian would do little things like write notes to Diane and give them to Janie Bradford to deliver to her. Before long, of course, everyone at Hitsville knew what was up and Brian's wife Sharon soon got wind of it, too. Diane and Brian saw each other from late 1962 through late 1963, and Sharon made her displeasure about the subject quite public. She would come to the studio and say, "I know Diane Ross is messing with my husband, and if I catch her, I'm going to kick her butt!"

Sharon was not a small woman, and one night at the Twenty Grand, she decided to make good on her threat. We were all on our way in to do our show, when Sharon accosted us, the Velvelettes, and my friend Alice Fletcher. Sharon was shouting obscenities at Diane, and we all circled around Diane, with Flo stepping right in the middle. Sharon kept saying she was going to kick Diane's butt, and for a few minutes, we had to hold Diane back—she was raring to go. We could see that it would be no contest, but we were also concerned that Sharon might take a swing at one of us. We were relieved when finally, we got Diane in the car and away from Sharon. Soon thereafter, Diane stopped seeing Brian.

Though we hadn't yet scored the big hit, a few of our records did get regional and a little national airplay. In January "Let Me Go the Right Way," which Berry produced, went to #90, and "A Breath Taking Guy," one of Smokey's tunes, topped at #75 late that summer. As we traveled across the country we met countless people who were working hard on our behalf, the record promotion men and disc jockeys who liked our records and did everything they could to bring them to the public's attention. Among them were Bob King at WOOK, Bill

Johnson of WUST, Al Bell (who later founded Stax) of WUST, Kelson "Chop Chop" Fisher, Al Jefferson, Paul "Fat Daddy" Johnson, Long, Tall, Lean, Lanky Larry Dean, Butterball, Robin Seymore, Dave Shaffer, Eddie Castleberry, Bill Williams, and scores more. They would also see that our records got plenty of airplay right before we came to town, and as a result the crowds always knew our songs and made us feel welcome.

Eddie Bisco was a white record promoter based in the Baltimore-Washington area who worked especially hard on our behalf. When we met him in 1962, he was around our age, and we knew he had a crush on one of us; it turned out to be Diane. Because Marvin Gaye's family lived in the area, Eddie had become good friends with Marvin, and Marvin's father, the Reverend Gay (Marvin added the *e* to his name when he became a performer), often had Eddie to his home for dinner when Marvin was in town.

In late 1963 Marvin married Anna Gordy. News of the impending marriage came as quite a shock to all of us. I felt very close to Marvin, and we were all hurt and confused when he began avoiding us. Shortly before the wedding, our conversations with him started to center on business and recording; there were no more leisurely afternoons spent around the piano. Of course this match was the talk of Hitsville, for not only was Marvin marrying the boss's sister, but she was seventeen years older than he. Though we no longer enjoyed our special relationship with Marvin, he still liked us very much. When he found out that Eddie had a crush on Diane, he arranged for Eddie to come up to York, Pennsylvania, where we were all playing, and stay with him and Anna.

We were all delighted to see Eddie; whenever we got together, we'd sing a new song for him or try out new bits of choreography, and he would tell us what he thought. After this particular show, we were all walking back to the hotel. Diane and Eddie were holding hands. We were crossing a street when a car suddenly swerved, missing Diane and Eddie by just inches. It wasn't an accident, either; the driver didn't like the idea of a white boy walking with a black girl.

Being white, Eddie was sometimes stuck in the middle. There were still plenty of restaurants and hotels that didn't allow blacks, and black establishments that didn't want whites. These restrictions reflected the local attitudes, but rarely in our travels did we see these barriers carried over into show business.

Once back at the hotel, Diane and Eddie, Flo and Paul Williams, and Eddie Kendricks and I went back to our room to talk and listen to records. The single room was divided into three sections by curtains hung from the ceiling; it was hardly the place to get intimate, with four other people just feet away. But when Mrs. Edwards burst in, we could tell she didn't see things that way. According to the rules of the road, none of the boys should have been in the room, and we all deserved a good talking to, but Mrs. Edwards ignored Paul and Eddie Kendricks and zeroed in on Eddie Bisco.

"*You* don't belong here. Young man, you are in trouble. I suggest you get back to Washington, D.C., as soon as possible."

We were all embarrassed; Eddie was getting the brunt of it because he was white. He ran back to Marvin and Anna's room. They suggested he stay overnight with them and try to talk with Esther in the morning. When Eddie apologized and promised it would never happen again, Mrs. Edwards was all business: "Well, I hope not, because your distributors could possibly lose the line," she warned. Fortunately, nothing came of her threats, and I've often wondered if the incident was ever reported to Berry.

Diane and Eddie continued their long-distance romance for nearly a year; she would call him collect, until his parents put a stop to that. Whenever we were in his area, we'd get together with Eddie, and he became our cohort in devising schemes to sneak out of our chaperone's sight. We never did anything bad; after working all day, just being able to go to a restaurant, bowl a few frames, or play cards in our dressing room was bliss. Diane kept in touch with Eddie for years, and he was one of our greatest boosters, encouraging us to forge on even when things looked dim.

That fall we'd made our first record with HDH, "When the Lovelight Starts Shining Through His Eyes" backed with "Standing at the Crossroads of Love" (a song HDH would rework into the Four Tops' "Standing in the Shadows of Love"). When "Lovelight" hit #23—our best showing so far—we thought we were on the right track, but when "Run, Run, Run" (b/w "I'm Giving You Your Freedom") just barely slipped into the Hot 100, we were distraught. We had been certain "Run" would be our big smash, and we began to doubt that this "marriage" would endure. After three years of recording we were dying to get that elusive hit. We liked Brian, Eddie, and Lamont and had a great rapport with them. They'd been doing great work with other artists lately—"Come and Get These Memories," "Heat Wave," and "Quicksand" for Martha and the Vandellas, "Mickey's Monkey" and "I Gotta Dance to Keep from Crying" for the Miracles, and

"You're a Wonderful One" (on which we did the backing vocals) for Marvin Gaye. When would our turn come?

One day we were working in the studio and Berry came in. He said, "I know everybody in the group sings lead, but Diane has the more commercial voice, and I want to use her as the sole lead singer."

We were all surprised to hear this; there wasn't even a discussion. Berry had made up his mind. We still believed that having three lead singers made the Supremes unique, but that didn't seem as important to Berry as making more commercial records. Of course, Flo and I were disappointed, but we never thought the arrangement would be permanent. Certainly, when a song came along that either of us could do very well, we'd get our chance. At that moment, all we knew was that we wanted a hit—desperately. If this was how we were going to get it, fine.

HDH had worked up some new tunes, including "Where Did Our Love Go," "Come See About Me," and "Baby Love," but we were quite upset when we heard them. To our ears, they sounded childish, with just a few words or phrases repeated over and over. Besides, we wanted to do something soulful, something with spirit, like the songs Martha Reeves was doing.

"Hey, we want hits," I told them one day.

"Yeah," Flo added, "stop giving us these songs you know won't be hits."

"Trust us," they said, laughing.

I couldn't, though. I went into their office to give them a piece of my mind.

Eddie tried to console me. "You don't like these now," he said, "but—just wait. You will."

All I could say was okay; we were lucky to get anything at this point.

One day in late March 1964 Eddie Holland wanted us to record "Where Did Our Love Go," which needed a subtle lead. Since that was my forte and I'd been doing the ballads for as long as we'd been singing together, I was certain it would be given to me. As was the usual procedure, he'd played the song for Berry, the Quality Control people, and a few other singers to get an idea of who might be best for it. Berry suggested that he try the Supremes on it. He offered it to the Marvelettes, but they turned it down, opting to record a song Eddie had written with Norman Whitfield called "Too Many Fish in the Sea."

To my ears, "Where Did Our Love Go" was a teenybopper song.

It had childish, repetitive lyrics ("Baby, baby, baby, baby don't leave me, please don't leave me . . ."), a limited melody, and no drive. It was too smooth, and I couldn't imagine anyone liking it. Still, this was probably going to be my lead, so I decided to make the best of it. But it was soon clear just what Berry had meant by his announcement. I later learned that Eddie wanted me to sing it, but that his partners had convinced him that Diane had the more commercial sound and, besides, wasn't she the lead singer?

Flo and I went along with them, and Diane did the lead. Little did we know that neither of us would ever sing lead on a Supremes single again. HDH hit upon a special formula for the Supremes and, after a few hits, Diane's voice became as much a part of the formula as the arrangements or any other HDH trademark. The bigger we got, the less anyone at Motown wanted to tamper with what was beginning to look like a sure thing. This changed our sound in other ways as well. On our earlier records, Diane would do her lead, then sing with us on the background, but eventually the backgrounds were done by Flo and me. Besides being upstaged, Flo and I also felt that the records suffered; our three-part harmonies were so beautiful; we should have recorded more of them.

From this day on, we'd spend almost every day we weren't on the road or involved in some other business recording with HDH. Although no complete record exists, I'd say we probably recorded at least five or six tracks for every one that was finally released, everything from show tunes to gospel. Motown was careful to release only winners.

In early 1964 the Supremes became one of the first Motown acts to perform outside the United States when we played the Clay House Inn, a classy black supper club in Bermuda. After months on the road we were ready for a vacation, and we had one in Bermuda. The people there loved us, and we took every opportunity to swim, bicycle, or just lie around, so we were in good shape when we got back to Detroit and learned we were booked for another tour.

We were flattered to hear that Dick Clark, the young host of TV's *American Bandstand*, wanted the Supremes for one of his Caravan of Stars package tours. Tours like these—a roster of stars from various labels traveling around for up to three or four months—could never be arranged today. Traveling is too expensive, the logistics are too complicated, and performers now have savvy managers whose various conflicts make the kind of cooperation we had back then impossible to achieve, unless it's for a good cause, like Live Aid. For just $1.50, kids got to see maybe a dozen of their favorite stars. Those days are gone forever, and I am happy that I was part of it while it lasted.

The tours would run from Memorial Day to Labor Day, and the other acts on the bill were the Jelly Beans, Major Lance, the Velvelettes, the Shirelles, Bobby Sherman, the Crystals, the Dixie Cups, Brian Hyland, Mike Clifford, the Ripchords, Gene Pitney, and Dee Dee Sharpe. Dick, who will always be one of my favorite people, was a great promoter, too. He gave us support and encouragement, and, unlike many other business people, never acted as if he were above us. He rode on the same cramped, dirty bus we did, and treated us all as equals.

Like the Motown tours, the Caravan went through the South. Whenever we came to a restaurant that would not serve blacks, Dick put it to a vote. Every time, our white colleagues voted to wait until we found a place that would serve us all. As a result, we usually ended up eating at the local Greyhound terminal, but we were all together.

All three of us made lots of friends on this tour. Mike Clifford was a white singer whose hits, "Close to Cathy" and "What to Do with Laurie," made him one of United Artists' most promising young stars. He and I spent hours talking, but I knew he really liked Diane. Many men were attracted to her even then. She had a certain air about her, a coy shyness that they found intriguing. Having known Diane as a little tomboy, I was amazed by this recent transformation. Her mother was chaperoning on this tour, and Diane stayed very close to her. Mike would ask her to eat out with him, but Diane would always decline, saying that she was going to have dinner with her mother.

Flo, on the other hand, was having a great time flirting with all the guys. It was obvious that she did this to be friendly and wasn't looking for a serious relationship with any man, but all the boys ate it up.

"Where are you from?" Flo would ask, and no matter what the reply, she'd come up with a funny line about their hometown that would have them rolling in the aisles. "Baby, I am from the Motor City. You ever been there?" And when they'd say no, Flo would do her best Mae West-cum-Edie Adams imitation, putting on the sexiest grin and saying, "No? Then why don't you come up and see me sometime?" At times like these, Flo was the life of the party, and everyone loved her.

My heartthrob on this trip was the star, Gene Pitney. I fell in love the minute I laid eyes on him and spent every moment I wasn't sitting beside him figuring out the best way to discreetly move over to his seat. Despite his having a string of hits behind him—including "Town without Pity" and "Only Love Can Break a Heart"—he was modest and polite. This was quite exciting, even though Gene was engaged, and we never so much as smooched the whole trip. When Diane noticed that I liked Gene, she pulled me aside.

"Why do you like that white boy?" she asked incredulously.

Why not? I thought.

A tour was a tour, but we felt we'd taken a step up with this one. Dick was an experienced promoter, and because of his reputation he was able to get us booked into places that were nicer than ones we'd worked on the chitlin' circuit. Some of these places were just high-school gymnasiums, auditoriums, or roller rinks without stages or dressing rooms, but they were still nicer.

A few weeks into the tour, everyone started getting bored, and the bus became the target of our frustrations. Garbage of all descriptions littered the floor. Sleeping was usually impossible, and so the three of us would stay up and practice our tunes. Those who wanted to sleep yelled at us to quiet down, and in Dick's book *Rock, Roll, and Remember,* he refers to "dummies" who sang all night. He was probably talking about the Supremes.

We would sometimes have to change—boys and girls together— in minutes under a makeshift stage, and sometimes we had to do our dressing, hair, and makeup on the moving bus. We soon got into sharing everything with everyone else—Mike Clifford liked using our Max Factor foundation, because he liked the tan look.

No matter what the circumstances, the Supremes always looked great. We were always well dressed, neat, color-coordinated and fully accessorized. Our image was important to us even then. Once, when an angry bus driver took off with the bus and our stage clothes, we weren't sure what to do. After discussing it with Dick, we went on in our street clothes. Our two most popular outfits were red sleeveless spaghetti-strap dresses with tons of fringe, and a silver spandex costume, complete with tight pants, halter tops, and high heels. We looked hot.

Tensions did mount, and sooner or later there'd be fights. Diane always made friends with everyone on the tour; she often would do their hair for them. But this camaraderie never stopped her when she felt she'd been wronged or slighted. When that happened, Diane pulled out all the stops until her opponent was forced to concede. Brenda Holloway and Diane were getting along fine on this trip until Diane insisted that Brenda had stolen her can of hairspray. Brenda denied the charge, but the two of them went back and forth about it until the Shirelles came to Brenda's defense, confirming that Brenda had had the same can of spray since the tour started. As much as I sympathized with Brenda, I knew that Diane was out of line, there was no way I, or Flo for that matter, was going to side against her. Mrs. Ross talked to her, and she finally calmed down, but she had been so clearly mistaken that we were all a little embarrassed by the situation.

One of the most dramatic spats involved Diane and one of my favorite Crystals, Delores Brooks, whom we called Lala. We all liked Lala; she was friendly and outgoing, and she had even made friends with Diane. Then one night while we were en route to a date, Diane accused Lala of stealing a pair of her shoes. Lala denied it, but Diane carried on about it, crying and playing the victim. Not everyone liked Lala; some people thought she was a real pain. When the argument escalated, Diane and Lala were ordered off the bus. We were all sure it was going to come to blows, and this worried Mrs. Ross, who jumped in the middle. Lala, a real sight in her four-foot-high beehive hairdo, was screaming at the top of her lungs and ready to belt Diane. By this time even Flo was set to defend Diane, and I was sure she was going to punch Lala any minute. Finally, Ed McAdam, the tour manager, intervened and told them both to shut up, get back on the bus, and sit down.

We were all embarrassed, but probably no one was as embarrassed as Mrs. Ross. She would talk to Diane, but Diane would still do little things that drove other people crazy. For example, we often had to dress for a show in a school locker room, where there was only one small mirror on the wall. One of the girls would be standing in front of the mirror putting on her makeup, and Diane would come along, smiling and acting very sweet, and sort of work her way around whoever was standing there so that she would be in front of the mirror. It was all done so casually that, by the time you realized what had happened, it was too late.

Diane always had a temper, and while some people might have seen her actions as the result of conniving, her behavior was actually more like that of a spoiled brat. Once she made up her mind about something, there was no reasoning with her, and even being her best friend didn't ensure that what you said would be taken as it was meant. In Diane's mind, anything that wasn't a compliment was a criticism, which hurt her deeply.

Diane would fight with anyone, and often she would take a minor issue and keep on it until you reacted. Knowing Diane as Flo and I did, we understood that the best way to deal with her in these situations was to ignore her. Diane was like a child testing a parent. Over time, her tantrums and shows of temper became like bad habits, and Flo's and my responses became reflexes. When we saw it coming, we just tuned out.

One day, for a reason so trivial I can't even remember it, Diane jumped on my back and started pulling my hair. She was punching me and screaming at me. Flo was within seconds of intervening when Mrs. Ross appeared and pulled her off me. One of Mrs. Ross' finest qualities was her sense of justice, and she never sided with Diane blindly.

Ironically, Diane made the only truly profound statement I ever heard her utter in the middle of one of these spats. She was carrying on about something, goading me to respond, and I just refused.

"Mary," Diane said in her crisp, high voice, "you better let it all out. Because if you keep it inside, it's gonna hurt you."

She was probably right. The statement also revealed to me one reason why she didn't hesitate to make a scene, which was something Flo and I just would not do: She saw it as quasi-therapeutic.

When the Dick Clark tour started, the Supremes got the usual polite hand after each number. Maybe a few people in the crowd would know "Buttered Popcorn" or "Lovelight," but the response we got was a mere whimper compared to the screams Gene Pitney or the Shirelles elicited. In our absence, Motown had released "Where Did Our Love Go" sometime in June. We knew it was out, but we weren't yet sufficiently interested in the business side of music to be reading *Billboard* or *Cashbox*, and without a radio on the bus we had no idea who had a hit.

Slowly, though, we began to notice the applause getting a little louder and a little wilder in each city. When the audience screamed for us, we stood in the wings paralyzed with disbelief. They really wanted us! By the end of August 1964, the "no-hit" Supremes had the number-one song in the country.

CHAPTER 14

We returned to Detroit in August, feeling like we had really made it at last. Having a number-one record proved to the world what Flo, Diane, and I had believed for years—we were the greatest. I couldn't wait to get back to Hitsville and find out how rich we were.

As long as we'd been with Motown I always seemed to be the one who spoke up for the three of us when it came to business. We couldn't wait to find out how much we'd earned, and I went to Esther Edwards' office feeling very proud. When I asked her how much each of us would get, she replied, "There is no money. Motown managed to get you on the Dick Clark tour only because he wanted Brenda Holloway. I told him to take you too, and he agreed."

"But, Mrs. Edwards," I said, "we've been on the road for three months, and most of the shows were sellouts. Surely, there must be some money coming to us."

"You were paid only six hundred dollars a week. Deduct from that the price of room and board and food for yourselves and Mrs. Ross and that leaves nothing." Then, as if to add insult to injury, she added, "It probably cost the company, but you needed the exposure." I tried to figure it out; where could the money have gone, especially when we so rarely stayed in a room anywhere?

I left the meeting crushed. Why did there always seem to be another hurdle? Up until now, we were having so much fun—it really was like living a fairy-tale. While most of our friends had gotten married, gone on to college, or were working at boring jobs, we were in show business and having the time of our lives. It seemed like we were living under a spell—and perhaps we were.

"Girls," Mrs. Edwards had said, "you know that what you're getting paid is important, but more important is how you project yourselves to people. When they begin to like you, they go out and buy your records, so think about your show."

Our "show" was our lives. We concentrated on what to wear, how to fix our hair, how to speak, what to say to journalists and other people we met, and so on. Even this early in the game, we were getting little messages that we wouldn't really understand until years later, like "Be careful about the guys you decide to marry, and make sure your husband has as much money as you. Because if he doesn't, he'll always be looking at your pocketbook."

The Supremes hadn't yet made their fortune, but judging by the way many of our colleagues at Motown (as Hitsville was now known) carried on, you'd think everybody else had. No one really knew how much anyone else was getting paid, but the general consensus was that the writers and producers were doing pretty well. I was sitting on the porch at Motown when I overheard this conversation:

"Man, I'll give you the money to buy a Cadillac," Brian Holland said to his brother Eddie. Brian had just bought his first Cadillac, and we were all admiring it.

"I don't want a Cadillac," Eddie insisted.

"Everybody here has a Cadillac. Don't you want one? I can afford to buy you one, no problem."

"I never wanted a Cadillac," Eddie continued. "I want a Buick Riviera."

"A Buick? Are you crazy?"

"That's what I want! I've never seen anything like it, and it's different," Eddie said finally.

This conversation took place against a backdrop that would be a familiar sight on West Grand Boulevard for years to come—a fleet of brand-new Cadillacs parked all over West Grand Boulevard. As soon as a writer, producer, or performer got his first check, it was as good as endorsed over to the local Cadillac dealership. Purchasers, intent on protecting whatever individuality they could enjoy when they were buying the same car everyone they knew had, would consult with one another about style, colors, and options, so that no two would be alike. Of course, no one would dare ask Berry about his preferences. One day Mickey Stevenson drove up in a Caddy the same color and style as Berry's new one, a light color, like gray. *Someone* would have to exchange his car; a few days later Mickey was tooling around in a black Cadillac.

All the money pouring in built the Motown machine. From the very beginning, Beans Bowles had made Berry aware that some of the artists on the roster, especially those with little or no previous show-business experience, needed some polish. Certain aspects of appearance, stage presence, and etiquette were not quite up to snuff, as far as Beans was concerned. Having worked with some of the classier acts, Beans knew what he was talking about. At a time when most record labels were content to just produce records, Berry wanted to produce stars. Eventually, the Artist Development department came under the guidance of Harvey Fuqua, who staffed it with the best people he could find.

Just what did Artist Development do for the artists at Motown? The most prevalent idea, which I like to call the Motown Myth, runs something like this: Berry took a bunch of ghetto kids with no class, no style, and no manners, put them through hours of grueling training in etiquette, choreography, and interview tactics, and then—voilà —stars rolled out of Hitsville like cars off an assembly line. Young "uneducated" blacks suddenly knew how to speak and which fork to use. And so the story goes.

Not only is this view incorrect, it's insulting. Yes, Artist Development played a role in preparing many of us to deal with a wide range of situations. However, in an age when top executives with graduate business degrees from Harvard are sent to special etiquette classes, it's safe to assume that most people—regardless of age, race, or class— would not know how to give a good interview or greet a president or a queen without some instruction. Motown's Artist Development department was patterned after the movie studio "charm" schools of the thirties and forties. In the sixties, when most young performers were rebelling against show-business conventions, Motown's approach seemed archaic.

The truth is that Berry never signed anyone to Motown who needed to be "remade." The uncouth, boisterous, and slovenly couldn't get a foot in the door anyway. Almost everyone who came to Motown wanted to move up in the world. None of us came from homes that didn't teach manners. We were all trying to get ahead, and it's always bothered me that some people have assumed that by accepting what some consider "white" values, we sold out. It's just not true.

Once we got back from the Dick Clark tour, Artist Development went into overdrive working on the Supremes. Although no one there knew how big a success we would become, Motown wanted us to be prepared for anything. The system was geared to give full support to whichever act was at the top then, so this month it might be the Supremes, and we would have first priority; next month it could be the Tempts or the Vandellas. All of us understood this, so there were no hard feelings, and everyone was very supportive.

One of our first chaperones, Mrs. Maxine Powell, was in charge of etiquette and grooming. She spoke and carried herself very properly. "Young ladies always . . ." was the stock opening phrase for Mrs. Powell's directions. Hats and gloves were mandatory attire for the girls around Motown, and she often lectured us about clothes. Since Flo, Diane, and I already had devoted years to creating our own unique and very sophisticated style, we quickly became Mrs. Powell's star pupils. Attendance in Artist Development was never mandatory. We went because we loved it. We spent only about six months working with Mrs. Powell, but anything that we learned would be incorporated into our behavior that same day. We would be out eating something, and if one of us accidentally picked up her chicken with her fingers, the other two would say, "Remember what Mrs. Powell said," and it would be corrected. It was like a little game to us.

Mrs. Powell was the expert in residence, and every day we reported to a studio that was set up in one of the buildings that Berry had just purchased adjacent to Hitsville. Mrs. Powell took her job seriously, and she would make us walk up and down the mirrored room while she critiqued our every move. She was always on the lookout for bad habits and would point out any flaw, no matter how minor. I can remember feeling her eyes upon me as I walked around with books on my head. Were my shoulders straight? Was my posture good? Was my makeup—the little I wore then—feminine and flattering—not too brassy? Which fork to use, how to greet people, how to hold eating utensils, how to enter a room, how to find a chair, and how to sit and rise gracefully were all part of the program.

Of course, not everyone was as receptive to the charm school course as we were. Those who were unaccustomed to thinking about their every move took any criticism personally, while others found the very idea of etiquette phony. There were some girls who thought that Mrs. Powell was just insensitive to their particular problems. Rosalind Ashford of the Vandellas, for instance, was left-handed, so she had problems following Mrs. Powell's right-handed instructions for handling flatware.

One thing that everyone working in Artist Development found, regardless of what they taught, was that some people just found learning these things much easier. Every group had one member who found the courses more difficult, and in the Supremes it was Flo. It wasn't that she didn't want to learn—she did. Flo's problem stemmed from her being a little awkward. She was always accident-prone, and she lacked what athletes call body sense. "Now, look, Florence . . ." became a familiar phrase. But Flo just worked harder.

Mrs. Powell's efforts paid some interesting dividends. Not only did we have a lot more self-confidence, but other people began treating us differently. This was true of all the Motown acts in general, but especially the Supremes. When Mrs. Powell accompanied us on the road, she would correct young men when they addressed us in a way that she felt was not quite proper.

Mrs. Powell had a great sense of humor. One day she was demonstrating to us the correct way for a lady to enter a car. She stood near a chair and pantomimed opening the car door, stepping sideways into the car, and sitting. When it came to the sitting part, she stuck her rear end out and said, "Now, girls, when you get into a car like this, *this*"—and she patted her fanny—"is what everybody sees. A lady, however, does it like this." And she showed us the proper way.

That afternoon, we were all standing on the porch when we saw her get into her car. The second she pulled away, we all fell down laughing, because Mrs. Powell had entered her car with her rear end protruding. Mrs. Powell was one of a few people around Motown, like Mrs. Ardeena Johnson, whose motto might have been "Do as I say, not as I do." Still, we liked them immensely and appreciated everything they taught us.

As beneficial as our grooming lessons were, there were some things that makeup and poise just couldn't help. Padded bras and falsies were all the rage, and even Flo, who definitely didn't need any more, was wearing them. Diane and I, still being beanpoles, used anything we could. Diane added hip pads, and I padded my backside as well. In my new curves, I was strutting around Motown with a vengeance. One afternoon I was chatting with some people in the lobby when, unbeknownst to me, Lamont Dozier stuck a long straight pin into what was supposed to be my derrière. When it was obvious to everyone that I hadn't felt a thing, they broke out laughing, and for a few seconds I fancied myself a very entertaining conversationalist.

A more serious aspect of Artist Development was the music classes we took with Maurice King, a veteran bandleader who'd worked at the

Flame Show Bar. Back when we were hanging out Milton's window, we would see Maurice, and later John O'Den snuck us into the Flame, where we met Maurice and Sam Cooke. John introduced us to Sam and Maurice as "his girls," and Sam Cooke wished us luck and told us to keep up the good work. We were so thrilled.

Maurice worked with most of the other Motown acts, including Mary Wells and the Temptations. We had worked with Maurice just prior to recording "Where Did Our Love Go." Maurice taught us various vocal exercises and more sophisticated arrangements. One day, we were working on "Where" when I said, "I hate this song!"

"Look, don't knock it," Maurice said. "Why don't you wait—you may be knocking something you will learn to love."

And, of course, when we got back from the Dick Clark tour, I knew what Maurice was talking about. After that I knew to leave picking the songs we recorded to those who knew best.

We also worked with choreographer Cholly Atkins, a well-known song-and-dance man whom we had met back at the Apollo in 1962. Cholly started in show business as a singing waiter in Buffalo, New York, and then worked with prominent stars—such as Bill Robinson, Ethel Waters, and Lena Horne—over the years. In 1945 he teamed up with Honi Coles, and the two of them worked as dancers with big-band leaders such as Duke Ellington, Cab Calloway, and Count Basie. He earned his reputation as a choreographer in New York, where acts would come to him so that he could "doctor up" their stage presentations. And that's how Harvey Fuqua met Cholly.

After Cholly joined Motown, he was very careful to always present a professional image, even in terms of his relationship with Berry. We were still a "big, happy family" then, but Cholly never attended the gatherings and Christmas parties. One day Berry asked Cholly why, and Cholly replied that he didn't see himself as being on the same social level as Berry, and that business was business, and personal time was personal time. I guess Berry respected Cholly's honesty.

Among the other people who worked with us in polishing our acts were Gil Askey, an arranger; and Johnnie Allen, a musician, arranger, and our rehearsal pianist. Cholly was in charge of scheduling, and he and the others kept copious notes and files on each group's progress.

Whenever we had time between recording and touring, we would be in the studio working out new steps, new arrangements, or anything else that needed practice. Flo, Diane, and I worked very hard, and it was clear to the people in Artist Development that we had something special. First, it was our music and our sound, which wasn't really rough or raucous and lent itself to the more sophisticated choreography and staging. Second, we had what Cholly called "built-in sophistication."

Motown's leading lady, Mary Wells, had just left Motown for a better deal with 20th Century–Fox, and Berry was looking for an act he would be proud to present anywhere in the world. Motown had already committed to a tour of Great Britain, which Mary was to headline; now, it was decided, the Supremes would assume what had been Mary's spot.

There was no question in anyone's mind now that the push was on the Supremes. Though we never attended production meetings, things that were said about us in them usually got back to us. Berry would say things like, "We're going to make a push on the Supremes," or "Hey, play the girls' record again," or "Well, the Supremes are who's going to make this company." And Berry meant every word of it. We were flattered to be "the girls" again.

We were local heroes. Wherever we went in our neighborhoods, people would call out to us and wave. In the Projects, "Where Did Our Love Go" could be heard coming out of every window. We gave copies of our hit to all our neighbors and relatives, and if one of our parents had a special friend over, we'd meet there and sing along to our record, doing our show in the living room. Everyone we knew was supportive of us. By now, even our siblings were friends: Roosevelt hung around with Fred and Arthur Ross and Billy Ballard, and Cat was friends with Rita Ross. They were all known in their schools for having a Supreme for a sister.

In August, we recorded a live album at the Twenty Grand Club, which was never released, and Motown released our second album, *Where Did Our Love Go*. The LP eventually went to #2, bolstered by our next two number-one singles, "Baby Love" and "Come See About Me."

On October 7, we embarked on our first English tour. The trip was off to a good start when we met Louis Armstrong at the Detroit airport. He gave us his autograph and then said, "I've heard so much about you girls. I hope I get to see you sometime soon. Good luck!" From the second we took off, things just kept on getting better and better. We knew our records were popular in England, but nothing could have prepared us for the reception we got at the airport from dozens of members of the Tamla-Motown Appreciation Society, which was headed by Dave Godin, a devoted fan who played a critical role in exposing our music to England. They carried placards bearing our photos and presented us with bouquets of flowers. We had all seen the reception the Beatles had gotten in New York earlier that year, and we were pleased to be so enthusiastically welcomed. This was the beginning of a romance with England and Europe that would last throughout our career and through my solo career, to the present.

During our two weeks in England, we did everything we could. Photographers and reporters seemed to follow us everywhere, and we were asked our opinions on everything from the British music invasion to fashion. The English press referred to us as "dishy," and their fascination with us was indicative of our relationship with the press for years to come. In the beginning they referred to the three of us as "Negresses," a term we had never heard. At first we were offended; we thought they had some nerve to insult us like that. As we began to understand the English, we saw that there was no offense intended. We were exotic darlings, sexy and cute, and all the more interesting because we were black and hailed from what the foreign press liked to portray as a rat-infested ghetto.

Every night, after we'd finished our work for the day, the three of us would sit in one of our rooms with all the latest papers and magazines spread out all over the bed. We would read some passages aloud and stare at the same pictures over and over again. It was incredible to us. Just a few months before, we were eating crummy road food in an old bus; today we were flying first-class, drinking champagne, and eating caviar.

After a week of touring, we were invited to London's Ad Lib Club as guests. Still young ladies ourselves, we were thrilled to meet Paul McCartney and Ringo Starr there. Earlier that day we had taped a spot for the pop music program *Thank Your Lucky Stars*, and by the time we left for home, "Where Did Our Love Go" was number two; by late November, "Baby Love" would top the U.K. charts.

We returned to the States, and within days flew straight to Hollywood to film the TAMI (Teenage Music International) Show at the Santa Monica Civic Auditorium. The show, which was directed by Steve Binder, stands today as one of rock's classics, with performances by us, the Rolling Stones, the Beach Boys, Marvin Gaye, Chuck Berry, Jan and Dean, Gerry and the Pacemakers, James Brown, Lesley Gore, the Miracles, and others. We performed "Where Did Our Love Go," "Baby Love" and "When the Lovelight Starts Shining Through His Eyes." The show was really great, but some of the best moments occurred backstage. The Rolling Stones and James Brown were both asking themselves and anyone within earshot essentially the same question about the scheduling: How did the Stones think they were going to follow Soul Brother Number One? The Stones weren't quite sure they could, and James Brown was pretty sure they couldn't!

Three days later, Motown released our third number-one single, "Come See About Me." When one of our promotion men, Jocky Jack, heard another version of the song by a group called the Nelodods, with exactly the same arrangement and backing, Motown rush-released ours. We were never sure if Motown knew that the Nelodods' producer was our friend, promotion man Weldon MacDougle.

Back in Detroit, we started recording A Bit of Liverpool, our "tribute" to the British Invasion. With this release and next year's Country, Western, and Pop, which we had recorded earlier, the Supremes started getting criticism for "selling out," because we weren't singing only "soul" music. In fact, we enjoyed singing all kinds of songs—everything from jazz to show tunes—and would do so throughout our career. We particularly liked the country material, since it lent itself to the complex three-part harmonies we loved to sing.

In December we returned to the West Coast to appear in Bikini Party, a movie that was never released. During our stay, Gil Bogas, a local promotion man, showed us the city. The big thrill of our stay there was having lunch with our idol, Sidney Poitier, at the Brown Derby. It had been arranged by a publicist, and we were as giddy as little girls, swooning all through lunch and making sure that he auto-graphed photos for us, our families, our friends—everyone we knew, it seemed.

This most auspicious year ended with the Supremes making the first of many appearances on The Ed Sullivan Show. After watching the show every Sunday night for as long as I could remember, I found it hard to believe that we were actually going to be on it. This was the best Christmas present in the world.

Although the program aired live, performers arrived in New York a week early to rehearse with the orchestra and tape their segments just in case they wouldn't be able to appear. As it came time for us to tape our segment, we dressed in short, blue, softly tiered sleeveless dresses, the most elegant in our stage wardrobe thus far. We were pampered by the makeup artists, who spent about half an hour on each of us, meticulously applying powders and liquids to make us look perfect for television. We had always done our own makeup, which we kept light, and we were leery of letting them do ours, but we were novices to television—they must know best. Or so we thought. When we took one last look before going onto the soundstage we were shocked. We looked like black-faced singers in a minstrel show!

"Honey, I'm not goin' out looking like this!" Flo exclaimed.

"Oh my god!" I gasped.

"Let's get this stuff off our faces before it's too late," Diane suggested.

We ran to our dressing tables and removed the dark pancake makeup as quickly as possible. Our self-taught makeup expertise would stand us in good stead in the years to come, since in 1964 few makeup people really knew how to work with black skin. All three of us were black, of course, but the nuances of our individual skin tones had eluded our artist, who'd covered all of us with a dark Egyptian tone. In minutes, we'd applied our own makeup and were ready to go on.

The afternoon's taped performance went smoothly. When Sunday night rolled around and our live spot drew nearer, we were very excited. Millions and millions of people would be watching us. We were so happy that we didn't even think about being nervous. I heard Mr. Sullivan welcoming us to his "shew." We stood side by side, with Diane in the middle, and shared one microphone. Cholly had worked out a very subtle but sexy little shimmy step that worked beautifully. We smiled demurely and sang perfectly. Within a few months, with a few more national television appearances behind us, we were America's sweethearts.

The dreams we had shared for so many years were finally coming true now—overnight. Our good fortune was the answer to all our prayers, and I believed that this would bring us closer together. Instead, our personal differences were suddenly cast in a new light. The higher we ascended, the more Diane wanted for herself. Around this time, she began dating Berry, and whenever she was unhappy about something, she would let him know. It had been hard enough dealing with her when all we had to face was her temper; knowing that even the most personal argument or discussion—even if it had absolutely nothing to do with our work—would be relayed to Berry fostered an atmosphere of distrust. Now Diane's little tricks—like checking what Flo and I would wear so that she could be sure to wear something totally different, or refusing to share her clothes with me after I'd lent her mine—took on a whole new meaning. These things were, on the surface, really quite petty, but what upset Flo and me wasn't what she did but what it all meant. We'd been friends—for life, we thought—but now our friendship was a means to an end, a license for Diane to behave exactly as she chose. And that hurt.

Flo and I had been parts of Diane's life—and she of ours—for so long now, we weren't just dealing with a friend but a family member. The Supremes became partners in a kind of marriage; each partner sees the others' flaws but tolerates them, because divorce is out of the question and fond memories of the courtship and romance refuse to die.

One day we were eating out when Diane suddenly became very angry with me. I have always been a very slow eater, and usually finish last, something Diane and Flo knew.

"Mary," Diane snapped, "you did that just to make us look bad."

Flo had a wonderful, mock-haughty look that seemed to say, "Well, who is this?" that she would give me at times like these. I couldn't believe my ears, and the look on Diane's face was hilarious. Would someone deliberately eat slowly to make someone else look bad? I didn't think so, and neither did Flo, but obviously Diane did. Flo and I just gave each other our secret look and kept on eating.

Diane was being regarded as Berry's other half, and Berry made the Supremes his number-one priority. He saw in the Supremes his vehicle to prominence, the golden key to any door he wanted to open. We were now BLAPs—black American princesses.

CHAPTER 15

Beginning in 1965, hardly a week passed that the Supremes were not featured on at least one television program. During the sixties, variety shows were extremely popular, and we appeared on just about every one of them. Motown had planned it so that we would debut our latest record on national television within a day or two of its release. We were seen on *The Ed Sullivan Show, Hullabaloo, The Hollywood Palace, The Tonight Show, The Dean Martin Show, The Red Skelton Show*, and countless specials. We usually did our latest release, which we often lip-synched—since it was the record being promoted—and then sang something else, like a show tune or a medley, live. Gradually, producers gave us more complicated production numbers, complete with intricate choreography and very sophisticated vocal parts. There weren't too many young performers interested in doing anything but their hits, so once the producers saw how much we loved doing these other numbers, they got more extravagant. We loved it.

Doing television was a lot of fun, and we met and worked with many great performers, such as Dean Martin and Johnny Carson. We always tried to look a little different for each appearance. Flo, Diane, and I loved to shop anyway, and now that we had to have not only new stage costumes but a large wardrobe of daywear for publicity appearances and luncheons, we took to shopping with a vengeance. Most of the television shows we did early on were taped from New York, so when we had even a two-hour break from rehearsals, we'd all jump into the limo and head over to Saks Fifth Avenue. We each had equal say in what outfits we wore onstage, and whenever any of us went shopping alone, she'd run into the others' rooms to show them what she'd bought.

The Supremes' image underwent its first major change at this time. Until now, we'd worn only the lightest makeup and maybe false eyelashes; Diane and Flo wore wigs. Soon after the first Sullivan show our itinerary was booked through 1965, so even I started wearing wigs. It was easier to change wigs than to change hairstyles. We each had dozens of them, all expensive, handmade human-hair pieces in a variety of styles ranging from Mod-ish Vidal Sassoon cuts to high, elaborate flips. In fact, the bulk of our luggage was made up of huge wig boxes, which were always carried on flights, never checked. Diane had been wearing long false nails for some time. Also, television work required heavier, pancake makeup, which we learned to apply ourselves. Soon the look involved more eyeliner, darker eyebrows—especially Diane's—and longer false lashes.

Next came the dressier dresses, which were still street length until mid-1965 or so, when we started wearing long evening gowns in performance. These first gowns were usually sleeveless, often with an Empire waist and made of soft fabrics, like chiffon or velvet. Motown went along with our sexy but wholesome image for the Supremes, but, contrary to what some people think, it wasn't foisted upon us. We really were those girls, and we never felt that what we were onstage was anything but an extension of our true personalities. When I had seen myself in the mirror years before in a homemade costume, I saw a girl every bit as glamorous as the one on television in 1965.

Of all the hosts we worked with, Ed Sullivan was my favorite. We were booked for his show so often that I began to think of it as *The Supremes Show*. Mr. Sullivan made no secret of the fact that he was crazy about us. The Supremes were the only act he let keep the special gowns from the production numbers.

Tapes of these early appearances reveal that while we were true professionals, there was still an innocence about us. Working in television and film gave us confidence and a chance to see how we looked. Strangely, because we traveled so much in those days, we rarely got to see ourselves on television, but when we did, we made mental notes about what looked good and what needed work. This was all great practice, and we applied to our live shows what we learned from seeing ourselves.

Motown was anxious to solidify its relationships with English and European record distributors, and so a tour was scheduled to begin in mid-March 1965. This was to become the infamous Ghost Tour. Though the Supremes had made a real splash in England just six months before, the Revue as a whole didn't fare quite so well. It was a strange turn of events for us. Just a year before, as the "no-hit"

Supremes, we'd been opening the Revue in the States, for the other acts—Marvin Gaye, Martha and the Vandellas, Stevie Wonder, and the Miracles—who'd all had huge hits. In England, however, it was another story: To date, only the Supremes had Top Ten hits there. Not surprisingly, some of the Revue veterans weren't entirely comfortable with the amount of attention the Supremes were getting. There were avid Motown fans all over England and the Continent, but it was clear that reporters in the smaller towns really didn't understand what the music was all about. And, for the first time in as long as many of us could remember, we were playing to half-filled houses.

The worst part of all, and the reason the tour was called the Ghost Tour, was what many of the foreign publications did to our photographs. One day we were scanning a local publication for a review.

"Oh, my God!" I exclaimed when I saw our picture.

"Who is that?" Flo asked.

"I don't know."

"We look like Martians!"

One of the Miracles looked over Flo's shoulder and remarked, "I think that's you, Flo."

"Me?" she shrieked. "Honey, I know I'm black, but this is ridiculous. We're all so washed out and smutty-looking, you can hardly see us. We look like ghosts."

Apparently the European photographer hadn't taken too many photos of blacks and the lighting was all wrong. We laughed about this the whole tour.

Beans Bowles and Mrs. Edwards, however, weren't laughing about much of anything. Financially the tour was a flop, but everyone at Motown saw it as a means of promoting the other acts and making the foreign distributors happy. We had left Detroit in high spirits, thinking that the Miracles, the Vandellas, the Temptations, and Stevie Wonder would conquer the English and European markets as easily as we had, but this was not to be.

Through it all, the Supremes received special treatment. Mrs. Edwards had divided all the travelers into three different groups, and we were in group A with Berry and his entourage. One of Mrs. Edwards' young protégés, Booker Bradshaw, knew England well, having attended Oxford, so he was put in charge of the tour.

We got a great welcome from fans at Heathrow Airport in London and then set out for the dates. We started out traveling by bus, but Berry got fed up with the length of time it took to travel through the

English countryside. When he complained about it, I said, "Now you know how we feel on those long tours."

He sort of grinned, then instructed his assistant, Don Foster, "Let's hire a limo."

So it was the Supremes, Berry, and Don traveling through Great Britain in a stretch limousine. We saw Bristol, Cardiff, Manchester, and Newcastle, and numerous small towns in between. The English cuisine was bland, as usual, and many of the fellows were surprised to find how easy it was to get drunk on warm ale. Whenever we asked for ice, people looked at us like we were crazy.

Though most of this came as no surprise to us, many of the other performers were appalled by such British things as the slick brown toilet paper, which was like heavy waxed paper. This wasn't anyone's idea of civilization, and people carried on about it like it was the end of the world. Now, after years of touring all around the globe, I shudder to think of their reactions had we been working the Middle East.

In London we stayed at the Cumberland, a luxury hotel near the Marble Arch, that offered a wide range of personal services, including overnight shoeshines. All you had to do was leave your shoes outside the door that night and the next morning they'd be back, nicely polished. Most of the guys put their shoes out one night, which inspired some wiseguy to go through the halls and switch everyone's shoes around. It took a couple of hours to get it all straightened out, and though we never knew for sure who the culprit was, James Jamerson, David Ruffin, and Bobby Rogers were prime suspects.

Everything moved rapidly. We barely became acquainted with one city before it was time to move on. The Supremes always got the biggest audience response. We had only three hits under our belts, and there was no guarantee that we'd do anything after that, so it's understandable that some of the other performers failed to see why we were getting preferential treatment. Frankly, I wasn't sure myself, and Flo and I did all we could to keep it from going to our heads.

Dusty Springfield, one of England's biggest female vocalists, was one of Motown's strongest supporters, and it was reported that she convinced the BBC to do a television special on our music. We taped "The Sound of Motown" during this trip. Dusty was the hostess, and I enjoyed working with her. She and the crew treated each one of us like a star, but it was clear that Martha and the Vandellas were their favorites. That was okay; I always thought there was room for all of us at the top.

For the opening number, we did "Shake" with the whole cast and wore those red fringed dresses Dick Clark loved. In our solo spot we did "Where Did Our Love Go," and later Flo commented on how square the English go-go dancers were. We then changed wigs, donned long white gowns, and sang "Stop! In the Name of Love." This number featured what is probably our most famous piece of choreography. Though no one recalls where the "stop" gesture came from, the Temptations worked with us perfecting the routine.

The finale included all of us and Dusty, with the Supremes standing alone on stage right. When the show aired in England the next month it received unanimous acclaim, and from that time on there'd be no more empty seats for any Motown act's show.

Soon after the show aired, Berry held a lavish birthday celebration for Diane. I remember this party especially because I was struck by how adeptly Diane played the star. Just months before we'd all been kids working at Hitsville. Suddenly Diane had ascended; she was now the first lady of Motown.

Following the TV special, we performed at the beautiful Wintergarden in Bournemouth. Berry was right there with us. This tour was a great opportunity for Motown and all its artists. We were getting booked in the most prestigious venues in the world, and we were all meeting important people from all walks of life. It was an exciting time.

Berry and I became very good friends. As we started traveling more, Diane chose to stay in her hotel room when we had time off. Berry and I would get up early and go out to see the city. We both wanted to learn as much as we could about everything we saw. For example, Berry and I would jump in a cab, then spend the whole ride asking the driver how to say things in the native language.

Berry and Flo also had a close relationship, but it was different. Berry was a different person when he wasn't being the president of Motown, and we liked him immensely. Flo, however, wasn't one to pal around, like I was. Her relationship with Berry was based on mutual affection and respect, and at this time we all felt like four very lucky good friends on a wonderful adventure.

Berry never let us out of his sight, and I began to think of him as the fourth Supreme. If he couldn't be with us, he had one of his executive assistants, such as Dick Scott or Don Foster, accompany us. We traveled with a huge entourage—a five-man band, a hairdresser, Gregory, and sundry personnel—and the logistics and business were complicated. Berry wanted to ensure that things would be taken care of.

We were all backstage in England one night when our publicist ran back to tell us that Lord and Lady Londonderry were in the audience, had loved our show, and invited us to visit their home. We were honored, and of course accepted.

"Maybe they live in a castle," I wondered aloud.

"Well, honey, if they do, it better be heated," Flo replied, "because some of these English places are too cold for me."

A few days later we rode in our limousine to the outskirts of London. When we arrived at our hosts' estate, I was dumbfounded. It was like something out of a fairy-tale; not exactly a castle but closer to it than anything any of us had ever seen before. The manicured grounds seemed to roll on forever, with beautiful gardens and a private lake. There was also a family chapel on the premises.

During our entire visit, Berry was right beside us. When we'd first met Lord and Lady Londonderry backstage, they were quite charming. His lordship was tall and handsome; I pictured him wearing riding boots and jodhpurs every day. But while the atmosphere at the estate was subdued, our hosts were very friendly and outgoing.

We stayed there a week and had everything at our disposal. We would leave at night to do the show, then return. One night we brought the English rock singer Georgie Fame back with us and had a blast. Our last day there we stayed up all night playing our records for them, and we even got them to sing along.

We were having the time of our lives. Back in Detroit, we were still living with our families in the Projects; here we were guests in a hundred-room mansion, dining amid antique china and crystal. Lord Londonderry got along great with Flo; she really kept him laughing the whole week we were there. Lady Londonderry seemed to like Georgie Fame, too. A few years later, she married Georgie.

This really was like living in a fairy-tale, not only for us but for Berry, too. We realized that we were going to make it—and bigger than we'd ever imagined. Berry never overlooked an opportunity; he had jokingly said that the Supremes would make Motown: now it was happening right before his eyes. Less than a decade before, Berry had been pushing his songs at the Flame. Now he was doing essentially the same thing, except the people he met were more important, the stakes much higher. How far could we go? No one knew. But we did suspect that there may not be a limit.

Even amid all this hoopla, I still cared more about the singing than anything else. Dozens of important people came to our shows, and the British press treated us like royalty. *New Musical Express* named the Supremes the number-three group in the world, and *Music Biz* named us the top female trio. We got a great reception in Germany and in France, where one of our more interesting adventures took place.

We were booked to play the Olympia Music Hall with the Miracles and Martha and the Vandellas. The show was going to be filmed for French TV, and, like most Motown shows from that period, it was recorded (and released in Europe as *Live in Paris*). Among those in the audience were Marlene Dietrich and singer Sarah Vaughan. That afternoon, someone came up with the bright idea of filming the three of us singing while skipping down the middle of Paris's busiest street, the Champs Élysées, during rush hour. Someone cruised ahead of us in a car, filming the action and blasting one of our records over a loudspeaker so we could get the lip synch right. The director didn't tell us that we didn't have official permission to do this, and after a few minutes of us merrily trotting down the street, traffic backed up for blocks.

Suddenly we saw gendarmes approaching us, yelling angrily. We didn't understand what they were saying, but the director kept screaming for us to keep going. We followed his instructions, and the next thing we knew, the policemen were grabbing at us and trying to forcibly remove us from the street. My arm was sore for days after, but as you can see in a film clip of the incident, we gamely proceeded as if nothing was wrong. Not knowing the story, you'd think it was staged.

After a few minutes we finally figured out what was wrong and that we might be headed to jail. The policemen weren't at all impressed with our explanation, and as we were being escorted away I said to Mrs. Edwards, "What are we going to do?"

"Yeah," Flo interjected. "If we go to jail, think of the bad publicity."

Mrs. Edwards replied, "It doesn't matter—as long as they spell your name right, there is no such thing as bad publicity." Fortunately we didn't go to jail, so we never found out.

In Paris Berry and Diane befriended a black French model named Ariane Sorps. Berry was taken with her, and Diane liked whatever Berry liked, so Ariane became her new best friend.

Berry always was a collector of interesting people, and Diane constantly craved new diversions. Ariane was different and exotic, and she was no doubt flattered by Diane's and Berry's attention. Whatever Ariane liked, Diane liked, and when we returned to the States, Ariane came with us. Back in Detroit, Ariane pranced around Motown like she owned the place. There was even a photo of her with us published in one of the local papers. A few weeks later, she returned to Paris, and I never heard of her again.

Coming home meant returning to a hectic schedule of appearances and recording dates and some great news: We had been booked to appear at the Copacabana in New York City, one of the most prestigious clubs in the country! Every moment of free time was devoted to preparation for this landmark event. In May we recorded several Coca-Cola commercials; one is based on "Baby Love," and there are two others, written by HDH, that incorporate musical phrases from other Motown hits. We were recording our hits in German and Italian, which we learned phonetically, recording new vocals over the original backing tracks, and were enjoying our fifth consecutive number-one hit, "Back in My Arms Again." *We Remember Sam Cooke*, our tribute to the recently deceased singer, was out (Flo was given the lead on "Ain't That Good News"), and we did several television specials, including "It's What's Happening, Baby," with the Vandellas, the Temptations, Marvin Gaye, and the Miracles, and a program about President Lyndon B. Johnson's War on Poverty. In May we were pictured on the cover of *Time*, and the following month we made the cover of *Ebony*.

Just eight months after our first big hit, the Supremes were Motown's greatest commodity. But as great as the Motown machine was, it could work only on a couple of acts at a time. As a result several other acts began receiving less attention than they deserved, especially since Berry was now spending so much time with us. Martha and the Vandellas, for example, saw their position erode at this time. Writers and producers still wanted to work with them, and they were still making great records. But Motown was still a small company, and our success was just too big for the setup. Before we hit, the company's promotional efforts would be concentrated on one act while it was hot; several weeks later, someone else would be hot. It all balanced out over the long run. The Supremes' constant success, however, threw a wrench in the works. I could see that it was happening, and I felt very bad about it. But I was too young to know how to approach my friends and tell them how I felt. It was all beyond my control.

Throughout; most of the artists had a genuine affection for one another; we really believed we were one big family. But success separated us from the other artists, and the industry started calling all the shots. We weren't just the Supremes—we were Motown's Supremes, not just the company's biggest act, but the company's public face as well.

In mid-1965, Flo, Diane, and I moved into homes on Buena Vista Drive in Detroit. Don Foster's girlfriend had done the preliminary search for us while we were gone, and when we returned we each made our final decision. It was only then that we learned that we'd all chosen houses on the same street. Having our own places was a dream come true, and the houses were tangible proof of our success. I bought one house for my mother, Cat, and Roosevelt, and a duplex for myself, half of which I rented out to Cholly and Maye Atkins. The house I chose was very modern, with a big backyard and spacious, open rooms, which I decorated in bright yellows and oranges. Flo moved many members of her family into a house a block and a half down the street from mine and across the street from Diane's. We both had our houses redesigned to include large kitchens. Flo's taste in decorating was classic, and she used lots of blue tones throughout. Diane didn't seem as interested in decorating her house. The one major renovation she made was to build a large mirror-lined room just for her clothes. Walking into this room was like entering a department store; all her clothes hung on professional racks, grouped by color. Diane didn't stay in her house long. While she was there, Mrs. Ross lived with her.

Berry, who had an almost sophomoric lust for competition, decided that we should hold a house-decorating contest, but we all declined; it seemed so silly. We were rarely in Detroit long enough to enjoy our places, but when we were, they were our private sanctuaries.

I first realized that the Supremes had grown bigger than the three of us after Berry heard through the grapevine that I was planning to install mirrors on my bedroom ceiling.

"I don't think it's a very good idea, Mary," he said. "It's not going to sound right."

Though I resented the idea of Berry having anything to say about what I did in the privacy of my home, I agreed with him. We often had journalists at our houses, and it would have looked bad. I knew then, though, that the Supremes were more than just another group.

The cost of purchasing, renovating, furnishing, and decorating our homes was certainly substantial, but I knew it represented only a fraction of what the Supremes had earned for Motown. Though Motown didn't submit its sales figures to the Recording Industry Association of America, the people who certify gold records, we knew that our records were selling in the millions worldwide. By now, we each received a weekly allowance of $500; anytime we needed more money, for example, to buy a car, we would tell Motown and it would be issued to us. In addition, our clothes and other travel expenses were deducted from our accounts. During my years at Motown, I never even saw my tax return. This would strike most people as hard to believe, but it was impossible to think that everything we were told wasn't true. If we hadn't made a fortune, how could there always be limos, champagne, thousand-dollar dresses, and a complete entourage at our beck and call?

The Four Tops—Duke, Levi Stubbs, Lawrence Payton, and Renaldo (Obie) Benson—had been together almost ten years when they signed to Motown in 1964. In the mid-fifties they'd recorded for several labels and, despite a lack of hits, they were always a popular supper-club act in Detroit and often played Las Vegas with Billy Eckstine. Around the time Duke and I met, Berry had matched the Tops up with HDH for their first hit, "Baby I Need Your Loving." The Tops were older than most of us at Motown, and they were always regarded as a class act.

When Duke and I had started dating in late 1964, he was separated from his wife and staying at Janie Bradford's house. Once my house was finished, he moved in with me, and we became known as the "sweethearts of Motown." Despite Berry's concern over what the public might think if I had mirrors over my bed, nothing was said about Duke and me living together. It was a time of true happiness. Duke liked the same things I did—entertaining, singing, decorating the house, collecting furniture, and having people around. Often other acts, such as the Miracles, the Temptations, and the Tops, would rehearse next door at Cholly's, then drop by.

Duke was a man's man, and many times when we were home he'd call and say, "Sweetpea, I'm bringing some of the guys over for dinner." I'd cook up a big meal, and we'd all hang out. Maybe a group would rehearse its new number in the den, and we'd all watch. Flo was at my house a lot then, and we had some great times. Duke was known for making a knockout punch, and we'd have what we called "sloopy parties." I can't count the mornings I woke up to find a guest lying face down on the black bear rug in the den. Diane rarely attended these gatherings; she kept pretty much to herself or spent her time with Berry.

We rehearsed for the Copa date for over four months. Our success there would be a milestone for Motown, and Berry wanted to be sure nothing went wrong. Once the Artist Development people finished with us, we were ready. Among the new tricks we learned was a classic hat-and-cane routine Cholly taught us for "Rock-A-Bye Your Baby with a Dixie Melody," which we loved doing. Cholly was also a master at devising routines especially so that we could all walk around the stage but never tangle our microphone cords.

There was some tension during these rehearsals. Both Cholly and Maurice thought that Flo and I weren't as ambitious as Diane, and we resented that. I caught on the quickest and once I learned something I knew it. Flo still would have to work at things to make them look smooth. If she made a mistake, it would upset her, but she would work at it until she got it right. Diane, however, proceeded very slowly and deliberately, and made sure everyone knew how hard she worked. Once on a television show she complained that she had a greater workload yet received the same pay Flo and I did.

For the Copa show, we all learned to twirl our straw hats. This was the trickiest part of the "Rock-A-Bye" routine, but we finally learned it and were all quite pleased. Diane, however, made sure that everyone knew she could do it. For weeks, she would stop anyone around the rehearsals and say, "Look!" and demonstrate the twirling.

As we got closer to the opening, Diane began refusing to comply with Maurice and Cholly's wishes. If they insisted that she do what they say, she would run to Berry. Before long, those working with us were handling Diane with kid gloves. We knew these people liked Flo and me, and I hoped they understood that it was Diane making the demands, not the Supremes.

Diane was making noises that she wanted to be set apart from us. She had Berry and never hesitated to hold that over the head of anyone who crossed her. What would come next was anyone's guess.

Flo, Diane, and I were being interviewed for an important European magazine feature when we heard Diane announce that her real name was Diana. This was the first Flo and I had heard of this. Apparently the name Diana was on her birth certificate, and she would start using it immediately. Flo and I couldn't believe our ears. We just stared at each other.

Flo and I continued to call her Diane. Of course, everyone has a right to change her name, and what Diane did was pretty minor. But I sensed that this was just one more step away from us, one more way of setting herself apart. The change bothered Flo most, not because of what Diane had done but because of the secret way she did it. Why surprise us? Why not just tell us about it privately first? It wasn't that big a deal. At this time, Flo and I were still hopeful that we might be singing more leads, or have solo spots in the live shows. Little did we know that our fates were sealed. The mass public that bought our hits never knew that Flo and I could sing.

Diane also started monopolizing interviews. Writers had always seemed to enjoy talking with all of us and writing about our different personalities. In the beginning we had been treated as three individuals and were quoted equally. Slowly, though, Diane started answering questions that were clearly directed at Flo or me.

During an interview in June 1965, the reporter said, "Florence, what's your most unusual experience while on tour?"

Flo said, "Hmm," and was getting ready to reply when Diane interrupted her and said, "She doesn't have to think long on that, because we know two that were really great."

This kept on until, after a year or so, no one would even bother to ask us, assuming that Diane alone spoke for the Supremes.

The company was buzzing with activity. The Copa's owner, Jules Podell, had booked our first appearance there for the summer, when most of the club's regulars were out of town. Most new acts were booked during this period; there was less money to be made—and lost —if they didn't work out. Though Ed Sullivan had predicted our success and we'd received nothing but raves for all of our shows, Mr. Podell took no chances. After all, the Supremes were the first black pop group of the sixties to play the Copa, and one of the youngest.

Having performed all over the world, we felt ready for the big time, but Motown wasn't taking any chances either. We moved into a New York hotel, joined by Cholly, music director Gil Askey, and arranger Johnnie Allen. We would get so tired, but we'd snap right to whenever Gil would say, "We have to work on this until we get it right." Cholly was more blunt: "I don't care if we work until we're blue in the face." We'd go back to the hotel for a few hours, then we'd be back at rehearsal. We sang the same notes, made the same moves, recited the same lines hundreds and hundreds of times.

Motown went into action like an army on maneuvers, and pretty soon everyone had something to do with the Supremes. Berry's youngest sister, Gwen Gordy Fuqua, helped with our wardrobe. After our sound, our clothes were the most important component of the Supremes style. We were still picking our gowns, but for this occasion a friend of Gwen's designed some special things for us. We—along with everyone else—approved the sketches but didn't see the actual dresses until opening night.

There were people all over the place, giving us instructions and taking our orders. I began to feel as if I could just stand still and everything would be done for me. All I'd have to do was walk onstage and sing. It used to be just the three of us; now we didn't have a minute alone without someone hovering around somewhere.

Opening night found me as excited as ever. I always thought going onstage was the greatest thing, and nothing ever flustered me. HDH called me "cool Mary." Backstage it was us; our hairdresser, Gregory; and a bodyguard, Joe Shaffner. When we realized that some of the people who were supposed to help us, including Mrs. Powell, were late, Diane started biting her false nails.

"Our new dresses are not here," she said.

"Well, some of our old dresses are here," Flo said, perusing the gowns, "but I know these aren't the ones we're going to wear tonight."

"I know they'll be here soon," I said, hoping.

"We've got to know which of these gowns we're supposed to put on," Diane insisted. Of course, we all knew that, but she was starting to get this wild look in her eyes.

We were relieved when Cholly's wife, Maye, came in and tried to help. She was like a mother to us, and she knew it was close to curtain time. As she was standing near the gowns, Mrs. Powell rushed in.

As always, Mrs. Powell had to be in control. She dismissed Maye curtly and started unwrapping the new dresses. With just minutes before curtain, we got dressed and were ready to go.

The club was packed. Eddie Bisco was in charge of making sure that everyone was comfortable and that the important people—disc jockeys, industry heavies, promotion men, press—had anything they wanted and good seats. He also had to be sure that everyone from Motown was taken care of. Among the celebrities at our debut were Ed Sullivan, columnist Earl Wilson, Sammy Davis, Jr., disc jockeys Murray the K and Frankie Crocker, and countless sales reps and distributors. And Motown spared no expense. Don Foster told me that the opening had cost Motown $10,000 (we were paid $2,750 for the week), and later Eddie Bisco revealed that he'd signed tabs amounting to $4,000 just for drinks.

It was a gala opening, and we started the show with "Put on a

Happy Face," which we sang in unison. The songs, dance routines, and patter went smooth as silk. We sang "Come See About Me," "Make Somebody Happy," "The Girl from Ipanema," "You're Nobody till Somebody Loves You," "Rock-A-Bye Your Baby with a Dixie Melody," "Somewhere" from *West Side Story*, and Cole Porter's "From This Moment On." The only problem was our stage gowns. The designer Gwen Fuqua chose usually made costumes for dancers, so these dresses were very soft and plain, in soft blue. They were nice, but we thought that the artificial flowers made of feathers were too much. Once we got onstage, we looked gaudy. For another show our gowns had feathers around the neck, which fluttered all over the stage whenever we moved.

"Get these feathers off my neck!" Diane panted as we entered the dressing room after a show.

"I think the flowers should come off, too," Gwen added, trying to be helpful.

"Do something," Flo said sarcastically as she stepped out of her dress. "Honey, these dresses are a mess, aren't they?" she asked me. I agreed.

Alterations were made, and, after a short rest, we were on for the second show. Since the Broadway shows were over, many stars were in this audience, and I felt like we were just getting better and better. All the hassles were forgotten, and even the gowns weren't a total loss; at least Motown knew to leave the costumes to us. We were cooking, and after the show we all hugged, knowing we had been a real smash. Now everyone in the entertainment world knew the Supremes had what it takes, and we weren't just girl singers anymore. We had arrived.

Right after the opening, Berry met with Harvey Fuqua and Mrs. Edwards and others. Berry wanted to see a few things changed and tightened up, especially our vocals, since he wanted to record a live album. Harvey then relayed Berry's instructions to Cholly and Maurice. Before, Berry would talk to everyone directly; now there was an official hierarchy and channels to go through.

Before we opened at the Copa, we had rehearsed two different openings for the show. Berry liked one of them, and Cholly and everyone else liked the other. But Berry was the boss and insisted that we do it his way first. After the opening night Berry decided that his way wasn't the best, and so we used the other. Regardless of what other people thought, Berry would always insist on seeing every second of an act, then he would make changes. The Artist Development people would go crazy, and we always wondered why Berry didn't make his changes earlier. But he didn't care; he wanted things to be perfect. Nine times out of ten, he was right. Also, I think he was trying to keep everyone on their toes, and he succeeded at that.

As the recording date for the live album drew near, we had to finalize our repertoire. Despite our joy at our success, Diane was becoming moodier. The pressure was really on all of us. Starting around this time Berry encouraged anyone in the Motown family— including relatives, road managers, and other performers—to keep a pencil and pad on hand and jot down anything they saw in the show that should be changed or improved. Berry would then come back and tell us what to change, often at the last minute. These switches would make Diane nervous, but she kept it to herself and did it.

Things came to a head, though, when it was announced that Flo would no longer be doing her solo number, "People," from *Funny Girl*. We had included the song in all of our nightclub appearances, and audiences loved it. Opening night at the Copa, Flo had just recovered from a week of the flu and was a bit hoarse, but she still sounded great. A couple of nights later, however, Diane was singing it. No one in Artist Development was ever given a clear explanation of why; Harvey Fuqua announced the change one day, and that was that.

We all suspected that Berry had taken the song from Flo, but Flo was thoroughly convinced of it and she was crushed. How much more of the spotlight did Diane need? Everyone knew that Flo was very sensitive and that this meant a lot to her. Berry's taking it away from her like this was just vicious. It was impossible to know for sure who had instigated it—Berry or Diane—but neither of them acted as if they were sorry. From that moment on, Flo regarded what was in fact the highest achievement of our career as a disaster. She was sad and moody, and I could see the three of us being torn apart.

I didn't have a featured solo spot, but, ever the optimist, I was still pestering Berry to let me sing a lead now and then, when one day he jokingly said, "Oh, Mary. You know you can't sing!" I was so devastated by his words that it would take me years of music therapy to overcome my gradual loss of confidence.

Flo responded to these events in a way that would become habitual for her. She would get defensive, and no matter what Berry said, she would disagree. Unlike Berry, Flo could not separate the personal from the professional. You were either her friend all the way in everything or you were her enemy; there was no in between. I couldn't beat this system, and, judging from the past few months, there was nothing the Supremes couldn't do. This whole situation would probably pass, or so I thought. Flo, however, was a firm believer in action, and she started bucking Berry at every turn. I wondered how long my two friends could keep this up. Certainly Diane would have to slow down some day, and things with Berry and her would cool off. I decided to wait until I had some answers.

But I was wrong. Diane was obsessed not with being *a* star, but *the* star. During the Copa date, she complained to Cholly about the choreography for "The Girl from Ipanema" because she didn't want to stand between Flo and me. Cholly refused to move her to the end and flew back to Detroit on business. When he returned to New York a few days later, Diane was on the end.

"Diane, you made that number look terrible. Go on back to the center," Cholly said angrily.

"No!" Diane replied. "You'd better talk to Berry."

Diane had called Berry, and he had agreed with her. The matter was settled, and when Cholly called Berry, he was told the same thing.

After our three weeks at the Copa, the Supremes were welcome to play any club in the world. Shelly Berger, a young Jewish actor turned agent, was hired by Berry and put in charge of us. He helped us in many ways: writing monologues, for example, and teaching us how to deliver lines. With his help, our fee for future Copa engagements would be raised each year until we were earning $20,000 a week, a sum equal to what performers such as Dean Martin and Sammy Davis, Jr., commanded. Because we never saw the accounts, we had no idea how much of the Supremes' fee was spent on drinks, complimentary tickets, and other promotional items. Shelly once said, "You couldn't pay enough commissions in four years to cover what Motown spends on you each time you play the Copa." Berry saw this as a trade-off—Motown had carried the "no-hit" Supremes; now the Supremes were going to carry Motown for a while.

But as the Copa had been the scene of several disappointments for Flo, it also put her into the spotlight. I heard through some of the agents that during a later show some movie people contacted Motown executives because they were interested in casting Flo in a film. Flo always had a natural flair for comedy and a wonderful delivery. Her lines, which she always rewrote from the script we were given, were classics: "Just give me the money, honey, and I'll do the shopping," was just one that had the audience screaming with laughter. Another of her famous lines was a reply to Diane's introduction of her as "the quiet one," was, "That's what you think." People laughed, but Flo, Diane, and I knew Flo wasn't kidding.

Standing onstage, I could see that many men regarded her as the sexiest one, and critics never failed to mention her beautiful voice or brilliant timing. Flo could have gone far, and she knew that. Looking back, I suspect that Berry and Diane saw it, too. But Flo needed support, and all she got from Motown were constant reminders to stay in her place.

To the world outside, the Supremes had everything, and Berry spared no expense in creating and maintaining that image. Berry instructed Motown employees to do our bidding and supplied limos, champagne, and unlimited funds. Money was no longer an object, and we never asked the price of anything.

CHAPTER 16

As long as I had known Diane, she would pursue her goals until she achieved them. With the Supremes' new stardom, this characteristic took on new proportions. When I'd see her threatening to tell Berry about something or hanging on his every word, I'd flash back to years before, when she'd said to me, "I'm going to get him." At that time, I didn't understand why she would want him; he wasn't sexy. But he had power, and as I would soon see, that is perhaps the strongest aphrodisiac in the world.

Diane stepped up her self-improvement program, but in secret. Instead of us all going out shopping for clothes together, Diane would go out alone and then refuse to show us what she had bought. She took makeup classes at John Robert Powers, and when Flo and I found out about it, tensions mounted. Again it wasn't what Diane did, it was the way she did it. The public's perception of us began coloring our personal relationships, and Diane kept stepping further and further away, returning to us only when there was no one else around.

Flo and I wanted to further our educations, and with more than just charm classes. We had all planned to attend college, but now that we were stars we had no idea when—or even if—we would get to go to school. As busy as we were touring, there were countless idle hours. We wanted to get our educations, and so I approached Berry about perhaps making some arrangements so that we could. I suggested that Motown contact Wayne State University and make plans to have professors join the entourage and tutor us privately. For example, a French professor might travel with us for a few months, then a physics teacher would come aboard, and so on.

For some reason, however, the plan never materialized, though Diane's "special" studies accelerated, and Berry was learning as much as he could about an array of subjects.

176

*   *   *

We were celebrities in our own right now, and meeting other stars soon became routine. When we were in London, the British rock group the Animals invited us up to their hotel. These boys were wild. I would go out alone, without a chaperone, and I dated Hilton Valentine, the group's guitarist. He took me to his apartment to listen to records, and I was amazed at his collection of American R&B and blues recordings. Strangely, he was just as amazed that I hadn't heard of most of the artists.

Times were really changing, and, compared to almost any other pop stars around, we probably seemed like nuns. We always felt a little out of place when we'd meet other stars who were either dressed like slobs, were stoned or drunk, or were using a lot of profanity. Knowing we were black girls from the inner city, many of our colleagues, especially those from England who liked to romanticize the plight of the disadvantaged, were surprised to discover that we dressed well offstage and comported ourselves like ladies. I shuddered to think what they were expecting.

One of the most memorable meetings took place in August 1965. We were in New York to tape Ed Sullivan's show, and our publicity people and the Beatles' publicity representatives thought it would be great to get the world's number-one and number-two pop groups together. When we'd met Paul and Ringo at the Ad Lib the year before, we hadn't really gotten a chance to talk with them in the noisy club, so we looked forward to a real meeting.

We wore smart, elegant day dresses, hats, gloves, high heels, and jewelry, as well as fur jackets—Flo in chinchilla, me in red fox, and Diane in mink. When our limo pulled up in front of the Warwick Hotel, the crowds of screaming girls—thinking we might be the Beatles—charged the car. Once we stepped out and they saw through our bodyguards that we were only the Supremes, they lost interest and went back to standing watch by the hotel door.

We entered the Beatles' suite, perfectly poised. Apparently other people had been up to visit them earlier, including Bob Dylan and the Ronettes. The first thing I noticed was that the room reeked of marijuana smoke, but we kept on smiling through our introductions. It was difficult to be gracious and friendly in the face of what we could only see as the coolest reception we'd ever received. We felt that we had interrupted something. Paul was nice, but there was an awkward silence most of the time. Every once in a while Paul, George, or Ringo would ask us about the Motown sound, or working with Holland-Dozier-Holland, then there would be silence again. Someone might crack a little joke, but we never knew what they were laughing about. John Lennon just sat in the corner and stared.

After a few moments, we wanted out. Years later, I was visiting George Harrison at his home in England. Recalling that first meeting, he said, "We expected soulful, hip girls. We couldn't believe that three black girls from Detroit could be so square!"

We were back on the road, booked to appear at the Michigan State Fair, on Dean Martin's show, and doing concerts at JFK Stadium in Philadelphia and the Safari Room in San Jose. Recording sessions, rehearsals, wardrobe fittings, interviews, and personal appearances were squeezed into every free minute. When we would sweat in some stinky bus or race through eight shows a day on the early Motown tours, we'd fantasize about how easy things would be once we made it. Well, here we were, working harder than ever—and I loved it.

Of course, most things were better—a lot better. Limos were now de rigueur, and there was always one waiting with its motor running. We seemed to always be racing for the airport; I never understood why the company didn't just give us phony schedules so we'd be on time even if we thought we were late, but they never did. Somehow, we always got where we were going. We had packing down to a science. Each of us always took along at least five pieces of luggage, but the only ones we couldn't live without were the makeup cases and wig boxes. Our arrival in any city would be quite a sight—us, the musicians, road managers, and the wardrobe and hair people (including our wardrobe mistress Miss Marjorie Wooden), each with a big wig box in hand. Days off would find me lounging around wearing a mudpack that would horrify anyone. Hours of flight time were devoted to manicures and pedicures.

Berry kept us pretty well insulated from the rest of the world and the business, it is said. But around this time, we stopped traveling with chaperones. Diane, tired of Mrs. Powell's lectures, had called Berry and had her taken off the road. Then Mrs. Ross stopped traveling with us. Before she stopped, she and Maurice King, our musical director on the road, made quite a pair. When we were in between shows or traveling, he and Mrs. Ross often played cards together.

Like her daughter, Mrs. Ross was quite a kidder, and if Maurice didn't look out, she'd hit him over the head. But Maurice seemed to enjoy it, and having those two with us made it feel like we were a real family. Mrs. Ross would talk to Maurice about Diane. Once she even told us, "Ever since Diane was a child, she's been stubborn and wanted her own way. Then when she gets her way, it isn't what she really wanted at all." Insights like these helped us all deal with Diane's tantrums, and Maurice seemed to have a way with Diane. She could be in the worst mood, and Maurice would still kid her, saying he'd spank her—even if they were sitting in an executive meeting. He was one of the few people around whom Diane would let down her guard.

The last of our chaperones was Doris Postle. Mrs. Postle was another Gordy family friend but quite different from Mrs. Powell or Mrs. Johnson. Mrs. Postle liked to have fun and she gave us free rein. "You young ladies are grown now," she'd say, "and I trust you."

"Yes, ma'am," we'd reply, all the while thinking of about a dozen reasons why she shouldn't.

Now we traveled with our own entourage of road managers, business managers, wardrobe people, and hairdressers. The days of scrunching up three to a lumpy bed, sleeping and changing on moving buses, and worrying about whether or not a restaurant would seat us were over for good. We had individual rooms in the best hotels, and we ate in the finest restaurants. When money was no object, neither was color. I found myself living in scenes that I'd only seen in movies. At every hotel, we'd open our doors and find baskets of fresh flowers and fruit, fully stocked bars, and every conceivable touch of luxury. The first thing I'd do was to unpack, then put out photos of my family and current beau, arrange all my makeup and perfume on the dresser, and try to make the room as much like home as I could, even though I knew I wouldn't be spending more than a few waking hours there.

Berry usually had a suite of his own near our rooms, and he kept an eye on us. Diane would have an adjacent room. Later the entourage was joined by Chris Clark, a white female singer Berry had signed and whom he was also dating. Often one of the road managers would really have to do some fancy footwork—including paying hotel guests to move to another room—so that Berry's room would be in between Chris's and Diane's. The road managers and musicians were my friends, so I got the scoop on these things.

In all-night towns, such as Las Vegas, we would party until dawn. The innocent image got harder to maintain as we traveled and met more men who were smitten by us. More often than not, once back from the show, I'd throw off the wig, peel off my stockings, wrestle my way out of the gown, and take off. No matter how hard we worked, I was determined to live my life. I had a boyfriend in every town, all around the world, and I couldn't wait to meet new people and really enjoy myself. What was the point of traveling around the world if you were just going to stay up in your room?

As curtain time approached we and our entourage would head for the dressing rooms to prepare for the show. We would decide on wardrobe changes, see that all the last-minute repairs had been made on our dresses and shoes, be sure that all the accessories were accounted for and that the flashy jewelry pieces were at hand. Our assistants had to be careful to hide our "beauty secrets"—the wigs, lashes, and falsies—which they smuggled in and out. Around this time, Winnie Brown, a niece of Flo's by marriage, began traveling with us as our hairdresser. Winnie was one of the few people whom Diane opened up to, and she was also the only person, it seemed, who could tease Diane out of one of her funks. She was a great storyteller and was known for her cute but naughty jokes. If she sensed some tension, she'd just come out with a line, and we'd all laugh. One of her favorite pranks was to walk to the wings with us, then when we were announced, to hold Diane's arm. We'd all walk onstage, but Diane would be held back by Winnie, who would be making faces the whole time. It was hard not to come on laughing.

There would be countless guests coming backstage to meet us, and no matter how harried things were, we were always gracious. Berry would also want to be back there, and always seemed to have some urgent news for us that had to be delivered when we were stark naked.

"I don't want to see what you have anyway, so you might as well let me in," Berry would say.

"Lock the door!" Flo always cried. "I don't want any dirty old man in here!" Diane would just giggle.

Berry was a riot at times like these. When my sister Cat and Diane's sister Rita graduated from high school, we flew them to New York to stay with us and see the show. Berry had them sequestered up in a hotel room one day, teaching them to sing and harmonize, claiming that he was creating "the little Supremes." Everyone got a big kick out of that.

Back home, we were really living in the material world. We could now indulge in our lust for clothes, and Saks Fifth Avenue in Detroit

Local girls make good: The Supremes return to the Brewster Projects.
(*Paul A. Begler Collection*)

From left to right: Florence, Diane, me, Sammy Davis, Jr., Cher and Sonny Bono rehearse for Sammy's March 4, 1966, show. (*From the NBC-TV/ Sammy Davis, Jr. Show archives, reprinted courtesy of Jeffrey Wilson's Hot Wax Music archives*)

Above: Recording "My World Is Empty Without You" at Hitsville U.S.A. studios in Detroit, 1966. The session was recorded for the TV documentary "The Anatomy of POP." Duke Fakir is standing in the doorway waiting to take me home. (*Allen Poe Collection*)

Right: In the 1960s we were "Berry's girls." (*Mary Wilson Collection*)

On our first trip to the Far East in 1966, fielding questions from the press. (*Mary Wilson Collection*)

No camera ever captured us like this!
(*Mary Wilson Collection*)

Here we are with the fourth Supreme: Berry Gordy. (*Paul A. Begler Collection*)

In a 1966 photo session with Berry Gordy. In the beginning, we all shared the leads, but Berry soon chose Diane—in more ways than one. (*Murray Laden*)

Facing page, top: After one of the shows at the Roostertail in Detroit with "the Motown family" in 1967. Left to right: (standing) Billy Davis, Gwen Gordy Fuqua, Mr. Edwards, Nate McAlpine, Levi Stubbs, and me; (seated) Mrs. Stubbs, Anna Gordy, Berry Gordy, Bobby Darin, and Diana. (*Mary Wilson Collection*) Near right: They called me "the sexy one." (*Mary Wilson Collection*) Far right: When the British Invasion hit our music charts, Diane, Flo, and I invaded the shops on Carnaby Street. (*Nick Strange Collection*)

Before we had sequinned gowns, we had miniskirts. (*Mary Wilson Collection*)

One of Flo's last photo sessions with us. We were still wearing our million-dollar smiles, but Flo and I were crying inside. (*Carl Feuerbacher Collection*)

Above: The first time Cindy stood in for Flo, at the Hollywood Bowl, April 1967. (*Mary Wilson Collection*) Below: Performing "Thoroughly Modern Millie" on *The Ed Sullivan Show* in 1967. (*Carl Feuerbacher Collection*)

On *The Ed Sullivan Show*, May 5, 1967. It would be Florence's last appearance on the show. (*From the CBS-TV/Ed Sullivan Show archives, reprinted courtesy of Jeffrey Wilson's Hot Wax Music archives*)

Tom Jones and me in Las Vegas. (*Allen Poe Collection*)

Cindy, Diane, and I exchange medleys with the Temptations on the Sullivan show, November 19, 1967. (*From the CBS-TV/Ed Sullivan Show archives, reprinted courtesy of Jeffrey Wilson's Hot Wax Music archives*)

The Duke and Duchess of Bedford show off their historic artwork, and Cindy, Diane, and I show off our Motown charm school stances . . . thanks to Mrs. Powell. (*Mary Wilson Collection*)

In the receiving line to meet the Queen Mother in 1968 with Diane (left) and Cindy (right). We are wearing our beaded gowns that Michael Travis designed, and they weighed 35 pounds each! (*Allen Poe Collection*)

At the funeral of Dr. Martin Luther King, in Atlanta, 1968. (*Nate McAlpine*)

Cindy, Diane, and me in our Michael Travis gowns on the "TCB (Taking Care of Business) Special" in 1968. (*Mary Wilson Collection*)

This was from my blond wig days. I think I saw too many Doris Day movies. (*Michael Ochs Archives*)

A never-released shot from one of our most famous photo sessions with
James Kreigsmann, 1968. (*Michael Ochs Archives*)

When we rehearsed "Love Child" for our appearance on the Sullivan show on September 19, 1968, Cindy and I were given "Love Child" shirts like Diane's. When it came time for the show, though, we were given street clothes instead. (*From the CBS-TV/Ed Sullivan Show archives, reprinted courtesy of Jeffrey Wilson's Hot Wax Music archives*)

How's this for impersonal? (*Mary Wilson Collection*)

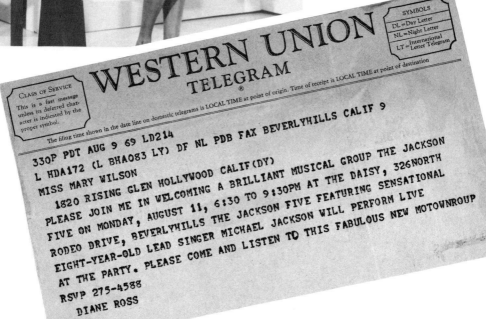

WESTERN UNION
TELEGRAM

SYMBOLS
DL=Day Letter
NL=Night Letter
LT=International Letter Telegram

CLASS OF SERVICE
This is a fast message unless its deferred character is indicated by the proper symbol.

The filing time shown in the date line on domestic telegrams is LOCAL TIME at point of origin. Time of receipt is LOCAL TIME at point of destination

330P PDT AUG 9 69 LD214
L HDA172 (L BHA083 LY) DF NL PDB FAX BEVERLYHILLS CALIF 9
MISS MARY WILSON
1820 RISING GLEN HOLLYWOOD CALIF(DY)
PLEASE JOIN ME IN WELCOMING A BRILLIANT MUSICAL GROUP THE JACKSON
FIVE ON MONDAY, AUGUST 11, 6:30 TO 9:30PM AT THE DAISY, 326NORTH
RODEO DRIVE, BEVERLYHILLS THE JACKSON FIVE FEATURING SENSATIONAL
EIGHT-YEAR-OLD LEAD SINGER MICHAEL JACKSON WILL PERFORM LIVE
AT THE PARTY. PLEASE COME AND LISTEN TO THIS FABULOUS NEW MOTOWNROUP
RSVP 275-4588
DIANE ROSS

Toasting the end of a dream. After the "farewell" show with Diane at the Frontier Hotel in Las Vegas. (*Mary Wilson Collection*)

Embarking on a solo career in 1979. (*Mary Wilson Collection*)

Me in the 1980s. And I've never felt better! (*Marc Raboy*)

would open especially for us and have special shoppers accompany us through the store. During this time, I began treating myself to jewelry, like the dome-shaped diamond cluster ring I bought in New York City and wore on every single album cover. Being back home was great, because it was now almost the only place left where we could walk around and go about our business without being accompanied by security.

That summer, we released "Nothing but Heartaches" and *More Hits by the Supremes*. In September, NASA's mission control played "Where Did Our Love Go" for the *Gemini* V astronauts, Pete Conrad and Gordon Cooper, as they orbited the earth. By the end of the month, we were back in Europe.

We attended the Grand Gala du Disque Festival, an international music event held in Amsterdam, Holland, as the official United States representatives to the celebration. A Dutch disc jockey named Peter Fellerman was our host and escort, and we had a wonderful time. He took Berry and us all around and told us about his country's history and culture. Like us, he was open and curious about things, and we remained friends for many years. By now we were all but ready to move to Europe for good, something I still think about.

One night in Holland, Diane, Flo, and I dined together in one of our rooms.

"And what will the mesdames have this evening?" the waiter asked.

"Chateaubriand, please," Diane answered, "Well-done."

"And you, madame?"

"The same, please," I replied.

Before he could ask Flo, she said, "I think I'll have this steak. Tartare?"

"Certainly." The waiter smiled and took our menus. For a second we wondered why he hadn't asked how Flo liked her meat cooked, but we figured they knew what they were doing.

A while later, the waiter returned to our suite with a rolling cart on which were placed a little mound of fresh raw ground meat, some finely chopped vegetables, an array of seasonings, and an egg. He put on quite the show, adding ingredients and stirring the concoction with all the flair of a magician pulling a rabbit from a hat. I began to wonder if I shouldn't change my order. Flo's dish looked great. Just then, Diane and I were served, and Flo's waiter molded her meat into a little patty with a "nest" in the middle, and then he broke the egg into it and proudly placed the dish before Flo.

"What's this?" Flo was mortified.

"Your steak tartare, ma'am." The waiter was as confused as we were.

"You don't expect me to eat it like that!" Flo was incredulous.

"Well, madame, that *is* steak tartare."

"Honey, you better take this stuff back and cook it!" Flo exclaimed.

Diane and I died laughing. After the waiter returned with the meat cooked, Flo said, "That's better."

A few days later we went to Brussels, then on to England, where we taped segments for *Top of the Pops* and *Ready, Steady, Go,* then traveled on to New York, where we appeared in Sybil Burton's "Very, Very In" at Arthur's. Two days later, we became the first pop group to play New York's Philharmonic Hall in Lincoln Center. The Spinners opened for us there, and the poster, designed by Eula, is now a collectors' item.

In November we did a benefit at Madison Square Garden called "USO A-Go-Go," with Sammy Davis, Jr., Joan Crawford, Carroll Baker, Robert Vaughn, and Johnny Carson. That month, "I Hear a Symphony" was at number one, and we returned to Europe with the Motown Revue for a show at the Olympia Music Hall.

Back in the States in December, we performed at the opening of the Houston Astrodome. Also on the bill was one of my childhood idols, Judy Garland. Though we had met many famous people, it was always different meeting someone who meant something to you. We couldn't wait to meet her, but every time we'd ask someone when we could, they'd just tell us "later." We snuck around, and finally she stuck her head out of the door of her dressing room and said, "How are you? It's nice to be on the show with you," then went back inside. I'd seen *The Wizard of Oz* dozens of times, and it was strange to meet "Dorothy" and see how frail and sad she was. We also got to meet a number of the astronauts, and after the show we went to a club where Glen Campbell was playing and sang a couple of songs. The day before we had appeared on Larry Kane's show, a local television program. We hadn't discussed wardrobe, and were surprised when we got there to see that Diane had really outdone herself, with big earrings, long fake lashes, and a big wig, while we were in our usual attire— considerably more modest—for daytime publicity appearances like this.

At the end of the year, we were guests at the Orange Bowl Parade in Florida, where we were booked to play in Miami, which became an annual tradition for us. That Christmas, Berry gave each of us a fur coat. We had a party in Berry's suite at the Eden Roc, and Aretha Franklin and her husband attended. It was a blast.

Professionally things just got bigger and better every day. Privately, though, it was a different matter. In just over a year Diane had become a new person, and with an entourage to do her bidding, there was no reason for her to think about anyone but herself. Road managers would bear the brunt of Diane's demands from now on. Once when we were in New York she told a new road manager, Phil Wooldridge, that she was hungry and wanted pizza. It was one in the morning, and Phil ran all over New York until he found a place that was open. When he got back to the hotel, though, Diane was asleep.

Another time, Flo, Diane, and I were playing Las Vegas but had gone to Los Angeles for dental work. Flo and I were already back in Vegas, and Diane was having special work done to close a gap near her left upper molar. Don Foster was to pick her up from the dentist's and take her to the airport for the flight back. Diane was still recovering from the dentistry and wasn't quite herself. Everything was running smoothly until she and Don went to check in. Western Airlines refused to let her bring on a huge wig box as carry-on luggage; she would have to check it. Diane had a fit and made such a scene that the airline refused to let her on with or without the box.

Don did everything he could, including bribing the counter attendants with the promise of free tickets to one of our shows. Finally they relented and Diane and the box got on the plane. The minute she was gone, Don ran to the phone to call Joe Shaffner, the person who would be picking up Diane in Vegas, to warn him.

"Listen, Joe, be at the airport—at the plane—on the tarmac, because when Diane gets off—she's mad as hell and she's all upset, and whatever she wants . . ."

Joe got there, but it was too late. Diane had landed and called Berry. Though it was clear to any logical person that Don made the best of a bad situation he'd done nothing to create, Diane was not happy, so Berry was not happy, and no explanation could change that.

"You're ridiculous," Berry told Don, using one of his favorite words. "What do I have you out there for if you can't handle things?"

After this, Don stopped traveling with us, but he was in charge of whoever did. He called constantly to be sure things were all right, because he knew that if one little thing went wrong, Diane would be on the line to Berry and that would be it. Sometimes it was quite embarrassing to be around her when these things happened, and we felt the way parents feel when their child throws a tantrum in public. We were public figures now, these scenes made us all look bad.

Shortly after it was announced that we had been booked to play the Flamingo in Las Vegas, rumors began flying that Diane would leave the Supremes. The first time we heard them, Diane was as upset as we were. We knew we weren't as close as we used to be, but we thought that we'd always be together. Well, maybe not always; we used to talk about which of us would marry first (me), and who would have the most children (me), and how it would be to settle down. They all thought that I was so boy-crazy that it was only a matter of time. But all that was in the future. As always, we looked to the future to fix what was wrong with the present. We'd still be happy when a show went well, and cry together when something went wrong. But these days less and less went wrong, and the fairy-tale got grander every minute. I took my place between my two best friends, waiting for one of them to give and for this phase to come to an end. Everything was so good now, certainly everything would be fine. Soon.

CHAPTER 17

We started 1966 with "My World Is Empty without You" in the Top Ten, a Grammy nomination for "Stop! In the Name of Love" (which we didn't find out about until months later), and a short tour of West Germany and Scandinavia. We maintained our usual frantic pace, appearing on a television special called "The Anatomy of Pop" and returning to the Copa for two weeks in March.

Things could not have been better, except that my relationship with Duke was ending. The Four Tops were doing very well, and after living with me for about two years Duke decided that he should give his marriage another try. At this point our schedules were always in conflict and sustaining a relationship with both of us so busy was nearly impossible. I respected his decision; he had a young daughter to think about. Still it hurt me deeply to lose him. We would see each other now and then, but it was never the same. Around this time Flo was ending her on-and-off relationship with another Top, Renaldo "Obie" Benson. We each provided the other with a shoulder to cry on.

Though none of us was really happy with what was going on inside the group, we still managed to have plenty of fun touring and performing. When we appeared on Sammy Davis, Jr.,'s show, we did a number with the Andrews Sisters. When we were all little girls we'd loved their songs, and I remembered sitting down in the basement on Bassett Street, singing along to their records. The producers had us perform a medley together, in which the Supremes sang such Andrews chestnuts as "Don't Sit under the Apple Tree," while they sang "Baby Love" and "Where Did Our Love Go."

We liked one another immediately, and we paired off: Maxine with Flo, Patty with Diane, and Laverne with me. In rehearsals, we had a great time. They taught us their parts and how to sway gently, and we taught them our routines. If someone made a mistake, everyone on the set would crack up. In fact some of the goofs were so funny —especially when they would tackle our choreography—that Sammy would make them repeat the mistake for anybody who dropped by. We seemed to be laughing the whole time.

Later that spring Supremes White Bread went on sale in the Detroit area. Some people thought this was an odd product for the Supremes to lend their name to, and it looks even stranger now that the expression "white bread" has come to mean "plastic" or "phony." At the time, though, these connotations weren't yet widespread, and besides, decisions about product endorsements were made by management. Certainly we would not have endorsed anything we deemed offensive, and loaves of bread seemed pretty innocuous. At this point we had done the Coke commercials as well as spots for public-service organizations. Our next venture into advertising would be an Arrid deodorant commercial, featuring our armpits.

Through everything, what really kept us—especially Flo and me —going, were the fans. In the days when we traveled so much, their methods of finding us were ingenious. Only years later would one fan reveal to me the intricate work involved in finding us.

A few days before we would arrive in New York, a series of phone calls would be placed.

"Hello, Waldorf-Astoria Hotel. May I help you?"

"Yes," the fan would say. "I'm calling from the Supremes' office and we would like to cancel the reservations they are holding."

"Just a moment, please. I'm sorry, but I can't find a reservation for the Supremes."

"Oh, excuse me. There must have been a mix-up here. Good day."

Then another call.

"Hello, Sherry Netherlands."

"Yes. I'm calling from Motown Records, and we have decided to change the reservation you are holding for the Supremes."

"Just a moment, Miss. I'm afraid I don't see them listed here."

"Forgive me. I've just remembered that they have been changed. Sorry to bother you. Good-bye."

Then another call.

"Thank you for calling the Warwick."

"Yes. This is Motown Records and we have to change the arrival time for the Supremes."

"One moment. Yes. They are to arrive here on Sunday, the fifteenth. What date would you like to change to?"

"Hold on one moment, please. Could I get back to you on that? In the meantime, please just hold it as is."

And so it would go. I don't know how many telephone calls were made, but the feminine voice was neither from Motown, nor was it female. It was Tony Turner, an eleven-year-old boy whose sleuthing led him to us whenever we were in New York.

"How did you know we'd be here?" we would scream when we saw him in the lobby. He'd just smile. Tony had fallen in love with the Supremes after his parents took him to see us at the Apollo. Though he loved us all, he was devoted to Miss Flo, as he called her. Tony was not the only one who could find us every single time, and of course he was not the only one trying. There were hundreds like him all over the country.

Though Motown kept up a tight security system, fans like Tony —who were always well behaved—were permitted to see us. There was a lot of competition among the fans, and the fact that it was friendly made it no less serious. The fans divided themselves into two groups: the B fans—just anyone—and the A fans, like Tony, who always got through. Within the fan community the As were stars in their own right (so the As told us), and one reason they were allowed to be around us was that it was known that a good A fan would throw the other fans off our trail. We were rarely mobbed, but could always count on a lively, vocal contingent of kids and teens waiting for us wherever we went.

I was touched by these shows of affection, especially from the little ones. It took a lot of stamina to stand outside a stage door, sometimes in freezing weather, just to catch a glimpse. All of us would sign autographs, but Flo and I would stay out and talk to the fans. Flo also made the younger fans her little pals, and soon Berry was criticizing both of us.

"Mary, you know I think you're making yourself too available," Berry said. I knew he wasn't referring only to the fans; he thought I had too many boyfriends, too.

"I like to be out," I replied.

"You should be more like Diane—untouchable, unreachable. You're getting too familiar."

But Flo and I didn't see any harm in what we were doing. Hundreds of times I saw her standing outside a stage door while a limo was waiting, motor running. She'd have her hands on her hips and be chatting away. "How are you all doing?"

"Fine," they'd all reply.

"How long you kids been standing out here? Probably all day, huh? You must be hungry. Let's go get something to eat."

Then she'd lead the kids down the street or around the corner to the nearest fast-food place. Flo would always be beautifully dressed, and on winter days her long fur coat would sort of billow as she marched along briskly, looking like a Pied Piper with a couple dozen young kids jogging behind her. She'd quickly get the proprietor's attention, order pizza or burgers and sodas or cocoa for everyone, then sit with the kids for a while. Once they were engrossed in their snacks, she'd slip out the door.

Sometimes she'd bring Tony or some other starstruck kid up to her room. On days when she was tired or didn't feel well, Tony would stand outside her door, and she would pass autographed pictures and dollar bills for treats to him, making him always promise not to reveal her room number and to bring back her change. This kind of accessibility, as limited as it was, irked Berry no end. The more Flo and I dealt with the fans, the more Berry complained about it, but he couldn't stop it and he didn't try. Once, when we were rehearsing for Ed Sullivan's show, dozens of kids were standing under the window of the studio screaming for us. When Flo saw what was going on, she threw a paper bag full of money down to them from a third-story window. It was about $20, which in those days bought a lot of hot dogs.

Another time we were taping a segment for the Sullivan show on West Fifty-seventh Street. Across the street from the studio was a large building under construction. When the workers on the site saw our limo waiting, they assumed someone famous would be coming out, so they kept watching. When they saw the three of us emerge, they started screaming for us. Diane, of course, rushed into the car, and I had started to get in, when Flo suddenly strutted into the middle of the street. She stopped right on the white line and raised her arms up as if she were on a stage. Everyone on the street, even people in cars, were cheering for her. Their love for Flo was so obvious. The minute Diane heard everyone applauding Flo, she tried to get the driver to take off and leave Flo standing there.

In May 1966, *Look* magazine profiled us for a feature entitled "From Real Rags to Real Riches." Each of us was interviewed separately for our profiles. Though this feature story should have been one of the high points for us, Diane managed to taint it by stating for publication that her mother had had tuberculosis. Diane didn't mean it maliciously; she loved her mother dearly. But Diane always was a chatterbox; she simply loved to talk, and it wasn't always clear how many of her slips were inadvertent. This time, though, she'd gone too far. When Mrs. Ross confronted her, she was hurt and angry beyond words. In those days having had tuberculosis still carried a stigma, and there was no reason for Diane to have mentioned it at all. Berry was also furious.

"Now," Berry said to Diane, "maybe you will learn to think before you open your mouth!" Ironically, Diane is quoted in the same piece saying, "Everyone knows to this day they can tell me secrets and I won't tell."

Along with this jet-set life came the jet-set life-style. Wherever the three of us went, we were fêted in grand style—at lavish receptions, gala parties, meals in the most exquisite restaurants. Of course, no occasion would be complete without the best liquor and the finest champagne. None of us had ever been what you would call a drinker, but once we had really made it, there was nowhere we could turn without finding someone poised to refill our glasses. During our first trip to England in 1965, we were introduced to fine sherry, and we adopted the custom of sipping a glass whenever people were drinking just to appear more worldly.

Diane and I could drink without suffering any ill effects, but Flo's tolerance for alcohol was almost nil. After just one beer, she would be unsteady; any more than that and she was clearly intoxicated.

As our schedule of club bookings, international tours, television appearances, and recording dates accelerated, so did tensions within the group. By now Diane was given her own dressing room, while Flo and I shared one. Seeing Diane and Berry together, I never knew exactly who was directing whom; when changes occurred, we never knew which of them had instigated them. But Flo and I could see that whatever Diane wanted, Diane got. In Flo's mind this was unfair, and her resentment began to consume her.

Despite this internal turmoil, the three of us never let the public know about our problems. Part of the Supremes' magic came from our ability to make the real world and its problems stop at the edge of the stage. When we sang together—no matter what had happened backstage or in private—we were as close and as happy as we had been singing in the Projects or sitting in the Hitsville lobby. Although I had believed that the group would survive anything, seeing the friction between Flo and Diane and Berry, I began to have my doubts. Sadly, Flo found it harder to ignore Diane and Berry's maneuvers and more difficult to maintain the façade.

Around this time Motown began engineering appearances to emphasize Diane's role and diminish Flo's and mine. In the beginning the three of us would enter a room together, followed by Shelly Berger or Berry. Before long, though, it was Diane who walked in first on the arm of a Motown honcho, while Flo and I followed behind like bridesmaids in a wedding procession. When Diane's name showed up in columns preceded by the words "leader" or "spokesperson," Flo and I were crushed. It was apparent that neither Diane nor Berry gave a damn about what we wanted, and Flo made no bones about feeling betrayed and lied to.

Things began to crack while we were touring the Far East that fall. We visited Tokyo, Okinawa, Taiwan, Hong Kong, Manila, the naval bases at Yokosuka and Kajikawa Naval Base, Medina Air Force Base, and the U.S.S. *Coral Sea*. We enjoyed touring the military bases, especially since earlier plans to do a tour of Vietnam had been canceled when the U.S. Government informed us that they could not provide adequate security. When we visited hospitals we were saddened to see so many young men injured, but grateful that our visits could cheer them up. Almost all of them had been in Vietnam, where my brother Roosevelt was stationed.

We made a special stop at a military hospital that had a large burn unit, where many of the most badly hurt soldiers were sent for treatment. Against the advice of our military escort we visited the burn victims. It was one of the most emotional experiences of my life; I had never imagined that human beings could be so brutally injured and live with so much pain. It was all we could do to keep from crying in front of them.

When we got back to the base to do our show, we were late. As we rushed to get ready, the military official in charge of the show told Don Foster that if we weren't ready to go on in five minutes—which was impossible—we couldn't go on at all, and we wouldn't be paid.

"What's your name?" Don asked.

"Why do you want my name?" the official replied.

"Because I'm going to go out there and tell the people who have been waiting for two hours to see the Supremes that the girls can't go on because they were late getting here, and that the reason they were late was that they were visiting those men's comrades in the burn center."

With that, the case was closed, and we went on to give one of our best shows ever.

Though we were world travelers, the Far East was so unlike anyplace we'd ever been, we were instantly captivated. Berry commissioned Milton Ginsberg to make what amounted to a very expensive home movie of our trip. Included in this footage (which remained in Motown's vaults until the mid-eighties) are some of our numbers and the usual posed stuff, like the three of us dressed as geishas (how telling!), talking to people working in rice paddies in the countryside, and pulling rickshaws into the above-ground sewage ditches.

There are also some behind-the-scenes sequences. Though neither Diane nor Berry could have foreseen this, the "intimate" scenes are by far the most revealing. One scene takes place in our dressing room. Diane languidly lays her head down and pretends to be sleeping, all the while keeping her face to the camera. Flo and I are chatting in the background, then Flo sits down to brush her hair. From the look on Flo's face, you know that she sees through Diane's ploy, and she proves it by acting like she's about to throw her brush at Diane. Of course Diane immediately picks her head up and opens her eyes in alarm. Then the film cuts.

In another scene, a reporter at a press conference asks us to sing "You Can't Hurry Love" a cappella. Berry very nicely says that he doesn't know if we can do it, since we've never done it before, but Diane says that she thinks we can. Once we indicate that we're game, Berry tries to help us along by snapping his fingers to the beat. We were prepared to do anything for the public, no matter what.

Back home, we continued with our itinerary, opening at the Flamingo in Las Vegas toward the end of September. By now, anyone who'd missed our shows could see us—and Berry—at the gambling tables. Gambling fever had always been rampant among the men at Motown, where there were probably as many all-night games upstairs at Hitsville as there were on the Strip. As the money had started rolling in, most of the male producers, writers, and performers took their turns being high rollers, usually with disastrous results. Women were rarely admitted into this male bastion, so we only knew what we heard, but it was no secret that money it had taken—or would take—years to earn was disappearing at the turn of a card. The stakes were also pretty outrageous—the keys to a brand-new Cadillac, thousands of dollars, and once even the right to produce an up-and-coming female lead singer, bet by a producer and won by Berry.

Sitting at a table, Berry was in heaven. Flo never especially liked to gamble, but Diane and I would go out with Shelly Berger's wife, Eleanor, and take over a table. Losing $5,000 a night wasn't unusual. We were all pretty lucky—blackjack was my game—but Berry and Diane did take some pretty big losses. I remember walking into Berry's suite after he'd had a particularly bad night and seeing everyone in his entourage acting like they were at a wake. When the boss was unhappy, everybody was unhappy.

In late 1966 I began to notice that Flo's drinking was becoming a habit. She never drank before a show, but after we finished our set we would change and go out to partake of the local nightlife or attend private parties. This was when Flo drank. A normal person leading a normal life could have slept it off and carried on. But we were not leading normal lives. After a show we might fly to another city to finish a recording or prepare for our next engagement or television appearance. Virtually every new record release or promotional appearance was preceded by a press conference and interviews, followed by a luncheon with local politicians or record business people, then rehearsals, then hours in makeup and wardrobe, then the show, then the parties, then the same thing all over again. Many nights we were lucky to get two hours' sleep before facing the public again. And we were never less than perfectly gracious and beautiful. To the public Flo was still the same.

But Diane and I knew differently. We tried to influence Flo to limit her drinking by curtailing our own. We would nurse a single glass of sherry for hours. Flo wasn't dumb, and she was touched by our efforts. "Don't worry," she'd say, "I'll be all right." As time passed, our little ploy became less effective. Though we were too young to consider it then, it is clear to me today that the unresolved emotional problems Flo suffered after the rape were making it more difficult for her to cope with what was happening now. She was sinking. Everything in her life seemed to be coming apart at the seams. Flo's rage over having her solo spot taken from her and the public's new Motown-inspired obsession with Diane was consuming her. Diane's blatant scene stealing could not be ignored, and my two best friends were starting to act as if they hated each other.

In the fall of 1966, while touring to promote our latest album, *Supremes A-Go-Go* (which featured my lead on "Come and Get These Memories"), we did a record signing at Stern's department store in New York City. The room we were in was divided in the middle by a models' runway that sloped upward at the back. We were seated at the top, and the fans gathered at the other end of the runway, held back by ropes and several security guards.

After we'd signed a bunch of records, the master of ceremonies, a local disc jockey, urged us to get up and walk down the runway so that the fans could get a closer look. When I hesitated, Flo got up and strolled down the runway, smiling politely. The fans always loved Flo, and as she neared them they reached out to her and applauded. After Flo sat down, I walked about halfway down and got my share of wolf whistles and applause. But when Diane's turn came, she held back, coyly shaking her head no and acting as if she hadn't a clue what the fans could possibly want. She kept it up until the fans were screaming wildly. In a flash, she jumped up, dramatically spread her arms so that the wide dolman sleeves of her sweater resembled a giant bat's wings, and charged down the ramp, flashing a brilliant smile. She turned and ran back up the ramp. The crowd tore through the ropes to get at her. The security people rushed to protect Diane, but she reassured them, cooing, "That's all right. They love me!"

Flo and I gave each other our secret look. I just let a smile freeze on my face, but Flo made no secret of her displeasure. This did not endear her to the fans, who were mesmerized by the Ross razzle-dazzle. Later, when Flo and I were alone together, she cried to me, "I can't take it anymore! Why does Diane always do this?"

During our trip to the Far East, Flo and Tommy Chapman had fallen in love, and they were now as inseparable as our schedule would allow. Flo now seemed happier when she was away from the Supremes. Tommy was very nice; he seemed to empathize with Flo, and he loved her. But people at Motown talked; in their eyes, Flo was one of the label's three leading ladies, and Tommy was just Berry's chauffeur.

Knowing how difficult it was for Flo to be intimate with a man, I was happy that she had Tommy. Whenever Tommy was around, she stopped obsessing about Berry and Diane, whom she'd come to regard as a single entity. As Diane moved further toward the front, Flo became not only defiant but bitter. Diane and Flo's bickering had become incessant, and I knew there was nothing I could say or do to revive our childhood friendship. Flo would be late for press conferences and rehearsals, and while I understood Flo's problem, we were all on the same crazy schedule. She was not only making us look bad, but hurting her own cause. I tried to reason with her. These things often happened early in the day, but rather than confront Flo then and risk a scene before a show I'd wait until we were off and back at our hotel.

"Flo, why were you late to the press conference today?" I asked. One look and I knew she was already on her second beer.

"Honey, I am not working myself to death to make Diana Ross a star." We always referred to Diane as Diane, and when Flo said "Diana" the bitterness cut through me like a knife.

"But, girl," I said, "can't you see that you are only making yourself look bad? You should have heard Diane carrying on. She was trying to get Berry on the phone, and you know she's going to tell him everything. Why are you doing this to yourself?"

"Because I don't give a damn about Diane or that jive Berry!" Flo screamed. "And don't think for a minute that they give a damn about me or you!"

Flo believed Diane and Berry were using her to make Diane a star. Unfortunately the only way Flo knew to fight back was to fight in any way she could. When Flo thought she was right, she was right, even if what she did was wrong. If she felt she was justified, that was it. An injustice was being committed, and Flo wasn't going to tolerate it.

Her defiance was coming to be regarded as a serious problem by Diane and the higher-ups at Motown. Though she would get much heavier over the next few months, she had already gained a little weight, which was enough to affect how our stage costumes fit. Sometimes Diane would want to wear one outfit for a show but couldn't because Flo's no longer fit her.

One night Flo ran into Berry at the Twenty Grand. In front of a bunch of people from Motown and some of the other performers, Berry said, "I agree with Diane. You have to do something about your weight. You are much too fat."

"I don't give a damn what you think!" she replied. Then she threw her drink in his face and stormed out of the club.

Though Flo had never been comfortable maintaining the Supremes' glamour-girl image, she had enjoyed it at first. Lately, however, she had come to regard it as phony and fake, and the rigors of touring, of being a star, seemed to overwhelm her.

"Mary, I can't do those interviews again and fly out tomorrow," she said. "Are those fools crazy?"

"I'm pretty tired, too," I would admit.

"I'm telling you, we need a vacation," she'd say emphatically. "And I'm telling Berry that. Who does he think he is, Napoleon?"

In these complaints, I could hear the first clues that Flo wanted out—out of the Supremes, out of this life. I would try to calm her down. Her concerns were valid, and I was worried too, but I knew that even if Diane left, we could go on, and if we did go on, Flo would probably be the lead singer. I would try to tell Flo these things, in the hopes that she would cool down and stick it out a little while longer. But as time passed it became increasingly evident that she would not.

Strangely, even when Flo was angry with Diane, she still worried about her, thinking, for instance, that the reason Diane was so thin was that Berry was working her too hard. Though Flo and Berry had gotten along, they now seemed to clash, and she alternated between seeing Berry as the force pulling Diane away from us and as Diane's ally in her power plays. Once Flo said, "Why doesn't she leave him? He doesn't care about her. She doesn't get anything that we don't get." Flo paused, then added, "Well, almost."

Still, Flo kept her sense of humor, especially onstage. It was around this time that she began replying to Diane's stage patter line, "Thin is in," with "Yeah, but fat is where it's at," which always brought down the house.

In their desperation, both Diane and Flo established lifelines to the outside world. Diane had Berry, and when he wasn't around she was on the phone with him, telling him who was doing—or not doing—what, and getting his advice and assurances. Flo had her family, whom she would call every day from wherever she was. She would talk with them for hours and tell them all her problems. Sadly, her family could not offer much constructive advice, nor give Flo sorely needed perspective. Her complaints about Berry, or Diane, or touring, elicited only support and encouragement. They believed she should express herself and not let "them" push her around.

That fall we had another number-one hit with "You Can't Hurry Love," and were booked up for the next year. We cut records whenever we could, and sometimes we did our vocals on different days. Though the records were still important, they were not our primary concern. The Supremes had transcended the "pop group" categorization and were now firmly embedded in the entertainment establishment. We were secure, and without having to worry about whether or not we could maintain our position, it seemed likely that we could finally concentrate on some of the internal problems that needed fixing.

Then the final wedge was driven. In our travels we talked to countless journalists. Toward the end of 1966 they all seemed to be asking the same question: Was it true that we were changing our name to Diana Ross and the Supremes? Flo and I always denied it. No one from Motown—not even Diane—ever said a word to us about it.

Over time we learned that the name would indeed be changed, and, when it seemed certain, Flo went over the edge. The underhandedness of it all was more than she could bear. She missed a couple of shows. To her credit, she never came onstage drunk, and, as always, we were consummate pros. When Flo didn't make a show, Berry would send out Marlene Barrow, one of the Andantes, and, frankly, few people in the audience were ever the wiser. But something had to give.

"You can't do this, Flo," I told her once after she missed a show.

"I don't care," she replied, lying. "Berry hates me, and I hate him. That fool!"

Flo was getting further and further away from me, and I found myself anxiously awaiting each day. Would she make the show? And even if she did, would she plummet back into this self-destructive depression afterward? Flo was threatening to quit the group. I could see that she didn't care what happened to herself. Flo was not a small woman, and with the drinking, she continued to gain weight. Soon the svelte, revealing stage costumes were tight and unflattering. Flo had always cared so much about her appearance that, when I saw that she was just letting herself go, I knew something was seriously wrong.

There wasn't much anyone could do. When Berry wasn't around, Diane would corner me and try to get me to side with her against Flo.

"Did you see how Blondie looked at that last show? I called Berry and told him. Flo makes us look bad, and I'm not going to stand for it!"

It had gotten to the point where Diane and I were hiding bottles from Flo, and the road managers saw to it that my room was always next to Flo's. Diane and Berry started avoiding Flo, which only enraged her. I sat in Flo's room with her all the time, it seemed. Flo would start griping about Diane and Berry, then she would threaten to call them and give them a piece of her mind. I would talk her out of it and stay with her. I'd tried to reason with her, but it was impossible.

For my part I just wanted to keep the group intact and keep Flo from going to pieces. Coming from my background, I never thought to suggest to Flo that she needed a psychiatrist. Perhaps if I had, things might have been different. We needed each other, but while I saw the situation as something that might be resolved one way or another, Flo saw it as the last straw. I knew that I needed an ally and I tried everything to get Flo to stay, but she wanted to go.

Weeks later in early 1967 Berry held a meeting with some upper-level people at Motown, Diane, and me. It was decided that the search for Flo's replacement would begin. Cindy Birdsong of Patti LaBelle and the Blue-Belles was everyone's choice, largely because she and Flo had a similar look, and she was contacted. In the meantime Flo stayed on the road, but things were touch-and-go. I never knew for sure if Flo knew about Cindy; if she did, she wouldn't have let on, I'm sure. I still prayed Flo would straighten up, but as the days passed, the possibility of that happening seemed less and less likely.

Our lives at that time were such that, even though we met hundreds of people, we really saw only each other. I had witnessed Flo's deterioration and it had been so gradual that I really had no idea how bad it was. One night I was walking back to my room with Stevie Wonder's drummer, Hamilton Bohannon. Flo opened her door and was so drunk she could barely stand. Hamilton was amazed. "What's wrong with Florence?" he asked. I knew then that it was all over.

It all blew up in Memphis. We were doing a series of one-nighters and were leaving for New Orleans, where we were scheduled to appear that evening. We were all sitting in the cars, ready to go, but no Flo. When she didn't come downstairs to leave with us that morning, Don went up to check on her. He found her sitting up in her bed drunk. She'd been talking to her family long-distance all night, and refused to go with Don. He got her up, washed her face, helped her dress, and finally got her into the car. As we drove to the airport, Diane was furious, and I was sad and disappointed. Flo was digging herself into a hole so deep she would never get out.

All during the flight, Flo refused to speak with us, and as I watched her from across the aisle, I could see how desperately she wanted out of what she viewed as an impossible situation. She knew that if she walked out she'd have to bear the responsibility for what might happen to the group, so she chose another way. Her attitude was, "Let them put me out!" And she made it easier and easier for them to do just that. She knew what she was doing, and there was no way anybody could stop her. Diane called Berry the minute we checked in at our hotel. Berry then instructed Joe Shaffner to send Flo home.

It had finally happened. It had been one thing for her to show up late for rehearsals and interviews, but that she'd allowed herself to lose so much control that they would take her away was incomprehensible to me. Before she left she was saying things like, "I know everybody is looking at me, and I don't care," but I knew she did. Where was my best friend, who was tough, strong, and proud? My friend whose dreams had all come true? Why was she throwing herself right into their hands?

As they bundled her up and got her ready to catch a plane back to Detroit, I took one last look at her. She gave me a big smile, and then laughed, as if the joke was on them.

That night Diane and I were the Supremes. We put on our best smiles and carried on as a duo. I was so shaken by the day's events, I could hardly think, but the show went on. Marlene Barrow was flown in for other shows. When Flo was back on the road with us, things weren't much better. Now it was worse than before because Flo wouldn't even pretend that she wanted to be there, and Diane wasn't pretending that she wanted her there. The minute Flo took a drink, Diane would be on the phone to Berry. I knew this couldn't go on forever.

And it didn't. One day in mid-April we were all summoned to Berry's home on Outer Drive. As I drove there, I recalled the past months' events and hoped against hope that Flo would say something or do something this afternoon to save herself. She'd given Berry, Diane, and me every reason to want her out of the group, but I believed she still might be the old Flo I knew and fight for her place in the Supremes.

When I arrived I found Flo and her mother, Diane, and Berry. We sat in the living room, where there was a huge grand piano. Diane and Berry sat together, Flo and her mother sat together, and I sat to one side by myself. With one look at Flo, I knew that dreams don't die, people just stop dreaming. As I sat there staring at Flo, Berry spoke calmly but firmly about how important the Supremes were, and how important each of us was to the group. Then in a somber tone, he told Flo that she had been messing up and was not upholding her end of the deal. Berry limited what he had to say to the facts. There were no insults or accusations; he knew better than to provoke Flo. She had a violent temper. It was clear that he just wanted to get it over with. Flo said nothing.

Then Flo's mother said, "But Mary still wants Flo in the group," and looked straight at me.

Suddenly everything got tense. I realized that Diane and Berry had come to this meeting not knowing what I was going to say or whose side I would take. For a second I thought to myself, why doesn't Flo speak up? Then I realized that Flo was waiting for me to rescue her, waiting for me to tell Diane and Berry how they'd mistreated Flo, and how wrong they were. But to what end? While Flo no doubt would have appreciated me defending her, she had refused to defend herself. She wanted out more than anything else, and she knew that I knew it.

As I stared at Mrs. Ballard I drew upon every ounce of courage I had. I loved Diane and I loved Flo equally, more than anything else in the world. But my two best friends had each taken a different course, and this is where it led. It hurt me, but I said, "Mrs. Ballard, Flo no longer wants to be in the Supremes. Yes, I want her with us, but she no longer wants us."

In those few seconds, I saw nine years of work and love and happiness fade away. Although I was an adult, the Supremes still stood in my mind as a dream from childhood, a wonderful dream that had come true. I believed the Supremes would last forever. Now I knew that even dreams that come true can change.

The real meaning of changing our name to "Diana Ross and the Supremes" became clear to me as I looked across the room at Berry and Diane. All of a sudden, I was alone. There wasn't a group anymore. This was the worst thing that had ever happened to us, yet Diane and I would never speak about it. Though Flo would do a few more dates with us, on a kind of probation, this was the last time the three of us were really the Supremes.

Flo's response was frighteningly cold and distant. She was detached, yet seemed satisfied with the outcome. Flo and her mother left, with Mrs. Ballard in tears. I stood at the window and watched them get into Flo's Cadillac and drive away. Turning my attention back into the room, I saw that Diane and Berry both looked relieved. In fact, within minutes, Diane was almost giddy, and she looked uncannily like she would onstage during our tribute to Martin Luther King, Jr., when she'd cry, "Free at last, great God Almighty, free at last." No one said a word about Flo; she was gone. I wondered, How could they be so happy?

Within minutes of Flo's departure, Cindy Birdsong came into the room, and we started making plans for rehearsals with the new Supreme. If I was going to stay with the Supremes—which I was—there was nothing for me to do but dig in and get to work. Suddenly I didn't feel like just one of the Supremes—I felt like the only Supreme.

CHAPTER 18

Of course no one could ever replace Flo, and I admit that at first my feelings toward Cindy were neutral. For Cindy, becoming a Supreme was a great opportunity, and she worked hard to fit in. Berry and Diane liked her a lot, and her jovial air was a welcome change, but instead of cheering me up, it only reminded me that Flo wasn't there.

We were scheduled to play a benefit sponsored by radio station KHJ for the United Negro College Fund at the Hollywood Bowl on April 29, which was only a few days away. Flo's fate was still up in the air—maybe she would be back; maybe she would not. What we did know was that Cindy would be singing at the Bowl, and so we got right to work, rehearsing and going over vocal arrangements for hours each day. Diane had not rehearsed with us in a while now, so the job of getting Cindy ready fell to Cholly and me. In Berry's living room, though, Diane stood up and started to show Cindy the steps Flo and I did, but it was obvious she didn't know what they were. Since Cholly still lived next door to me, we set to work at his place, and Cindy stayed at my house. Cindy was a fast study, and we were pleased with her progress, but we knew the real proof would be in the performance.

The Hollywood Bowl show went like a dream. Because the stage is so far from the audience, it was even harder for people to see that Cindy was not Flo, and in fact many reviewers were fooled. Cindy was very excited. We had also worked very hard to get our sound right. Flo was a first soprano, and Cindy a lower, second soprano, so I had to make some adjustments in my singing. The night before the show, Cholly made a point of telling Diane not to mention to the audience that Cindy was replacing Flo.

The show was such a success that the next day the three of us went on a shopping spree. An exclusive Rodeo Drive shop in Beverly Hills opened up just for us. Diane and I strolled through, picking up anything that caught our fancy, but Cindy just watched us. Though

Cindy had been performing for many years, she was still a little awk-ward around us, especially Diane.

Though it seemed that Cindy would be joining the Supremes, she was committed to the Blue-Belles for the next several months. Soon after the Hollywood Bowl show, Cindy left us to meet her other group, and so Flo was back. Flo's pride wouldn't let her beg for her place in the Supremes, but I could see that she was glad to be given a second chance. I believed that once Motown made it clear that they meant business, Flo would either leave for good or shape up.

Rumors that Diane would be leaving the group were now com-mon, though like the name change, it was never discussed with any of us. It was obvious that her being thrust to the forefront was part of that plan. Though I knew better, in my heart I still retained the small-est hope that when and if Diane left, Flo would be made the lead singer, and that was certainly worth holding out for. Flo, however, couldn't see that.

There were many other people whose interest in us was as great as Berry's, among them General Artists Corporation, our booking agents. Sure, the Supremes were the top act, but if we continued having to use stand-ins for Flo, or if we ever worked again as a duo, our image would be shattered. I did not want the name changed. Berry, sensing that I might be a problem on this issue, explained to me that the name change would benefit all of us because we would actually be two attractions—the Supremes and Diana Ross—and so would earn more money. "Don't worry about it, Mary," he promised. "*I will always take care of you.*" Believing Berry and feeling I had no choice, I went along.

In late May, when Flo was back with us for a few appearances, we made what would be Flo's last appearance on *The Tonight Show.* As always, Diane sat next to Johnny Carson, while Flo and I were relegated to the couch, and Diane did most of the talking.

In the course of the conversation Johnny Carson mentioned that there had been a stand-in for Flo at the Hollywood Bowl and asked if this meant we were breaking up. Of course we denied the rumors and made a few jokes. Carson then went on to another topic, but Diane interrupted him to say, ". . . just like in a Broadway play . . . we have a stand-in. The show must go on. Except for me. They can't stand in for me. But Florence and Mary, we have two young ladies that will stand in in their place."

That was news to me! I didn't know they had one for me, too. After this Flo monopolized the entire interview, interrupting Diane to give clever and honest answers to the rest of Carson's questions. The audience loved her, and for a minute I could see the old spunky Flo, but it really wasn't her. Though she didn't drink in public, she had been drinking so much and so often that her emotional problems got worse. It seemed that whatever bravado she got while she was drunk would carry over to when she was sober.

The times Flo was back with us, it was obvious how much she had changed. Her drinking had escalated. When we were on the road, she shunned the rest of us and stuck with Tommy. After our shows at the Copa, we would all ride back to the hotel in our limo, while Flo and Tommy walked back alone, holding hands.

There were other dramatic changes in Flo's behavior, such as her treatment of the fans, whom she now avoided, and her appearance. Flo's facial features were delicate and naturally beautiful. Suddenly she was wearing very harsh, dark eye makeup and keeping her sunglasses on all the time. She was also heavier than ever, and Diane, who was never known for her diplomacy, never let Flo forget it.

That July we played the Flamingo Hotel in Las Vegas. This was an important occasion for several reasons, not the least of which being that this was the first time the marquee would read "Diana Ross and the Supremes." Berry was in all his glory, and we knew there were many important people in the audience. For one of our first numbers, we wore two-piece tuxedo pantsuits. Unlike our long, flowing chiffon gowns, these fit very snugly, and Flo barely squeezed into hers.

For the first time Flo drank before the show and came onstage tipsy, with her wig awry and her costume too tight. At one point, Flo moved in such a way that the waistcoat of her outfit rode up over her belly and her flesh was exposed. Berry ran backstage the second the show ended and in front of a small crowd of Motown and Flamingo people, he calmly ordered, "Get her off the stage. Now."

Back in the dressing room I knew this was it. Diane, Berry, and I were upset, but Flo just acted like she didn't care.

"You're too fat!" Diane said to Flo. "Why don't you stop drinking so much? Look at yourself! You're as big as a house!"

Next to my size 7 and Diane's size 4, Florence's 10/11 looked huge. Worse, she was out of shape.

"Florence—" Berry said.

"Berry, you better get out my face!" Flo snapped back.

"Listen to me, girl. You look terrible onstage! Look at the other girls. You're not holding up your end," Berry replied.

"Oh, I don't care. Leave me alone!"

There was nothing left to say; Flo was told to leave. She packed and went back to Detroit, and Cindy, who had been discreetly sequestered down the street at Caesar's Palace, stepped in the next night, for good.

In July we released "Reflections," the first single released under the name Diana Ross and the Supremes. Because we recorded our singles so many months in advance of their release, this is the last hit single Flo appears on. We also played Forest Hills Stadium with Cindy. The announcement that Cindy was now a Supreme prompted much speculation from the press as to the exact circumstances of Flo's departure. Officially, Flo left because of exhaustion and a desire to settle down, and people seemed to accept that. The real story was kept under wraps, and Flo, despite everything that had happened, chose not to divulge the truth.

I stayed in New York for a couple days after the Forst Hills date. One day in early August I received a telegram.

Mary
Stick by Florence. It may happen to you. Think about it.
                                                        —*Tempts*

That August we were in Los Angeles, where we performed at a fundraising dinner for President Johnson. Though we had never met him, we were impressed by his social policies, especially in the area of civil rights, so we were happy to help him. After we had finished singing, we were getting into our limousine when we saw the president running toward us, leading a trail of Secret Service agents, and with his daughter Lynda in tow.

"I was supposed to rush away from here and head back to the White House before the show was over, but I refused to leave until I got to talk to the Supremes." He told us how much he liked "Somewhere," which contained a love monologue, and his daughter also complimented us. We were quite thrilled about this meeting, and it was reported in newspapers all over the country the next day.

Later that month we performed at the Steele Pier in Atlantic City, where Diane and Cindy were robbed of furs, jewels, and other items from their hotel room. Security was tightened up, and we carried on with our schedule, playing the Cocoanut Grove, the Michigan State Fair, and doing the now-routine guest spots on *The Ed Sullivan Show,*

The Hollywood Palace, and other television programs. By September, *Diana Ross and the Supremes' Greatest Hits* was the number-one album.

Motown was only too happy to broaden our audience and consolidate our show-biz appeal, and so we flew to Las Estacas, Mexico, in October to film an episode of *Tarzan*, a weekly series starring Ron Ely in the title role. In a case of truly bizarre casting, we were to play three nuns. Our makeup was so natural, it seemed almost nonexistent, and the long, dark habits were an interesting contrast to our usual stage attire. After the makeup people had finished with us, we'd sneak back into our dressing rooms and put on more makeup. Of course Diane had the most lines, but we all spoke, and even sang "Michael Row the Boat Ashore" and "The Lord Helps Those Who Help Themselves" (we had recorded some other gospel songs at Motown, but they've never been released). Also co-starring in this episode, "The Convert," was James Earl Jones. Berry, Shelly Berger, and Mike Roshkind, Motown's newest expert in corporate public relations, were also on hand.

Cindy was very excited about the show, and Berry seemed very attentive. He couldn't seem to compliment her enough. I was pleased that things were going so well for Cindy, but as time passed, I realized that she had come to the group believing—as did the public—that Diane was the leader. Nonetheless, Cindy and I gradually became good friends, and in her I had a confidante and buddy, which I needed very badly.

After Flo left, my relationship with Berry was a little strained. No one was quite sure what to say to me, or what I might do. Maybe I wanted to leave, too. They shouldn't have worried, though; I'd outlast them all. But we had a great time in Mexico, far away from the usual bustle, and Berry and I were pals again.

We became friends with the other cast members and crew, and Ron Ely and I were real chums. We were all staying in a beautiful hotel, where we'd lie around the pool on our days off, or go shopping in town. We all got Montezuma's revenge, and even that became a source of humor. There were plenty of reporters and photographers on the set, and they got some funny pictures of us, including one of me sitting with my habit pulled up over my knees, smoking a cigarette and drinking beer. When the show aired in January 1968, it was the highest-rated episode in the series.

*　　*　　*

Back from Mexico, we hit the road again. "In and Out of Love" had just been released, and in early November we played UCLA's Pauley Pavilion with trumpeter Hugh Masekela.

Cindy was many things—a great singer, a good buddy—but no ally when it came to standing up to Diane and Berry. I had no idea what they had said to her before she joined, but it was clear to me that she believed that just because Diane was the lead singer she called all the shots inside the group.

"She's not the boss. I've told you that. We're a group, and everything comes up for a vote, okay?"

"Okay," Cindy would reply.

"The same thing happened last week with the blue dresses. Don't just go along with everything she wants. If you don't want to speak up to her, wait until I get here."

"Okay."

"There won't be any group if you and I don't stick together. Please, Cindy."

"Okay."

Suddenly the Supremes seemed bigger than all of us. I began to feel like that little girl on Bassett Street, waiting at the picture window for somebody or something. Until then, I just drew into myself. I wasn't depressed, but I knew things weren't as good as they could have been. But how to change it?

Throughout 1967, one of our booking agents, Norman Wise, had been telling me about this wonderful new singer he thought I should get to know. Each time Norman mentioned him, I sort of half-listened. I had been pursued by countless men, and at that point Norman's latest choice—a guy named Tom Jones—struck me as just another celebrity who wanted to meet one of the Supremes. There were plenty of those. One day, though, when we were discussing a trip to Europe, Tom's name came up again. I had bought some of Tom's records and, besides being shocked to find that he was white, was impressed by his great looks. When Norman tried to play matchmaker again, I went along with it. He arranged a meeting between us, to take place in Munich, Germany, at the Bambi ceremony—the European equivalent of the Academy Awards—at which he conveniently booked us to perform.

As the date drew closer I became giddy as a schoolgirl. With Flo's departure I'd been thinking about my own life and career. Loneliness seemed to come with the turf. I remembered going to see Diahann Carroll when she was playing the Elmwood Casino in Windsor, Ontario. After the show, I went backstage to invite her to a party, and that night we talked a lot about how lonely life could be for a female performer. It was about ninety-five percent hard work and five percent glamour, but I still loved every minute onstage. When I was singing, I saw my purpose and direction clearly. Offstage, though, I felt very much alone. Since my breakup with Duke, I had dated a bodyguard from Puerto Rico, Brian Holland, Fuller Gordy (Berry's older brother), and a wonderful English producer named David Puttnam. This little rendezvous was just what I needed.

Shelly Berger arranged to go with us on the trip, and I let him and Cindy in on my little secret. She was as excited about it as I was. Diane and I were no longer chitchatting about everything like we used to, and I feared that if she knew the real reason we were going, she'd refuse, so I kept it a secret from her. This was unlike me, but I have to admit that after being in the dark about so many of her and Berry's plans, I sort of liked having a little intrigue of my own for a change.

The three of us and Shelly flew from New York to Milano, where we were to catch a connecting flight to Munich. Somehow, though, we missed our plane by fifteen minutes. I was crushed, but couldn't act too disappointed. Deep inside, I wanted to pound on the counter and get put on some flight—any flight—but that was not my way. We decided to stay over. Berry wasn't there, so Diane was talking to us, and we were having a great time.

That night we dined at Alfio's, an Italian restaurant we'd discovered on one of our previous trips. We each ate a dozen escargots and drank lots of red wine. On the way home, our cab driver insisted on keeping all the windows open. It was freezing, and in my broken Italian (based on my broken Spanish, which sounded like German and Japanese), I tried to convince him to close the windows, saying "Cerra la ventana" and pantomiming the motions for him. All he'd say was something that sounded like "ajo." Finally it dawned on me what he was trying to tell us: He had to keep the windows open because we all reeked of garlic. We laughed all the way to our rooms, then settled in for a night's rest.

The next morning I was up bright and early, rushing everyone to make our flight to Munich. Once we arrived there we had to head straight for our dressing rooms, since we had missed our rehearsals. I tried my best to stay calm as we got dressed. Every once in a while I'd catch Cindy's eye, and we'd both grin. Diane was taking her time getting ready, oblivious of the fact that I was ready way ahead of time, which was rare. She was barely dressed and didn't even have her wig on when there was a knock at the door.

"Who is it?" I asked, my heart pounding.

"It's Tom Jones," he replied in his beautiful Welsh accent.

Diane screamed, jumped up, and ran into another room. I had been waiting for this moment for weeks and wasn't going to blow it. I opened the door and there he was, dressed in a ruffled white shirt, black tuxedo, and—of course—skin-tight pants. Sparks flew; he was gorgeous. Why had I waited so long?

"What's the matter with her?" he asked, gesturing toward the door where Diane had disappeared. "I didn't come to see her anyway."

Fortunately Diane was out of earshot. I introduced him to Cindy, and we spoke for a few moments, making plans to meet after the show at a dinner party. When he left, I was speechless. A second later Diane huffed into the room, obviously miffed.

"Did you guys know he was coming?" she asked.

"No," Cindy lied.

"No, we did not," I added, pretending to be insulted that she would suggest such a thing. Apparently it worked.

The show went well, and though I was into it, my mind was on Tom. At the dinner I saw him seated across the room from me at a table of beautiful women. I tried not to be too obvious, but every time I looked over at him, our eyes would meet. He sent messages to me through the waiters, saying that he was sorry for the delay, but he would speak with me as soon as he could. When he finally made it over to my table, he said, "Look, I'm going to be traveling in a limousine with Richard Burton and Elizabeth Taylor, so we can't go together to the next nightspot, but go on, and I'll meet up with you."

When I arrived at the next destination, he had already left, but there was a message waiting for me, telling me where to meet him. I got there, only to find another one: "I'm on my way! Don't leave! Tom." After waiting a while, I decided to go back to my hotel. I should have been disappointed, but I wasn't. I was already in love, and I knew that somehow we'd be together.

Back at my hotel a grand celebration that involved every guest there was in progress. People were drinking champagne by the bottle. I went into one of the large rooms and joined the fun, drinking champagne and having a ball. Suddenly he entered the room, and for a moment I felt like we were living out a scene from a musical, with "Some Enchanted Evening" playing in the background. Within moments we were throwing back glasses of champagne and having a wonderful time. I could see instantly that Tom was like no man I had ever met. He was extremely down-to-earth and passionate. We talked, then we cuddled, then we kissed, and by the time the evening had ended I knew I was in love. When we finally parted to go back to our separate rooms I was already thinking about when I would see him again.

This was really love at first sight, but much more. Tom loved women, and his reputation as a sex symbol preceded him, but he was a man's man. Despite his recent ascent in show business, he retained the basic values of his working-class Welsh upbringing and always spoke his mind, no matter who was around to hear it. I think that many other stars, after years of being surrounded by people who worshipped them, found Tom's attitude refreshing. Elvis Presley, for one, always sought Tom out and spent as much time as he could with him. These characteristics also made Tom a great friend, in addition to being a fine lover, and our relationship was wonderful. It was wildly romantic, and yet we could spend hours and hours just talking, which is something Tom rarely did with a woman, or so he said.

After that night I was consumed by thoughts about our next meeting. Since we both had hectic schedules, we would fly to each other whenever we could. I truly believed I had found my love at last.

During this trip we also went to England, where we appeared on the Palladium television show (which also included Tom). It seemed that every time we went to England we were treated better and better. This time the Duke and Duchess of Bedford held a party in our honor at a Chelsea restaurant/disco called the Club Dell'Aretusa. Among the invited guests were Vanessa Redgrave, Mick Jagger, Marianne Faithfull, Brian Jones, John Paul Getty, Michael Caine—Cindy's idol— and Tom. We were later also invited to the Duke and Duchess's estate, Woburn Abbey, an ancient home filled with antiques, art, and other treasures. We were tickled when they told us that they kept entire sets of our albums at both Woburn Abbey and their Paris flat.

A few days later, in early February 1968, we played what was the English debut of Diana Ross and the Supremes at London's Talk of the Town. Cindy and I rehearsed as much as possible, and the show was really tight. Gil Askey was there and we had our own rhythm section, which seemed to impress many of the British pop singers, who didn't have these luxuries. Our band included Bob Cousar on drums, Jimmy Garret on bass, Napoleon "Snaps" Allen on guitar, and Bobby Jenkins on percussion. The show was structured around several medleys—"Thoroughly Modern Millie," a tribute to Sam Cooke, and our greatest hits—and included "Unchained Melody," "You're Nobody till Somebody Loves You," "Michelle," and "Yesterday." The latter two we especially enjoyed singing, since Paul McCartney was in the audience that night. Also there were Samantha Eggar, Michael Caine, Laurence Harvey, Tony Blackburn, Engelbert Humperdinck, the Shadows, Cat Stevens, Shirley Bassey, and Sharon Tate and Roman Polanski.

We went onstage after having been up for two days without sleep and having just arrived in London from Cannes. We were a smash. The British press loved us and made a point of mentioning our rendition of "Somewhere" and Diane's monologue. Frankly, I found it a bit on the mushy side, but the audience always ate it up.

Following the show, Paul McCartney joined us and others at the Speakeasy and we celebrated until four in the morning. Paul was always one of my favorite people and we became friends. Despite being a big star, he was always very sweet and open. In fact, when it was later officially announced that Diane would leave the group, Paul telephoned me to ask how I felt about it.

The next day we had a press conference at EMI, the English distributors of our records. There were at least fifty photographers and writers, all asking us the kinds of questions we had never been asked before: How were our love lives? What kind of pajamas did we sleep in? What were our exact measurements? What did we think about the Vietnam War? The Black Power movement? And what was the truth behind Florence's leaving the group?

We weren't sure what this was all about. It wasn't that we minded answering questions. But before this, the press had gone along with the Motown PR program, sticking to such topics as the music, our gowns, whom we had met recently, what our homes were like, and so on. The next day we saw the headlines: SUPREMES MOBBED AT EMI, and the answers were in the copy. Though some critics called us "sensational," others were claiming that we had gotten away from our "roots." "Get back to church, baby!" one writer pleaded.

At this point, the English journalists were far more critical than Americans about what they perceived as our "selling out." The English held on to the misguided notion that a black who was singing and didn't sound like Aretha Franklin or Otis Redding must have been corrupted in some way. And what was this church business? None of us had ever sung in church. This segment of the press completely disregarded the fact that our roots were in American music—everything from rock to show tunes—and always had been. We weren't recording standards because they were foisted upon us by Motown; we loved doing them and had since we were fourteen years old.

But the times were definitely changing, and being accomplished, world-famous black women, the Supremes were caught in a cross fire between standard show-business conventions and new, more radical ideas about performers as political spokespeople and leaders. And, of course, now everyone was a critic. Though we'd never shunned political or social issues, we were starting to take a beating for being glamour girls in a "relevant" age. The press would accept some other pop stars' cries for revolution at face value, never bothering to note that these stars lived as lavishly as we did. But the Supremes were right out there, and before long we'd be attacked in the press for not being "black" enough. I still wondered what exactly they had meant. Did they mean to say that blacks could only sing "soulful" music? Or that to sing Cole Porter, you could only be white? These kinds of ideas struck me as a new kind of racism, but no matter. It would soon be clear that being the Supremes wouldn't be enough.

CHAPTER 19

Soon after we returned to Detroit I learned that Flo had married Tommy Chapman in Hawaii on February 29. It was a civil ceremony, with no guests. I was very happy for Flo. Things seemed to be looking up for her, and about two weeks after the wedding she signed a two-year recording contract with ABC Records.

As part of her settlement with Motown, she was forbidden to even mention that she had been in the Supremes. It seemed petty and ironic, since everyone knew she had been a Supreme and she had picked the name. With Tommy acting as her manager, Flo hired an attorney named Leonard Baun, who negotiated a better deal for Flo than what she was originally offered in July. Just before the wedding, Motown gave Flo approximately $160,000, which represented all of her earnings for her work with the Supremes. She and Tommy turned this money and some other funds over to Baun, who was supposed to oversee them for her. With some of the money Flo rented an apartment in Manhattan, and she and Tommy started a management firm, with Flo as the sole client.

As always, we were busy, but in the few weeks since I'd met Tom I managed to fly to London, New York—anywhere to be with him. Only later did I discover that Tom was married. I couldn't believe it. Maybe Tom figured that since every other woman in the Western world knew that he was "unavailable," I should have, too. At first I felt like a fool, then I felt betrayed, as if I had been the one cheated on. My pride wouldn't let me be treated like this; I didn't have to be any man's mistress, and after my experience with Duke I had vowed never to get involved with a married man again. I resolved to break it off the next time I saw Tom, but when that time came, I realized that I couldn't. It was too late.

Tom was living in London at this time, and whenever I could manage four or five days off, Cindy, Dick Scott, and I flew there and stayed at the Mayfair Hotel. Tom would come to my suite and spend think too much about me being a Supreme or a star. We would just get together whenever we could and have a great time doing those things that girlfriends do. If I were playing in the New York metropolitan area, I'd call Margie to come get me, and we would go out or go see Tom's show, stopping en route at a McDonald's. For the first time I realized how far I'd gone beyond what anyone would consider a normal life.

In February 1968 Motown released "Forever Came Today," the first in a series of Supremes songs I did not sing on. When the song was recorded in mid-1967, we were so rarely in Detroit that we heard little of the company gossip, but it was clear that HDH weren't entirely pleased with their deal there. Motown was changing. Berry had his sights set on the West Coast; he wanted to get into movies and television, and he liked hanging out with the entertainers, such as Sammy Davis, Jr. and Sidney Poitier, and other VIPs he'd met. He was spending less time in Detroit, and some people—particularly those like HDH who'd thrown their lots in with Berry during the lean years— now wanted to share in Motown's success. It was no longer enough just to be part of the company: This was especially true for those who had built the company, many of whom remembered Motown's promises of profit-sharing plans and other "extras."

The issue had been raised in 1966, when Clarence Paul held a meeting of disgruntled Motown artists and producers at his house. They discussed ways to get together and support one another in dealing with Motown. All of that went the way of the wind when people heard rumors that management people were sitting in parked cars, taking notes on and photographs of who went into Clarence's house. But Motown's success then was nothing compared to what it was now. Motown had expanded into several other buildings and had even taken over another black-owned label, Ric-Tic/Golden World.

HDH had tried to get a better deal from Berry, and when things didn't work out to their satisfaction, they instituted a work slowdown. HDH were determined to get what they wanted from Berry or not work for him at all. So few artists succeeded after leaving Motown that many people there saw Motown as all-powerful. But Eddie, Brian, and Lamont's situation was different. They were an integral part of the Motown machine, and Eddie felt that he knew the business inside-out. That was one reason they wanted to be more involved on a corporate level, which Berry refused to consider. Their contribution

the evening, then go home in the morning. Traveling
world to meet my lover for just one night was the height o
When I'd come into London, Tom would send his Rolls-Ro
me up. Any time I met him in a large city, where there mig
of press around, I dressed plainly and kept my sunglasses on.

I treasured every moment with him. We would laugh a
and just be so happy to be together. The way he pronounced m
in his Welsh accent, rolling the *r*s, made it sound like music. H
to take me to his favorite pubs in London, and later, when w
bolder, we ventured out into some of the nicer restaurants, like
Chow's in London. Eventually we were spotted, and it made the go
columns, but no one at Motown ever said a word to me about it.
the fan magazines I was the femme fatale tearing Tom's home apa
But at this point, I didn't care about what anyone thought. I w
young and in love. Whenever one of us would think about the othei
the phone would ring; it was as if we could read each other's minds
across the miles. If one of us missed the other's call, we would leave a
coded message saying that a "Jimi Hendrix" had called, which must
have kept people in our entourages buzzing.

It was nice to be with someone who thought the world of me.
When we were together, I was in heaven, but when Tom was away, I
would wonder if I had not traded one problem for another. Not only
was Tom married, but he had a child, and even if he'd been single, I
would have had the gaggle of other women who followed him wherever he went. And Tom loved women too much to say no.

Whenever I could I went to his shows, and Tom would always
sing songs just to me. In Las Vegas he once sang "Green, Green Grass
of Home," then segued into "That Old Black Magic." I was both
flattered and embarrassed to have such a private tribute paid so pub-
licly.

Whenever Tom and I talked about singing, which was often, I
would urge him to give up the sex-god shtick and play it straight. He
had one of the most beautiful voices I had ever heard, and I often told
him that he had the makings of the next Sinatra. Of course these
suggestions weren't especially appreciated by Tom's manager, Gordon
Mills, but I didn't care. Gordon wasn't crazy about me anyway. The
more I talked to Tom about his singing, the more I thought about my
own, and so I started taking vocal lessons from Teddy Hall in New
York. It was at Teddy's studio that I met Margie Haber, a wild Jewish
girl from Long Island who soon became my best friend.

Margie became my lifeline to the outside world. She didn't really to Motown's success—and the Supremes'—was incalculable, and when it was clear that they had stopped working, Berry went into action.

In August Motown sued HDH for $4 million in damages resulting from their not writing and producing hits. Motown also sought to restrain HDH from going to work for anyone else. HDH countersued Motown for $22 million. The cases dragged on for years and were finally settled privately, out of court. But long before that, as early as spring 1968, the damage was done—at least as far as the Supremes were concerned.

The sound HDH created for us was what set our records apart. Their songs were made for us, and after this we bounced from producer to producer. When "Forever" hit in April, at #28, our lowest-charting single since 1963, it was our last HDH hit.

Though the Supremes were at the top of Motown's roster, other acts were doing well. The Temptations and Marvin Gaye were soon playing the Copa and the Latin Casino, and Berry started talking with people in television and working on plans for producing television specials. Although Berry had long employed whites in upper-management positions, around this time he started signing more white artists as well. The most profitable black-owned business in America was also one of the most thoroughly integrated.

Despite some of the criticism the Supremes got for being too "glamorous," we were fortunate to come along when we did. Blacks and whites were making efforts to change things, and music helped bridge the gaps. Touring the South had opened my eyes to racism, and as the Supremes got bigger, we would be confronted by people saying the funniest things. Of course they meant well, and, fortunately, we knew where they were coming from, but these comments said a lot about what the Supremes meant. In Miami, where we usually performed over Christmas and New Year's Eve, a middle-aged Jewish woman came up to us and said, "You know, I usually don't let my children watch Negroes on television, but the Supremes are different." We were living examples of the slogan "black is beautiful."

We were playing the Copa on April 4 when we learned that Dr. Martin Luther King had been assassinated in Memphis. Like so many Americans, we were stunned. We canceled our show, and the next night appeared on *The Tonight Show*, where we talked about Dr. King. Many performers were going on radio and television to pay tribute to

Dr. King and to do whatever they could to inspire people to channel their grief and anger into something positive. This evening we performed "Somewhere," which had long been in our repertoire, substituting for the "love" monologue a short, dramatic speech about unity that Diane, Berry, and Shelly Berger had written. Unfortunately, efforts of this type couldn't quell the violent riots that broke out in several major cities, including Detroit. Dr. King was a man of peace, and it saddened us to see his death used as an excuse for rioting and looting.

We made arrangements to fly to Atlanta immediately, where along with such celebrities as Marlon Brando, Sammy Davis, Jr., Eartha Kitt, Diahann Carroll, Harry Belafonte, and others, we were to walk those last miles with Dr. King.

As we rode into town with Junius Griffin, an associate of Dr. King's who also worked with Berry, we noticed a commotion in the street and saw a man up on a telephone pole. We couldn't figure out exactly what he was doing, but one of us mentioned that we thought he was cute. Junius replied, "Oh, that's Jesse Jackson."

The funeral arrangements were made by a committee of prominent blacks, including the Reverend Ralph Abernathy, Jesse Jackson, Sidney Poitier, and Julian Bond. Harry Belafonte was chairing the meeting, and when he was called away by other business, he asked Berry to keep things running until he got back. Apparently when Harry returned about half an hour later, the meeting was in chaos. When we later heard the various accounts of who did what and what was said, we were embarrassed that such a solemn occasion was marred by such pettiness, since we were all representing peace.

On the day of the funeral, Diane, Cindy, and I walked with thousands of others, and as we made our way to Dr. King's final resting place, I hoped his work would live on and that every person there would keep his memory alive.

Not long after the funeral, Mrs. Coretta Scott King organized the Poor People's March on Washington, D.C. Mrs. King asked Berry if he would provide entertainment at a benefit in Atlanta, where the march was to begin. Junius Griffin helped Berry get this together. Mrs. King called Berry on Tuesday, and by that Thursday, it was all arranged down to the last detail. The Supremes, Stevie Wonder, Gladys Knight and the Pips, and the Temptations performed for over thirteen thousand at the Atlanta Civic Center. At the end of the show, the Reverend Ralph Abernathy of the Southern Christian Leadership

Conference presented Berry with a plaque. Mrs. King then gave Berry a leather-bound set of Dr. King's books, which she had inscribed. It was a proud moment for all of us.

Back in Detroit, though, the rioters had done incredible damage, and this event marked a turning point for Motown. The Supremes had been recording so frequently in Los Angeles that I was spending more time there than at home, and I had considered moving there. After the riots my decision was firm. Every time I was on the West Coast, I'd scout around for the perfect house.

On July 23 we endorsed Democratic presidential candidate Hubert Humphrey. We had met him earlier and were convinced that his policies were sound. Humphrey's platforms included a continuation of President Johnson's social policies. Though it didn't always make the front page, the Supremes had long been contributing to Democratic causes, usually as performers at fund-raising functions. For example, we sang at a benefit to clear Senator Robert Kennedy's campaign debts after his assassination. The Gordys were always politically active, especially Esther Edwards, and when the idea of endorsing Humphrey was presented to us, we thought it over carefully and were glad to do it. We certainly could have refused, and we would have if we had been asked to endorse someone we did not believe in.

For some reason, though, the press had a real field day with our endorsement, and some writers treated it as if it were a joke. In several published accounts, more space was devoted to what we wore than what we said. Humphrey wasn't the most popular candidate to come along, and his sincerity was ridiculed. We were hurt by this, but thought better of speaking out. We just hoped that we had helped his cause. The next day we performed at a fund-raising dinner for him at the Waldorf Astoria.

Despite knowing that it was hopeless, my affair with Tom was more intense than ever. We were staying at his cabin in Bournemouth when his wife called. She told Tom she suspected that he had a woman there and that she was coming up to see for herself. Tom and I decided that I should leave. He put me in his limousine and kissed me good-bye. I cried all the way to London. Ironically, Tom's devotion to his wife and child was one of the things about him I admired most. Never once did he even hint that he would leave her, but I couldn't let go. Sometimes I'd been so foolish, going so far as to telephone his home in England, only to hang up when his wife would answer.

Between all our work, I kept in touch with Flo through my cousin Josephine, who was living in my house in Detroit and had been friends with Flo for years. Flo was expecting her first babies—twins—and her record, "It Doesn't Matter How You Say It," had been released in the spring. She was still my best friend, and I wasn't comfortable with the way things had been left between her and Diane. She was out of the group now and never coming back. I felt it was time that things be settled. Everyone at Motown loved Flo, and I thought it would be good for her to see them. Berry was holding a huge party at his pool-house, and I had been invited. This was, I thought, the perfect chance for Flo to see some of her old friends from Motown and see how much she meant to them. Her departure had been so abrupt; no one had really said good-bye.

When I suggested the idea to Flo, she flatly refused. As the day drew nearer, I kept insisting that she go.

"Mary," Flo said, "you know this is a bad idea. You know Berry and Diane won't like the idea of me coming there. Forget it, will you?"

But I continued pestering her until she reluctantly agreed to go with me. We drove up together in my car. Flo was a little nervous, but everyone from the company welcomed her so warmly that we both forgot about Diane and Berry. We were having a great time, but there was an undercurrent of tension, and I knew that Flo and Diane were each watching every move the other made.

Finally Diane left Berry's side and sauntered over. She wasn't especially warm to Flo, but she was pleasant, and they talked for a while. Then she left and went back to Berry. A while later Diane came back to Flo and asked, "How have you been? What have you been doing?" Things seemed to be going very nicely, and I was pleased with myself for having engineered this meeting.

Several minutes later Diane came back over and made a comment about Flo's weight. Flo bit her tongue, and we kept talking. Diane went back over to Berry, then came back again. Each time Diane would walk toward us, I could see Flo tense up, and as the evening wore on, Flo drank a little—which was all it took—and the exchanges got louder and less pleasant. The last time Diane ran back to Berry, Flo turned to me and said loudly, "What does she keep coming over here for?"

Everyone stopped talking and looked at Flo. I knew then that Flo had been right: She shouldn't have come. All I could think of was getting her out of there as quickly and gracefully as possible. But once Flo got to drinking and things got hot, she was the last to walk away from a good fight, and the last time I saw Diane coming over, I knew that was exactly what was in store. Flo had had three or four drinks by now and could barely stay on top of her stool.

"If she comes back over here one more time," Flo proclaimed loudly, "I'm going to kick her."

I could tell that everyone felt sorry for Flo. They looked from Diane to Berry to Flo. Something had to give.

"Flo," I said quietly, "I think it's time to go."

"No, Mary. You stay; I'll go," she replied.

A second later Berry said, in a voice that everyone could hear, "Who brought her here?"

Berry knew damn well who did, and I knew I'd have to go, too. "Get her out of here," he said calmly but sternly. We left.

The minute we got into my car, Flo turned to me and said, "Mary, I told you I shouldn't have come. I don't know why I let you talk me into it." Flo didn't let me forget this night for a long time. Diane and Berry, on the other hand, never mentioned it.

Regardless of Diane's or Flo's motives for behaving the way they did, it took me months to get over my own anger. I was still singing with Diane, and Flo was still my best friend. I was miserable, but maybe I was just being selfish. I had always been in the middle, and here I was again, trying to make us all friends again. I had always admired Flo's outspokenness and Diane's aggressive nature, but things would never be the same. We had all suffered wounds that would not heal.

In addition to the changes I had witnessed in Diane, I could see that Berry was a new man, too. The roles were clearly shifting, and, at least in public, Berry seemed to be doing Diane's bidding as often as she did his. Sometimes, though, Berry surprised her.

Once when we were in Miami Billy Davis, Berry's personal aide and a friend who traveled with us (and no relation to Berry's early songwriting partner) and I stayed out all night long. We walked back to our hotel along the beach, certain that we were going to run into Diane and Berry on their way to breakfast. When I got upstairs I breathed a sigh of relief. I had just put my key in the door when Diane popped out of her room and said, "Well, where have you been all night?" I walked into my room and closed the door.

That night my singing wasn't great, and after the show Diane,

Berry, and I were in the dressing room when Diane decided that Berry should know why.

"Mary, you see? That's what happens when you're out all night. You lose your voice."

"Look, Diane," I replied, "I do my job here, and as long as I do, my private life is none of your business!"

Berry never said a word.

Diane now really was the star of the Supremes, and this was something of a problem when we started working with new producers. Even people we had worked with before, such as Smokey Robinson, approached the Supremes differently, choosing to emphasize a lighter, middle-of-the-road style, and Diane's voice at the expense of any good harmonies. Nick Ashford and Valerie Simpson had been successful with a series of duets they'd written and produced for Marvin Gaye and Tammi Terrell—"Ain't No Mountain High Enough," "Your Precious Love," and "Ain't Nothing like the Real Thing." But the song Diane cut with them (using the Andantes, not Cindy and me, on backing vocals), "Some Things You Never Get Used To," barely scraped into the Top Thirty.

Berry was always fascinated by people, and every once in a while he'd bring someone new into Motown. While we were in New York, working at the Copa, Cindy introduced him to her friend Suzanne de Passe. Suzanne was the talent coordinator for a New York club called the Cheetah, and she and Berry hit it off right away.

Before long Suzanne was walking around wherever we were working, with a little notepad and pen in hand, jotting down notes. She made suggestions to Berry about everything. She soon became one of his top assistants, but unlike so many bright newcomers Berry would hail as geniuses and then discard after he realized they were as foolish as everyone else had known they were from the start, Suzanne stayed.

Things were changing, and I felt like I was in limbo. I had no real home and felt that I needed to get away. I said to Berry, "I need a vacation—a real one. Not one of those little breaks you give us, where we still have to come in to record or do publicity. I've been working too hard."

"Mary, you had better work while you can," he replied in that paternal tone of voice he liked to use. "There may come a day when you will wish you had taken advantage of every working day offered to you."

"But, Berry, I deserve a real vacation."

"Mary, we're getting ready to write and record a new single. Don't you want to be in on it? It could be important."

"I'm going for only a week, and you know I have business on the West Coast. Can't you wait until I get back to record? I'm not a writer; you don't need me for that anyway."

My arguments didn't seem to be working. Berry acted as if I were doing something foolish, but he knew that I knew that they didn't need me to write a song. This was just a game. I took the time off and went to Los Angeles to take care of some details regarding my upcoming move there and then went on to Acapulco. Duke's marriage had ended, so we decided to give it one more chance, just to see if we could make things work.

I found my home, a large, modern place in the Hollywood Hills, complete with pool and sauna, and we had a wonderful time in Mexico. I came back to Detroit refreshed and ready to get to work, only to find that they had gone ahead and recorded the new song without me. Berry had wanted a song written, so Pam Sawyer, R. Dean Taylor, Frank Wilson, and Deke Richards had composed "Love Child." Although I was angry and hurt by being left out, I did like the song. Though its story line was not autobiographical for any of us, we knew girlfriends and relatives who had babies out of wedlock, and we knew what a hardship it was. "Love Child" was quite explicit, and the message was, I felt, important. It would be our only number-one record in 1968, and the first major hit I had not sung on. When we performed it on Ed Sullivan's show in September, we lip-synched; still, the words caught in my throat.

After Flo left, HDH had begun recording Supremes records with just Diane and someone else on backing vocals to keep to the release schedule when we were touring. What happened with "Love Child" seemed designed to send Cindy and me a message; namely, that Diana Ross was all that they needed. Diane and Berry were together all the time, usually working on something. It was impossible for me to know what they were doing when, and by now it was clear that they didn't want me to.

Looking back, I suppose I shouldn't have been surprised that things turned out the way they did. But I also knew that I had worked hard, and the Supremes were still the hottest thing Motown had. I knew Diane would leave the group eventually, but in the meantime it seemed stupid of Motown to make things harder for us as a group.

After all, the name would have a value for years to come, and up until then, most artists who left groups to go solo usually failed.

That fall we were also working on our first television special, "TCB," which starred Diana Ross and the Supremes and the Temptations. Since our appearances on *Tarzan*, Berry had been cultivating a working relationship with people at NBC, so this was quite a coup for him. It was produced by Motown Productions in conjunction with George Schlatter and Ed Friendly, who were responsible for *Laugh-In*. Mark Warren was the director, and Donald McKayle, who had worked on *Hullabaloo*, was the choreographer. The set was a modern, multilevel Plexiglas platform, and we wore beautiful gowns, designed for us by Mike Travis.

We all knew there would be at least one solo spot for Diane, so that didn't ruffle anyone's feathers. However, once we got down to rehearsing and taping, it was clear to all of us that seven of us were extras. It was "Miss Ross this" and "Miss Ross that." Paul Williams grumbled, "This must be the Diana Ross show." "Where will Miss Ross be?" was the only thing the crew seemed to care about. It was bad enough that none of us had any input regarding the show, but the fact that a newcomer had more influence than we did indicated how drastically things at Motown were changing. Suzanne de Passe didn't mind telling us what to do, but she didn't dare cross Diane. At one point, designer Mike Travis and Diane were discussing gowns when Suzanne burst into the room, frantic about something.

"Wait just a moment," Diane said. "I am talking to Mike and I will talk to you later."

"Sorry, Miss Ross," Suzanne replied, embarrassed.

I wasn't sure if Diane was as confused about Suzanne as we all were. Of course this was another little game; Diane and Suzanne couldn't be nice enough to each other when Berry was around.

The Temptations were as upset about things as Cindy and I were. One of them even remarked that, since Motown knew the Supremes weren't really accepted by blacks and the Temptations were, they were being used to draw black viewers. We felt better when Otis, Eddie, Cindy, and I were featured in a production number of the Brazilian hit "Mas Que Nada." We did a good job, but then one of the production people came over and told us that it might not be in the show. And, no surprise, it wasn't. Why put us through all the work, then? The whole situation was a mess, and it seemed to get worse every day.

I'd read the script, so I knew Diane had a special spot, the "Afro

Vogue" number. I didn't realize just how special it was, though, until I saw the set. The entire background was made up of hundreds of still photos of her, and she had several costume changes. Diane was great, but I couldn't stop thinking about how little any of the rest of us knew about what was going on.

Having worked with Diane for so many years, I knew she'd be tense and anxious. No matter how she might have acted toward other performers, she always carried her weight and worked hard to see that everything she was responsible for was as close to perfect as she could make it. The Tempts, however, hadn't worked with her as closely, and since some of them had known her as a kid, they found the "Miss Ross" business ridiculous. They weren't going to defer to her; they thought it was a joke.

Besides being one of my biggest heartthrobs, Eddie Kendricks is one of my best friends. He and Diane had been buddies from way back too, but as the plans to launch her solo career starting taking form, some of her earlier Motown friendships had lapsed.

During a break one day, all of us went out to eat, except Diane, who rarely went with a group of us, and Eddie, who had something he wanted to do. Although Eddie hadn't asked anyone to, someone in the group was thoughtful enough to bring back some food for him. When Diane found out about it, she walked up to Eddie and said, sarcastically, "Oh! How do you rate that?" It was absolutely absurd; we couldn't believe our eyes. A minute later, she came over and playfully slapped Eddie across the face. Ever the gentleman, he did nothing. Having an attitude was one thing, but this had gone too far. It was getting harder and harder for me even to want to be around her.

Amazingly, the show was great. When we were all singing together it was just like old times. When it aired in early December, we got rave reviews, and an album we cut with the Temptations was on its way to the top of the charts, along with a single, "I'm Gonna Make You Love Me." Despite all the tension and unhappiness, the special was a great boost to all of us, and plans were put in motion for a second program with the Supremes and the Tempts.

In early November we traveled to Stockholm, Sweden. There Sweden's Princess Christina came to each of our shows at Bern's Cafe, bringing along lots of her friends and even dancing on the tables. After the shows she would hang out with us at one of her friends' homes. Berry, who was with us, of course, seemed especially to like these meetings. After Sweden, we went to Copenhagen, Brussels, Hamburg, West Berlin, Munich, Frankfurt, and then London, where we did a show at the Palladium. The real highlight of this trip was the Royal Command Performance we gave before Princess Margaret and Lord Snowdon, the Queen Mother, Princess Anne, and Prince Charles at the London Palladium.

In the middle of "Somewhere," Diane gave the little monologue we had been doing since Dr. King's death:

"There's a place for us. A place for all of us. Black and white, Jew and gentile, Catholic and Protestant. So was the world of Martin Luther King and his idea. If we keep this in mind, then we can carry on his work."

A tear rolled down Diane's cheek as we picked up the song again. After we'd finished, there was a two-minute standing ovation, and the Royal Family cheered wildly. Though the British press still adored us, a few writers were critical of our having subjected the Royal Family to something so "political." But they had loved it, and in interviews for a long time thereafter Diane eloquently defended the speech.

The event also had its lighter moments. Though we had enjoyed doing the show, because we were meeting royalty and had memorized all the protocol, we weren't exactly loose. Everything was quite proper and formal; we knew not to speak until spoken to, and not to address a royal, and so on. We stood in line, with Diane first, then me, then Cindy. Princess Margaret walked up to me, extended her hand, then —so quietly that no one else could hear—she whispered in her prim, high-pitched voice, "Is that a wig you're wearing, Mary?" I did all I could to suppress a giggle. When I realized that she was very serious about it I thought how bizarre it was that a member of the Royal Family could be so candid. Here I'd grown up in the Projects and I had more sense than to ask someone a question like that. But then I thought how great it was to have these experiences, and how glad I was to be a Supreme.

CHAPTER 20

In November of 1968 Flo gave birth to her twins, Nicole Renee and Michelle Denise. They had been born prematurely, but they were healthy, and Flo seemed anxious to get her career going. I had heard her first single, and though I loved Flo's voice, I didn't think the material was right for her. I hoped she would find success.

Nothing that had happened in the last year could erase my years of friendship with Diane, and I decided to let things ride. I knew she would be leaving the group soon, and I wanted the Supremes to go on. I would be the last original member, and I wasn't about to throw everything away, like I was beginning to fear Flo had. The Supremes were going to continue, and I tried to prepare myself for what lay ahead as best I could.

The success of "Love Child" prompted Berry to want another release in a similar vein. I didn't sing on "I'm Livin' in Shame," which I thought was melodramatic and lacked a message. From this point on, I would not be on any other singles except those we recorded with the Temptations. "The Composer" and "No Matter What Sign You Are" are surely among the worst things ever released under the Supremes' name, so not singing on those wasn't too bad. That these records charted so poorly compared to our biggest hits was due in part to the fact that, as several critics have since pointed out, they did not sound like "Supremes records." However, when the Supremes' "farewell song," "Someday We'll Be Together" was recorded without Cindy or me, I knew it really was over.

On February 1 we opened at the Frontier Hotel in Las Vegas. As Diane's leaving the group drew near, everything seemed to revolve around her, and Cindy and I became "just" the Supremes. When I read interviews where Diane said things such as "I am leaving the Supremes," it hurt.

One night during this engagement I was standing backstage when

225

I happened upon Diane and Berry. They didn't notice me, and, as I stood there, Berry said to Diane, "Now, Diane, you go out there and ignore everything. Forget about the girls—all of it—and just think about yourself."

I could tell by the look on Diane's face that she was shocked, and in that moment I was reminded of the Diane I knew and loved. For a moment I believed she still did care about me. It was one of those rare instances when I could see that she must have wrestled with her conscience, too.

Despite this, though, she did exactly as Berry said. From the moment we were announced, she ignored us. There was none of the usual interplay, and she barely made eye contact with either Cindy or me. I understood her so well, perhaps too well. Maybe if I'd reacted the way most people would have, things would not have gone this far. This slight was the last blow. I suspected that things would probably get worse before they got better, and I'd either have to ride it out or leave. My friends from the Club Bravo (Dionne Warwick, Leslie Uggams, Mira Waters, Lola Falana, Yvonne Fair, and Nancy Wilson, with Lena Horne as den mother) often gave me refuge.

My friend Nancy Wilson was also performing in Las Vegas, and when she heard that we were in town she invited me to dinner at her hotel suite. I was grateful to spend some time with another woman whom I didn't see every day. Of course I didn't discuss any of my problems with Nancy; that was group business. When I got there, Nancy's beautician had just finished doing her hair. I asked if she could do mine, and she happily obliged. She gave me a hair-relaxing treatment and seemed to know what she was doing. Later, when she rinsed off the solution, my hair started falling out, breaking off near the root. I was mortified, and the poor beautician was afraid she'd done something wrong.

"Oh my God! I'm so sorry," she kept saying. "I only did what it said to do. I've done this so many times. I don't understand—"

But I couldn't be consoled. I was hysterical, crying, "What am I going to do? I've got shows to do! What am I going to do?" I knew that my hair was falling out as a result of stress and exhaustion. Nancy didn't know what to say. She took me back to my hotel, and someone in the entourage sent for my mother and my doctor, who both flew in immediately.

When my mother got there she didn't say a word; she just held me and I cried my eyes out. This was the first time I really thought everything was getting to be more than I could handle. When my friend and doctor, Herbert Avery and his wife, Monaloa, arrived from Los Angeles, we talked. I told him all about what was going on with the Supremes and my personal life with Tom. I'd been running around the world, having the time of my life, I thought. This episode made me realize how much of a mess my life was. Dr. Avery gave me some advice, and I resolved to straighten things out. I knew the relationship with Tom had to end and that I had to stop holding everything inside. There was only a short while to go before Diane left. I had to hold on.

I threw myself into decorating my new home in Los Angeles, giving parties and entertaining friends whenever I had a chance. Cindy moved to L.A., too, and we became closer than ever. The two of us would go to private clubs in Beverly Hills, such as the Daisy, the Candy Store, and Pips. We were at one of these clubs when I met a new neighbor, Jim Brown, the football player. He introduced me to a young basketball player from UCLA named Mike Warren, and the two of us hit it off right away. He was still in college when we met, but that didn't stop me from falling in love with him. He came into my life like an angel.

I had just brought my adopted son, Willie, out to live with me. Willie is my cousin Christine's eldest child, and, ironically, I adopted him under circumstances similar to the Pippins' taking me. Christine had several children, and she and I agreed that Willie would have more opportunities living with me than were available to him in Detroit. Besides, I had always loved children and had a strong maternal streak. I was happy to have Willie, but it was quite an adjustment. Mike was there with me every step of the way.

"Mike," I often said to him, "with your good looks and charm, I think you have the potential to make it in this business."

"Do you really think so, Mary?" he would ask shyly.

"Heck, yeah. You should give it a try. You have charisma. You'll find your niche. Wait and see."

Now, whenever I see Mike on *Hill Street Blues*, I always think that few people are more deserving of success than him.

Diane and Berry were still an item, though it was hard to see where the relationship was going. They didn't seem any closer to marriage, and yet they still seemed fascinated with each other. This didn't stop Diane from seeing other men. For a while she was dating Tim Brown, a football player with the Philadelphia Eagles. Whenever we would play in the area, he would come to see Diane, sometimes he would bring along one of his teammates, and the four of us would double-date. Everyone in the entourage knew about Tim, except, I assume, Berry. Of course, Berry had been having his fun, too, bringing Chris Clark on the road while he was seeing Diane.

Years before, Flo and I had started traveling with our dogs. When we were out on tour once, we had seen two little Yorkshire terrier puppies from the same litter, and we each took one. They were our constant companions and soon became as good as traveling as we were. I had never known Diane to be particularly fond of animals, but when she saw the amount of attention ours got she decided to get not one but two dogs, a Maltese named Tiffany and a Yorkie named Little Bit. When Cindy joined the Supremes, she got a Boston terrier. It was quite a menagerie.

Cindy and I kept our dogs on their leashes at all times, or locked in the hotel or dressing room. Diane, however, preferred to let her dogs roam free, no matter where we were. We had all of the dogs with us at the Latin Casino in June 1969. This was one of our bigger engagements, and the dates had been sold out for months. There were plenty of industry people and celebrities in the audience, and the show was a success. The standard procedure was that we would do our "last" song, then Diane would exit to one side, and we would exit to the other. After a few moments of applause, we would return to do the encore.

As Cindy and I were making our false exit, we heard Diane, who we thought was standing backstage, let out a blood-curdling scream. I rushed backstage to see what had happened. The audience had also heard the scream, and they immediately expected the worst. Before I got to Diane's dressing room, I heard someone ask, "Is there a doctor in the house?" Had something happened to Diane? From backstage I could hear people in the audience talking.

"Something must have happened to one of the girls."

"Oh, no! This is awful! I wonder what it was."

"Are they coming back?"

As I ran to her dressing room, I could see people standing around and Diane in the middle of the crowd, jumping up and down and screaming at the top of her lungs. At her feet Tiffany and Little Bit were walking very shakily and vomiting violently. By now a crowd had gathered around, and in the chaos people were calling out suggestions.

"Let's get them to the hospital."

"Joe," Diane screamed at our road manager Joe Shaffner, "this is your fault! You should have kept an eye on my dogs!"

"Let's just get them to the hospital," the first voice said again. "We're wasting time."

"They must have eaten the rat poison that was out," another voice added.

"Yeah," someone else said. "She should have kept them on a leash."

At that, Diane started screaming again, "I'm going to sue this place if they've poisoned my dogs! How dare they lay poison down when animals could be around!"

Everyone was doing their best to calm Diane down, but she just got wilder by the minute.

"I'm getting out of here and I am never in my life going to appear here again. I want to leave at once!" She ran into the dressing room, and a group of people followed her. A few made timid suggestions, but nothing was really getting accomplished. The dogs had been rushed to a hospital, and Diane was yelling, "Pack my things! Let's get out of here!" as she flung gowns around the room.

"I want to be taken to the hospital where my dogs are! Immediately!"

As people were talking, trying to decide who would travel in which car, someone from the club said, "Now the other two girls can go on without her."

"Oh no," someone from Motown replied, "you cannot send them on alone."

And this went on for several more minutes. The phone rang and Diane answered it. Everyone fell silent. Diane said, "What's going to happen? I don't know . . ." We figured that the dogs must have died. A second later, she said, "We are leaving!"

One of the club owners, Dave Dushoff, had heard enough. "Well," he said, "I don't see why you can't do the show. We had a very famous singer here recently, and his mother died and he still did the show. It's only your dogs. Come on."

"I'm canceling the show," she proclaimed, "and we're going to sue this club. And we'll never be here again!"

"I've never heard of such a thing," someone else from the club said. "You shouldn't have let your dogs run loose."

"Well, *you* should have had signs up!" Diane retorted.

"You let them roam! And it is not our fault if they got sick."

This was a mess. Berry was right there, but he did nothing to stop Diane. Berry and Diane were getting ready to leave when she spotted Joe.

"This is all your fault," she screamed. "It's your responsibility to look after my property!"

Joe was silent. Diane was furious, and I could see that there was more going on than just the dogs. Several people suspected that Berry had found out about Tim. Unfortunately, it wasn't just Diane who was canceling, it was the Supremes. I was ashamed at how unprofessional it looked to everyone.

"Miss Ross has to leave. She is very upset," Berry told the club people as he helped Diane to the door. In front of us, he was kind and understanding. The next day, however, he was livid. He believed that Shelly Berger had straightened everything out with Dave Dushoff, one of the Latin Casino's owners. When the other owners heard about it, however, they refused to accept the cancellation. All four thousand of the house seats had been sold for every night of our two-week engagement. In addition, the Latin Casino was a supper club, so there were thousands of dollars in food that would go to waste.

During July we were booked at the Copa, so I had plenty of time to spend running around New York with Margie. I invited her to stay with me at the Sherry Netherland Hotel, and since Tom was also in town, we would go to see his show.

The night the Apollo astronauts landed on the moon, Margie and I were in Tom's dressing room, waiting for him to change so that we could go out for a bite. When he emerged from his shower, barely covered by a towel, he cried, "Oh, Mary," and started hugging and kissing me. I was so engrossed watching the moonwalk that I shooed him away. Margie later told me that the whole time I stared at the screen, Tom stood there staring at me. I was really in love, but I knew it had to end.

Whenever I could, I brought Margie along with me to all our shows. She would be with me as I dressed, would sit in the front row for the show, then come backstage, and we would usually leave together. Diane seemed to resent her, which I thought strange, since Diane and I weren't that close anymore. What was there to be jealous about? Still, Diane would make a point of being catty to Margie.

One evening we were riding in the limousine from Manhattan to the Westbury Music Fair on Long Island. On the way out, Diane was debating whether to come back into New York after the show or to stay overnight in a hotel near the Music Fair. Margie, who knew the area well and was trying to be helpful, said, "Even though it doesn't seem far away, the drive from Long Island to Manhattan can be very long, because the traffic on the expressway gets backed up."

After the show, we drove back to Manhattan, and the ride went smoothly. Diane, however, couldn't resist making a dig at Margie.

"It's so typical of you, Margie. There is no traffic problem. I knew we didn't have to stay overnight on Long Island. I'm certainly glad I never listen to you."

Margie took it the right way; she ignored it. But I couldn't. At the same time, I didn't confront Diane about her behavior, either. Looking back now, I've often wondered if I was such a good friend to her, never telling her off at times like these. It seemed to me that we were both locked into patterns that were unbreakable, and getting more destructive with time.

In October we hosted *The Hollywood Palace*, which meant that Diane hosted, and we just sang. On this show, Diane introduced the Jackson Five in their first national television appearance.

Everyone at Motown knew that Bobby Taylor of the Vancouvers had discovered the Jackson Five and had told Berry about them. Berry didn't have time to see them audition in person, so he had asked Bobby to take them over to the Graystone Ballroom, where Berry kept a whole batch of video equipment, and tape their act for him to look at later. Bobby taped the Jackson brothers, and Berry signed them immediately. Many artists had come through Motown, but few of the newer acts had made it big. Berry knew the Jackson Five would be big money-makers, and Motown set out to promote them from the very start. Part of the promotion was that Diane had discovered them. A few weeks later, Diane hosted a party in the Jacksons' honor for three hundred guests at the exclusive Daisy Club in Hollywood. I didn't know anything about it until I received my invitation via telegram.

Knowing that Motown's plans for Diane's solo career had been the force behind much of the unpleasantness of the first TV special made doing the second one a bit easier. We weren't treated any better, but at least we knew why. I also knew that this phase would end when Diane left, and that wasn't too far away now. None of us were upset at the taping of our second special with the Temptations, "G.I.T. on Broadway." Diane's departure was announced in early November; the word had been out around Motown for some time.

Strangely, we never talked about her leaving. I mean, Diane and I never said two words to each other about it. Like everyone else in the world, I read about it in the papers. Speculation was that I would be taking over her spot as lead singer; Diane had said so in interviews. But it was never really discussed, and if Berry had asked me to, I am sure I would have declined. I had been singing in the background for so long that I doubted I could sing lead well enough. My standards for the Supremes—whoever they were—were too high to let my ego run amok. After years of being denied the chance to sing more leads and being told over and over that I couldn't sing, my confidence was shot. I was taking singing lessons with the best teachers in the world, but in my heart I knew I wasn't ready to make that step.

Once it was an open subject, Berry and I discussed possible replacements, but there didn't seem to be too much of a rush to decide. Fan magazines were holding polls to see who readers thought should take Diane's place, and Tammi Terrell seemed to be their favorite. Sadly, Tammi was nearing the end of her long struggle with a fatal brain tumor and was never considered. Other names were suggested, but I was in no rush. If nothing else, the last three years had made me more determined than ever to keep the Supremes alive, with or without Diane. I was here for the long haul, and I had to feel comfortable with my new partner.

One day Berry said, "I found somebody." When I met Jean Terrell, the sister of the boxer Ernie Terrell but no relation to Tammi, I liked her immediately. She was a great singer, and her voice was higher and totally different from Diane's. She seemed happy to be in the Supremes, and I was happy to have a real group again. We started rehearsing for live shows together in the fall and had begun recording that winter. Though it was obvious from the beginning that Jean had a mind of her own and wasn't nearly as much a team player as Cindy and I were, I overlooked it. Things would be worked out, and I was just happy to know that the Supremes would go on.

My relationship with Tom was coming to a close. We both realized that our feelings were too serious for us to keep chasing each other around the world. We were at my home in Hollywood and I was throwing one of my usual parties. There were people all over the place, and Tom and I were alone in my room. We both knew what was coming. "Mary," he said, "I don't think this is fair to you. There is no future for us, and I think we should break away from this affair now."

I had to agree. He wasn't going to leave his wife, and I had always known that. I was crying, but when we said good-bye at my door, I knew we were doing the right thing.

After that, we kept in touch, and deep inside I still nurtured the faintest hope that things might change. I finally accepted that they never would when he brought his wife backstage after one of our shows and introduced her to me. She was very nice. After I was married and got to experience firsthand what she had gone through, I understood the pain and humiliation she must have suffered. Still, Tom remains one of the very special people in my life. I fell in and out of love after that, having affairs with Steve McQueen, Flip Wilson, and Jack Lucarelli.

In early December, Cindy was kidnapped from her Hollywood apartment by the building's maintenance man. She escaped from him several hours later by jumping from his moving car on a freeway. The incident upset all of us. I had to stop keeping my front door open whenever I threw big parties after a couple of suspicious characters turned up. While some of my nervousness probably had to do with the brutal murder of Sharon Tate, there was no question but that things were changing, and everyone I knew felt the same. (I had to use Lincoln Kilpatrick to house-sit while I was on tour.) The end of the sixties seemed to bring an ill wind. I sensed that this was the end of an era. As a Supreme I had spent so many years traveling with chaperones, bodyguards, and other people whose job it was to look after me, that I had rarely thought of being in danger. Cindy's kidnapping was just an extreme example of how mixed a blessing fame could be.

Later that month "Someday We'll Be Together" was at number one, and we were caught up in a flurry of "farewell" publicity. It was hard to know exactly what to feel.

On December 21 we did our last show with Ed Sullivan, performing a greatest-hits medley and "Someday." It was strange to think how far we'd come since our first appearance on that stage just five years before. By this time I had spent so much time with Jean and Cindy that, in my mind, they were the Supremes. This was just a formality. I felt like I'd said good-bye already. It was sad and yet triumphant at the same time, and as we walked down a ramp, Diane kept moving further and further away.

On Wednesday, January 14, 1970, Diana Ross and the Supremes gave their final farewell performance at the Frontier Hotel in Las Vegas. Looking back over the past couple of years, I could see that everything had been leading up to this, and, professionally, this was the only way things could go. Diana Ross was going solo, and the Supremes would continue—Jean, Cindy, and me. We even had our first single in the can, "Up the Ladder to the Roof," which I was sure would be a hit.

People must have asked us how we felt over a million times, and there were a hundred different emotions, but for me the main one was relief. In the public's eye, every group—no matter how "equal" the members—has its star, and that's fine. But in the day-to-day work, a group has to function as a team, and that was something we hadn't done for a long time now. Diane's status at Motown and her relationship to Berry made it impossible for things to be otherwise, and if she hadn't left the group, something would have had to change. Working with Jean and Cindy was a joy. Maybe we weren't as close as Flo, Diane, and I had once been, but we were starting fresh. After years of hard work, I felt I was embarking on another wonderful adventure. I had been blessed to have been in the Supremes the first time; now it could happen all over again.

Deep inside, in the part of me that still believed in dreams, I couldn't deny that I was also very sad. This was, I thought then, not the end of the Supremes, but the end of the dream Diane, Flo, and I had shared. The three of us were who we were today because of a dream we all had nurtured a decade before. There were plenty of people behind us; I wouldn't deny that for a second. But the three of us had created the Supremes; we'd made ourselves into our image of what we could be, in our homemade dresses and fake pearls. Now, here Diane and I were, dripping in real diamonds and adorned in black velvet and pearls by Bob Mackie. And this was the end.

The farewell performance was scheduled to begin at midnight. I sat in my dressing room, sipping champagne and quietly putting on my makeup, doing the same things I had done a thousand times before. As showtime drew nearer, I felt exhilarated, and I went out onstage determined to enjoy myself.

The moment I heard the laughter die and the applause begin, I knew Willie Tyler and his dummy Lester had finished their act, and within minutes we would be standing on that stage. I was reminded of our school concerts where Flo and I sang our opera solos; Willie Tyler and Lester were on those shows, too. It was so long ago. It felt funny to realize that though I was now, at twenty-five, more experienced, I still felt like the same little girl. I could hear the band—Gil Askey with Jimmy Garrett, Napoleon "Snaps" Allen, and drummer Curtis Kirk, who had replaced Bob Cousar and Bobby Jenkins. As I walked toward the backstage area, I felt looser than ever. This was it. Diane would be free to follow her own dreams, and I would be free to make the Supremes a real group again.

As we stood in the wings awaiting our cue, Diane and I just glanced at each other in silence. There were no "good-bye"s or "good luck"s; not even a hug. We could have done those things, but we both knew it would have been a farce. We had said our farewells long before this.

When the curtain went up, the roar of the crowd was so loud the floor vibrated under my feet like an electric charge. Though our arrangements were exactly the same, each note seemed to come zooming at me faster than ever. We started with a lengthy medley of hits, including "Stop! In the Name of Love," "Baby Love," "My World Is Empty Without You," "Come See About Me," "Love Is Here and Now You're Gone," and "I Hear a Symphony."

Diane did a bit of patter, then we sang a very suggestive version of "Hey Big Spender." I got my recent solo spot singing "Can't Take My Eyes Off You." I sang it with all my heart, thinking of Flo, and wishing she were there with us. Diane then did "I'm Gonna Make You Love Me," which she sang right to Berry, and he loved it. From this point on, she continued punctuating her performance with what one writer later described as "out and out hints about her close-guarded relationship with Berry Gordy."

I knew there would be no stopping Diane tonight, and I wasn't disappointed. She upstaged us, which was nothing new, but for the first time it didn't really matter, because this would be the last time. Throughout the show, she would step into the audience and sing to people. This was the only show we did where Diane got two solo spots. When she began "Didn't We," she almost broke down crying, and after the song she made a reference to the fact that Berry's family had "accepted" her. Her next song was another solo, the old torch song "My Man." Few people could guess how important this moment was to Diane. She was grateful to Berry—as we all were—and this performance was her way of saying thank you to him in front of the whole world.

When Diane got to "Aquarius/Let the Sunshine In," she walked around the audience, putting the microphone in front of people so that they could sing along. In the audience that night were Steve Allen, Jayne Meadows, Dick Clark, Lou Rawls, Bill Russell, Hugh O'Brian, Shirley Eder, and, of course, the Motown family, including Marvin Gaye and Smokey Robinson. Everyone screamed when Marvin got up to sing along. We had sung the chorus about fifty times before it finally ended. In the middle of it, Diane asked that our mothers stand up. My mother stood, then Cindy's, but Diane's was nowhere to be seen.

"Mother, where are you?" Diane cried out, looking crushed.

"She's probably trying to make it the hard way," someone at Berry's table called up, using a term familiar to anyone who plays craps. Everybody laughed, and Mrs. Ross later returned.

Finally the show was winding down. As the first chords of "Someday We'll Be Together" were played, Diane said, "We won't be together on stage as a team, but we'll always be together in our hearts." The three of us were teary. This was sad. For the finale, we sang "The Impossible Dream" to Berry. It was fitting.

After several standing ovations, the Frontier's entertainment director, Frank Sennes, presented us with a plaque from the hotel—the first for their Wall of Fame—and flowers. Diane's were said to be black roses from Berry. He read a telegram from Ed Sullivan and another from the mayor of Las Vegas; then he gave each of us a gold watch. The people at the Frontier had gone all out for this occasion. The room, which seated fifteen hundred, was packed to the rafters, and they had named drinks after us: Diana's Delight, Mary's Mystique, Cindy's Sin, and Jean's Jubilee.

At the end Diane brought Jean onstage and introduced her, touting her good looks and fine voice. She graciously conceded that the Supremes would go on without her. We received seemingly endless ovations. Then it was over.

Paul Block and the public-relations staff at Rogers and Cowan had really outdone themselves. The Frontier gave us a lavish party in their cabaret room which was attended by every celebrity in Vegas. There was also a large cake inscribed "Someday We'll Be Together." Right after we arrived at the reception the three of us and Berry and Pops Gordy sat together in a booth, toasting one another with champagne, while writers and photographers from around the world recorded every second of it. All the other Motown people came over and congratulated us, gave us hugs and kisses, and wished us the best of luck.

After a while, I quietly left the party to go to the tables. I loved gambling, and Margie and I spent a few hours there. I was being paged all the while we were gambling, but I just ignored it. I knew that they wanted me back at the party; there was probably more press or other celebrities on hand. Motown had worked overtime to make everything about the farewell and Diane's departure seem friendly, and I had cooperated. I was happy for Diane, but now I needed to be by myself, or at least with a real friend.

During the show Cindy was very excited and professional, and I had a ball, and reporters wrote about how I clowned around, and "teased Diana Ross, much like a sister would, toying with the spotlight —a demonstration of the girls' closeness." That the world still believed we were the best of friends seemed the perfect ending.

Margie and I went to my room with several bottles of champagne, and sat up until dawn, talking and laughing, toasting to happiness and freedom and true friendship. Every fifteen minutes, the phone would ring, and there'd be someone from Motown on the other end.

"Mary, why aren't you down here?"

"Because I'm in my room," I'd reply, giggling.

"Don't you want to come down here?"

"I'm having a party up here!" Then I'd hang up. Margie and I would laugh some more and then go back to our conversation.

When I couldn't keep my eyes open another minute, I crawled into bed, certain that I would sleep like a baby. Years of tension and stress had disappeared magically; tomorrow my career would be my own again, and a whole new chapter in the history of the Supremes would begin. I drifted off to sleep, feeling better than I had in months.

Just barely an hour later, the phone rang.

"Hello?" I mumbled into the receiver, which I couldn't even see. "Who is this?"

"Mary?" I knew it was Berry.

I couldn't believe my ears. He knew I slept late; what could he possibly want at this ungodly hour?

"What?"

Berry spoke briefly about the farewell celebration, then he dropped the bomb:

"I don't like Jean Terrell," he proclaimed.

"What are you talking about?" I had to be dreaming.

"I want to replace her with Syreeta Wright."

We'd been over all this already. Jean was in; she had been introduced to the world last night as the new Supreme. Was he mad? I had noticed that Berry was having a harder time getting Jean to follow his directions to the letter than he'd ever had with Diane, but he was in love with Diane. I didn't think Jean's attitude was that big a problem, and besides, I would be dealing with her more than Berry would anyway. What was wrong with him?

All I knew was that I couldn't let him get away with this. Our first single was set for release; the Supremes were what had kept me there all these years. Berry wasn't going to ruin it now.

"Mary, do you hear me?" Berry asked when I was silent for a minute. "I want to replace Jean with Syreeta."

"No!"

"All right," Berry replied. "Then I wash my hands of the group."

Berry hung up, and I decided that the Supremes were going to work. I'd make it happen.

EPILOGUE

Despite Berry's lack of interest in our career, the Supremes went on to have several more major hit records—"Up the Ladder to the Roof," "Stoned Love," "River Deep, Mountain High" (with the Four Tops), "Nathan Jones," and "Floy Joy." Cindy left the group in 1972 and was replaced by Lynda Lawrence. The next year, when Lynda and Jean decided to quit the Supremes, Cindy returned and Scherrie Payne (Freda's sister) took over the lead spot. When Cindy left for the second time, in 1976, Susaye Green stepped in. Finally, in 1977, the Supremes were officially disbanded.

Through the years, Flo and I kept in touch. I was living in Los Angeles with my husband, Pedro Ferrer, and touring the world with the Supremes, so I rarely saw her. We talked on the phone, and my cousin Josephine, who lived in my old house on Buena Vista, saw Flo often.

After her twins were born in November 1968, Flo did a few college dates and made a couple of television appearances, but her career hadn't really taken off. One of the last good moments was her performance at one of President Nixon's inaugural functions in January 1969. After that, things went downhill.

Though he loved her very much and gave it his best effort, Tommy Chapman didn't have the experience or the knowledge to guide Flo's career. After working with Berry for a while, he had surmised that there was nothing to it, and Flo had taken part of her settlement money from Motown and set Tommy up in his own management company, Talent Management, Inc. Cholly Atkins and arranger Fred Norman helped Flo put together an act. She was willing to play smaller venues, just to get her confidence back and to get used to working again. Though there was no way she could have been booked into the same places the Supremes had played, Flo should have been working small but classy establishments, not the little bar and grills Tommy booked for her. In some places, the bands were so bad that they could not read music, and one night in Atlantic City Flo was forced to sing tunes she had never sung before just because it was all the band there knew. Word around was that Tommy also made outrageous demands of ABC Records, which were not well received.

Flo was no fool, and certainly she saw that Tommy was nót qualified for the task, but it was too late. That March her attorney, Leonard Baun, informed her that all of her funds—the $160,000 settlement from Motown plus Flo's other assets—were exhausted. Flo was stunned by the news and would spend the next year, with the help of her brother Billy, trying to find another attorney to take her case against Baun. In the press, Baun called her charges that he had mismanaged her funds "ridiculous," then added, "She will be flat broke after she pays her taxes." Years later, Baun would be disbarred. Until then, no local or state government official Flo or Billy contacted about the case would touch it.

When Flo was with the Supremes, we would sing "You're Nobody till Somebody Loves You." When Diane sang the line, "Gold won't bring you happiness . . .," Flo would break in and quip, "Now, wait a minute, honey. I don't know about that." When I later read interviews with Flo, where she said, "One day you're on top of the world and the next day you're broke," that line came back to me.

By mid-1969, Flo was worse than broke; she had gained more weight and become so depressed by her situation that she refused to leave the house. She continued in this state for some time. In early 1971, she filed an $8.7 million lawsuit against Motown and the Supremes, alleging that in late 1967 Diane had "secretly, subversively, and maliciously" plotted to oust her. She also revealed that while she was in the Supremes she had received a $225 weekly allowance and had never seen an accounting of the Supremes' income. (I had never seen an accounting either.) Based on this lack of information, she requested that her earlier agreement with Motown—which forbade her to bring future suits against anyone or anything related to the Supremes or Motown, and in which she signed away her rights to any future income from the Supremes, such as royalties from records she sang on—be declared nonbinding. In 1973, the case would be thrown out of court.

She had also instituted another suit against Leonard Baun, charging him with gross negligence, malpractice and breach of fiduciary duties and obligations." No one in Flo's family is sure when or if she ever received any kind of settlement from this suit.

Flo had always been a fighter, but that never made the fighting any easier. Flo had given birth to her third daughter, Lisa, in 1971. My cousin Josephine often called me in L.A. to tell me how Flo was doing. She would bring her daughters over to visit Josephine almost every day. She and Jo would sit around chatting and drinking beer. Sometimes Jo would have to help Flo get home, then she would keep the girls until Flo sobered up.

After the management firm went under, Tommy went to work as a road manager for a recording group, then as a chauffeur for a local minister. In order to keep her house, Flo pawned her jewelry and other valuables, but finally she was notified by the bank that foreclosure was imminent. Flo went to another recording artist, who agreed to lend her $700. When she went to the artist's business office to pick up the money, she was told to sign an agreement outlining the method and amount of the repayment and several blank sheets of papers. Flo wisely refused, but the decision cost her the house.

"Why my house?" she would cry to friends. "Why couldn't I at least keep my house?"

Our houses were more than just homes; they were the symbols of our success, and owning a home meant that you were secure, or so we all thought. During this time, Flo and Tommy separated. At first he provided child support. No matter what happened between them, Flo always defended Tommy; she still loved him very much. After she lost the house, she and her three children moved into a two-family apartment with her mother and sister Pat. When Tommy stopped sending support money, Flo's sister convinced her to apply for Aid to Families with Dependent Children. Flo finally went. Later she said of the experience, "Being a star, going there would mean I'd reached the bottom. But the children are important. I had to think about the children."

Flo always felt responsible for everyone, and this was no doubt a contributing factor to her problems. When we were making money, she would instruct Taylor Cox to send money to members of her family from her account. Over the years, she took great pleasure in helping her family, and there seemed to be no end to their requests. She could never say no, and so withdrew far more money from her account than either Diane or I. Taylor Cox, who worked at ITM, would keep us up to date on our accounts. Word of Flo's financial plight didn't reach me until she had lost the house. She never asked for help.

One of the few people outside her family that she confided in was Maye Atkins, Cholly's wife. Cholly and Maye were still living in the other half of my house on Buena Vista, so they saw Flo often. Flo had gotten up to around two hundred pounds. Though she had lost most of everything else she owned, she held on to the Cadillac. When her kids were asleep at night, she would make herself up, put on what was left of her finery, and drive around Detroit for hours, singing along to tapes in the car. Many nights she would go to her old house on Buena Vista, which had not been resold and was boarded up and vacant. She soon lost the car, too, but she made regular pilgrimages to the house, often with her three children in tow.

One day before Christmas 1974, Maye saw Flo and the three girls standing in the snow outside the old house. She went out and asked Flo to come in. When Maye asked her what she was doing, bringing three little ones out in such bad weather, Flo couldn't give a coherent answer.

"I don't have anything for Christmas for my kids," Flo said. "You know, that's a shame, Maye. After all the money I made. I was a big star, and here I can't even afford a few gifts for my kids this year. When Christmas comes, I might be in heaven with my children."

Maye was alarmed by Flo's last statement. When some friends of the Atkinses dropped by, Maye asked them to give Flo and the girls a ride home. Flo agreed to go, but once she'd got into the car, she demanded to be let out. The couple gave Flo cab fare, but when Maye looked out again, Flo was sitting on the porch of her house.

Maye decided to make Flo's plight known, in the hopes that public interest might spur Flo to pull herself together. Maye told the story to a reporter from the *Detroit Free Press* on the condition that she remain anonymous and that Flo be treated with dignity. The next day the story was on the front page. *The Washington Post* picked up the story and sent two writers to Detroit to get an exclusive interview. Days later, the story of the ex-Supreme living in poverty was all over the wire services.

The story did what Maye hoped it would. Fan mail poured in from all around the world, Flo was asked to appear on several talk shows, and there were rumors that Flo had been offered a role in a Broadway play. A local day-care center wanted to employ Flo for $85 a week, and a New York club called the Riverboat wanted her to play there. Flo considered taking the day-care job but refused to perform. She was afraid.

In June 1975 she made her final concert appearance in Detroit at a benefit for Joann Little, a black female prisoner who was charged with killing a prison guard who allegedly had raped her. Also on the bill were comedienne Lily Tomlin and the feminist rock group Deadly Nightshade. Flo received a standing ovation. It was so obvious that the public loved her. Yet that just wasn't enough.

In August 1975 Flo came to visit me at my home in Los Angeles. We both felt it would be a good change for her. I knew of her performance in Detroit, and I set out to convince her during her stay that she should be singing. She helped me prepare a birthday party for my husband and never let my daughter Turkessa who was then four months old, out of her sight.

One night while she was there, Cindy Birdsong, Scherrie Payne, and I were playing Magic Mountain. Just before the last number, I said, "Ladies and gentlemen, I have a surprise guest—Miss Florence Ballard!"

The audience went crazy. Cries of "Flo, we love you!" went on for minutes. It had been eight years since Flo had stood onstage as a Supreme, and her fans' devotion was stronger than ever. Flo and I were teary-eyed, and I could see that Scherrie and Susaye were also moved. Even though she did not sing with us, I hoped this would show her how much the fans still cared. As we walked backstage, I could sense Flo's excitement. I decided then that I would tell Flo how I felt, no matter how much it hurt.

It was a very hot night, and we drove back to my house in silence. Once we got inside, I tried to express my feelings. We were sipping wine and had wound down from all the excitement.

"Flo, you see they love you. You can sing again."

"But, Mary, you just don't know."

"Girl, get yourself together. Florence, you are one of the finest singers I have ever known. Do whatever you have to do to get some work and maybe a record deal. At least try, Flo," I pleaded.

"I can't, Mary," she replied. "There's nothing I can do about it."

My plan had backfired; it seemed that the longer I talked, the more depressed Flo became. When we'd first arrived home, Flo seemed happy, but after a couple of drinks she was the saddest person I had ever seen.

"Flo," I said slowly, "you have got to do it. You love to sing, and you see the fans love you. You only need to find the right producer and some good songs. Flo, dreams don't just die—people can change them."

I believed in what I was saying, but when I looked into Flo's eyes, I could see that she didn't. There was no hope left in her, and for a moment I felt that my friend was gone, far, far away. She just looked up at me, like a child who'd been beaten. "Mary, leave me alone. Don't you realize that it's over? I don't want to do it anymore. Just leave me alone."

I wanted to shake her and scream, "Wake up, Flo!" I became angry with her for falling to pieces. "It's time for us to go to bed," I said.

"I don't want to go to bed!" Flo was like a stubborn child.

"Flo, if you break anything, I'm going to be upset." She could barely walk. "Suppose you were like this and you were alone with your children? What if you were at home and you accidentally started a fire? How are you going to help yourself or your children? Look at yourself, Flo!"

"Now, you see?" she cried. "You see?"

Flo went back to Detroit a couple of days later, and I didn't see her until Thanksgiving. When Flo heard that I was holding a family reunion in Detroit she knew she would be welcome. Everyone knew of her problems, but she maintained her dignity, always smiling and happy—the old Flo. That was the last time I ever saw her.

Sometime in late 1975, Flo received a large settlement from a lawsuit, mostly likely one she brought against the owners of a property where she had fallen on the ice and broken her leg the year before. Wherever it came from wasn't important. Flo and Tommy were back together, she bought a new house, and paid cash for a brand-new Cadillac. This seemed to be her second chance. Several people who knew her said that the minute she got the money, she went back into her "Supremes bag," by which they meant that she started taking care of herself again.

In 1975 Cholly and Maye moved to Las Vegas, where Cholly choreographed shows for the stars. Neither of the Atkinses had heard from Flo for months, when one night in February 1976, she phoned. It sounded to Maye as if Flo had been drinking, and all Flo seemed to want to talk about was the old days.

"Why did Diane have to act that way?" Flo asked Maye over and over. Flo had never got over that, and Maye just listened. Then Flo said, "Maye, I don't feel so well. I have a pain in my chest."

"Flo, baby," Maye replied, "you'd better get to the hospital."

"No," Flo said, acting as if it was no big deal, "I'll be all right." Then she hung up.

Five minutes later, Maye's phone rang. It was Flo. This time she wanted to talk about me and my mother.

"After they put me out," Flo said, "Mary was the only one who stuck by me." Then Flo started to ramble on, sometimes incoherently. Maye began to worry.

"Flo, honey," Maye said, "why don't you go to the hospital?"

"Yeah. Okay. Maybe." Then the line went dead.

A few minutes later, Flo called again.

"Thanks, Maye."

"Thanks? For what, Flo?"

"I know you called the *Detroit Free Press* about me."

"Now, why would I do that, Flo?"

"Because nobody else in Detroit cared enough about me, except you, Maye."

Flo hung up again. The more Maye thought about what Flo had said, the more worried she became. She decided to call Flo and see that she was okay, but then she realized that she didn't have Flo's new number.

At 3:30 A.M. on Saturday, February 21, Flo called her mother and told her she was experiencing shortness of breath. "Mama, if anything happens to me, I want you to keep the children," Flo said.

"Oh, baby, nothing is going to happen to you."

During the night, though, Flo seemed to get worse, and her daughter Nicole called Flo's sister Maxine to tell her that something was wrong. Maxine and some of Flo's other siblings dismissed Nicole's calls as another one of Flo's attempts to get attention. Tommy was at work, and Maxine's car wasn't running. She promised to come over first thing in the morning and check up on Flo then.

Years later Maxine said she had had a premonition of Flo's death. Two weeks earlier, Flo was visiting Maxine and her mother. The whole time she was there, she drank glass after glass of water.

"Why do you keep drinking so much water?" Mrs. Ballard asked.

"I'm hot inside," Flo replied. "I can't get rid of this hot feeling."

Flo had high blood pressure and was taking medication for that and more medication to lose weight, and her family might have assumed that her various aches and pains were caused by that.

When Maxine got to Flo's the next day, she found her lying on the floor, unable to move. She was paralyzed from the waist down and could barely speak. When she did, the words sounded like a mechanical whisper. Maxine and Flo's daughters managed to get her on a couch, and Maxine called an ambulance.

Flo was rushed to Mount Carmel Mercy Hospital, where she died the next morning of a heart attack, the result of a blood clot in a coronary artery.

I was at my assistant Hazel Bethke's house in Glendale, California, with Scherrie Payne and Susaye Green, picking out old Supremes gowns to take on tour. Hazel came into the storage room and said, "Mary, your mother just called. She said Flo passed away."

I couldn't move. All I could say was, "I knew it, I knew it," and cry.

My husband, relatives, and friends helped me pack for the trip to Detroit. Hazel took care of my travel arrangements. All I could think about was Flo and how much I loved her.

Once I got to my old house on Buena Vista, I had the comfort of my family, all of whom had known Flo for years. I called Flo's family and spoke with some of her sisters. Everyone was in shock; it had all happened so suddenly, and just when Flo seemed to be getting herself back together. Maybe she never would have sung again, but at least she could have been happy. Only then did I realize that simply being happy in life was more than enough.

Jesse Greer had married my friend Diane Watson, the girl I had wanted to replace Barbara Martin in the Primettes. Jesse and Diane drove me to the funeral home to view Florence the night before the funeral. Winnie Brown, our former hairdresser and Flo's niece and good friend, did Flo's makeup and hair. Flo was dressed in a flowing, light-blue robe. They had positioned her so that she appeared to be almost sitting up, and when I first saw her I was surprised at how heavy she was. Still, she was beautiful.

There were crowds surrounding the funeral home, and when we arrived and I was recognized, people started banging on the car. I was in the backseat with Diane Greer and could see people trying to get my attention. Inside, and outside the home, I heard people talking, blaming Diane and Berry for Flo's death. Though Flo had played along with Motown's version of her departure, things were out in the open after the 1971 lawsuit. But still no one really knew the full truth. Flo was the tragic heroine; I guess people had to find a villain.

The next day I was driven to the New Bethel Baptist Church in a Rolls-Royce. I never knew for sure who supplied the classic cars used in the funeral procession. My mother, my sister Cathy, and Diane Greer accompanied me. As we neared the church, we saw thousands of people lining the sidewalks. Policemen did all they could to keep the crowds back, but it was near impossible. Earlier that day, I had met with Flo's family. It had taken all I had not to break down in front of her three girls, but here, I knew this was the last time I would ever see Flo. I just wanted to be alone with her, but I knew that I would not be.

I spotted dozens of people I had known from the Projects and school. When Motown had moved to Los Angeles in 1975, part of Detroit had died. Today, though, the city was alive for one more day. People had started lining up in front of the church before dawn. Some of the mourners wore mink coats and evening gowns, while others were in housedresses and tattered streetclothes. There were over five thousand people standing outside when I got to the church. The police were trying to hold the crowd back, but every time a celebrity stepped out of a car, someone would shout, "Here comes somebody!" and bodies would press forward. When we arrived, we were asked to stand with Flo's family and my family in the line of mourners entering the church. A few minutes later, a limousine pulled up next to the church steps and Diane jumped out, flanked by four bodyguards. The crowd booed her, and I saw the pain on Mrs. Ross's face as she stood in the line with us. Diane looked stunning, and I watched as she was quickly ushered in. She came down the center aisle of the church, and people were pushing and shoving to get a glimpse of her; the scene caused quite a commotion. Diane was seated in front next to Tommy and Flo's mother and held Flo's youngest girl, Lisa, in her lap.

When I got in a few moments later, the first thing I was struck by were the floral arrangements. Every act from Motown had sent one, as had Berry. Diane's said, "I Love You, Blondie." I took my seat a few rows back from Flo's family, but this wasn't like any funeral I had ever attended before. The crowd was wild, and there were flashbulbs popping every other second.

Reverend Franklin nearly lost his patience, asking people to sit down, be quiet, and show some respect for the dead. I was listening but thinking about Flo. For some strange reason I recalled this gorgeous white fox stole Flo had. She knew that I loved it, so whenever she wore it I'd always say, "Flo, if you ever die, will me that coat, honey." And then we'd laugh. Why was I thinking about this now? Because I never thought Flo would ever die.

Right after the reverend finished, Diane jumped up and said, "Can I have the microphone, please!" Then she said, "Mary and I would like to have a silent prayer."

At first, I was stunned, then shocked. Diane and I hadn't spoken to each other in months. I was furious that I was being dragged into this. My grief was personal and private. I didn't want to get up, but I was so taken aback by Diane's words that I felt I had no choice. Declining would have made a bad situation worse. There were things I wanted to say, but to Flo, by myself. But I got up and stood beside Diane, who said, "I believe nothing disappears, and Flo will always be with us." Then she handed me the mike. "I loved her very much," was all I could say. Diane and I walked past Flo's coffin, and I looked down at Flo and gently touched her cheek. She looked so pretty.

As we filed out, the organist played "Someday We'll Be Together" —a Supremes hit neither Flo nor I had sung on—over and over. We got into our cars to go to Detroit Memorial Park for the burial. The pallbearers—Duke Fakir, Obie Benson, Levi Stubbs, Lawrence Payton, Marv Johnson, and Thearon Hill (Stevie Wonder was an honorary pallbearer)—had to be ushered out by attendants. At the sight of Flo's coffin, the crowd got even wilder, and in an attempt to keep onlookers away from the coffin, all of her floral arrangements were thrown out to the mob. Within minutes, the only proof that the flowers had ever existed were the bare wire and Styrofoam frames left lying on the sidewalk.

When we reached the cemetery, it was just Flo's family, the pallbearers, the Four Tops, and me. After Flo's body was lowered into the ground, everyone made their way back to the cars. This was it. Suddenly I realized that Diane wasn't there. Regardless of what had passed between us, we were the only two people who had shared Flo's greatest moments. For that reason alone, Diane should have been there. But she was gone.

A wind blew through the cemetery, and in just a few moments a thousand thoughts came to me. How did three talented little girls come to this? What turn of fate made one friend a household name, while the other struggled for years in poverty? When did our dream die? And what else could I have done to help Flo? I thought back to the night after Magic Mountain, when I looked into Flo's eyes and realized that she was beyond all of this now. There probably weren't any answers to my questions, and if there were, they came too late.

I finally threw my flower down on Flo's coffin.

"Don't worry, Flo," I said aloud, because I knew she could hear me, "I'll take care of it." Then I repeated one of Flo's favorite lines from our happy days: "Honey, we is terrific."

APPENDIX I:

A SUPREMES ITINERARY

Here are some of the highlights of our career, as compiled from my personal diaries and scrapbooks. Asterisks indicate information that is missing or unknown. All chart positions are from *Billboard* magazine.

1961

January 15	The Supremes sign with Motown.
March 3	"I Want a Guy" backed with "Never Again" released (recorded late 1960).
July 21	"Buttered Popcorn" backed with "Who's Loving You" released.
September*	Recorded "Those DJ Songs" (on *25th Anniversary*, 1986).

1962

May 8	"Your Heart Belongs to Me" (recorded December 1961) backed with "He's Seventeen" (recorded August 14, 1961) released, #95.
November 5	"Let Me Go the Right Way" (recorded August 30, 1962) backed with "Time Changes Things" released, #90.

1963

February 2	"My Heart Can't Take It No More" backed with "You Bring Back Memories" released.
June 12	"A Breath Taking Guy" backed with "(The Man with) the Rock and Roll Banjo Band" released, #75.
July*	Recorded "Come On Boy" (on *25th Anniversary*, 1986).
October 31	"When the Lovelight Starts Shining Through His Eyes" backed with "Standing at the Crossroads of Love" released (recorded October 1963), #23.
December*	*Meet the Supremes* released.

1964

*	Recorded "Penny Pincher" (on *25th Anniversary*, 1986).
February 7	"Run, Run, Run" backed with "I'm Giving You Your Freedom" released, #93.
May*	Recorded "Send Me No Flowers" (on *25th Anniversary*, 1986).
June 17	"Where Did Our Love Go" released (recorded April 8, 1964), #1.
July 3	Recorded "With All My Heart" (unreleased).
July 6	Recorded "The Truth Does Hurt" (unreleased).
July 24	Recorded "In His Eyes" (unreleased).
August 13	Recorded "Darling Baby" (unreleased).
August 17	Recorded *Live! Live! Live!* (unreleased).
August 18	Recorded "Ooowee Baby," released on *The Supremes 25th Anniversary* (1986).
August 20	Recorded "Put Yourself in My Place" (released on *A Go-Go*, 1966) and "Across the Road" (unreleased).
August 31*	*Where Did Our Love Go* released, #2.

Summer	Dick Clark's Caravan of Stars tour with Gene Pitney, Brenda Holloway, and others.
September 17	"Baby Love" released (recorded August 13, 1964), #6.
September 12–21	Brooklyn Fox Theatre, New York, New York, with Dusty Springfield, the Shangri-Las, the Temptations, Jay and the Americans, the Contours, the Ronettes, Martha and the Vandellas, Little Anthony and the Imperials, Marvin Gaye, the Miracles, Millie Small.
September 29	Recorded "Blue Memories" (unreleased).
October 7	Leave Detroit for English promotional tour.
October 15	Met Ringo Starr and Paul McCartney at the Ad Lib Club, Birmingham, England.
October 24	Filmed *The T.A.M.I. (Teenage Awards Music International) Show*, Santa Monica Civic Center, California (filmed in electronovision) with the Beach Boys, Chuck Berry, James Brown, Marvin Gaye, Gerry and the Pacemakers, Lesley Gore, Billy J. Kramer, the Miracles, the Rolling Stones, hosted by Jan and Dean. Released 1985, Media Home Video.
October 27	"Come See About Me" released (recorded July 13, 1965), #1.
November	*A Bit of Liverpool* released, #21.
November 14	Dick Clark tour, Holy Cross College, Worchester, Maine.
November 24	Recorded "The Only Time I'm Happy" and "Who Could Ever Doubt My Love" (on *More Hits by the Supremes*, 1965).
December 1	Recorded "I'm in Love Again" (on *More Hits*, 1965).
December 12	Recorded "Bikini Party" (unreleased).
December 16	Recorded "Take Me Where You Go" (on *From the Vaults*, 1979, 1982).
December 24	Rehearsal for *The Ed Sullivan Show* (CBS) *The T.A.M.I. Show* movie shown in Michigan Theatre.

December 25	Motown Revue, Brooklyn Fox Theatre, New York, with Marvin Gaye, the Miracles, the Marvelettes, Stevie Wonder, the Temptations.
December 27	First appearance on *The Ed Sullivan Show* (CBS), performed "Come See About Me."

1965

January 8	Recorded "I Just Want to Make You Happy" (unreleased).
January 11	Rerecorded "Take Me Where You Go" (unreleased).
January 11/13	In England *New Musical Express'* readers voted the Supremes the #3 group; *Music Business Magazine* names them the #1 female group.
January 18	Recorded "You've Been a Long Time Coming" (unreleased).
January 25 or 26	*Hullabaloo* (NBC).
February 2	"Battle of the Stars," recorded 3 sides live (unreleased).
February 8	"Stop! In the Name of Love" released, (recorded January 5, 1965), #1.
February 17	Recorded "Big City Babies Don't Cry" and "Fancy Passes" (unreleased cuts).
February	Nominated for Grammy Award for best R&B Vocal Performances, "Baby Love."
February 18	Filmed *Go-Go*, in Palm Springs, California; a Dick Clark production.
February 23	Recorded "There's No Love Left" and "It's All Your Fault" (on *25th Anniversary*, 1986).
February 27	*The Hollywood Palace* (ABC).
March	*Country, Western and Pop* released (recorded February 6, 17, and 26, 1963), #79. Recorded "Sleepwalk" (on *25th Anniversary*, 1986).

March 3	Recorded "Rock-A-Bye Your Baby," "You're Nobody 'til Somebody Loves You," "Little Miss Loser," and "Something for My Heart" (for unreleased *There's a Place for Us* LP).
March 12 to mid-April	Motown Revue in Europe with the Temptations, the Miracles, Martha and the Vandellas, Stevie Wonder.
March 18	Motown Revue taped *The Sound of Motown*, BBC special, London, England. Hosted by Dusty Springfield, air date April 21. Released on Sony Video, 1985.
March 21	Winter Gardens, Bournemouth, England.
March 26	The Venue ABC, Kingston on Thames, England (Motown Revue first U.K. visit), with Martha and the Vandellas, Stevie Wonder, the Miracles, Earl Van Dyke.
March 30	Manchester, England.
April	*We Remember Sam Cooke* released, #75; *Elegant Teen* cover story "Supreme Supremes."
April 1	Recorded "Love is like a Heat Wave" (on *The Supremes Sing Holland-Dozier-Holland*, 1967).
April 15	"Back in My Arms Again" released (recorded December 1, 1964), #1.
April 19	Recorded "He's All I Got" (on *I Hear A Symphony*, 1966).
April 21	"The Sound of Motown," BBC special airs in England.
April 27	Rerecorded "Put Yourself in My Place" (on *A Go-Go*, 1966).
May*	Steele Pier Memorial Day show this month. Recorded a tribute to Berry Gordy, "We Couldn't Get Along Without You" (special lyrics to "My World Is Empty Without You," on *25th Anniversary*, 1986).
May 2	Leave for New York to tape *Hullabaloo* (NBC).

May 7	Recorded "It's the Same Old Song" (on *The Supremes Sing Holland-Dozier-Holland*, 1967).
May 12	Recorded two Coca-Cola commercial themes ("Baby Love" and "When the Lovelight Starts Shining Through His Eyes" variations).
May 21	*Time* Magazine cover story with other pop artists.
May 25	Recorded "Love You Forever" (unreleased).
June	Cover of *Ebony* Magazine.
June 2	Recorded "Mother Dear" (on *More Hits*, 1966).
June 10–11	Taping President Lyndon Johnson's "War on Poverty" special, CBS Greenfield Village.
June 16	Rerecorded "Fancy Passes"; recorded "Sincerely" and "Mr. Sandman" (unreleased).
June 25	Recorded "Don't Let True Love Die" (unreleased).
June 28	"It's What's Happening Baby," special (CBS) with Johnny Mathis, the Temptations, Martha and the Vandellas, Marvin Gaye, the Miracles, airs.
June 28	"War on Poverty," special (CBS) airs.
July	*More Hits by the Supremes* released, #6.
July 7	Recorded "Too Much a Little Too Soon" (unrecorded).
July 16	"Nothing but Heartaches" released (recorded May 13, 1966), #11.
July 21	Tape *Jackie Gleason Summer Show with Al Hirt*.
July 24	*Al Hirt Show* airs (CBS).
July 28	*The Tonight Show* (NBC).
July 29*	Copacabana debut, New York, New York, recorded *Live at the Copa*.
August	Bill Billikin Parade, Chicago, Illinois.
	Recorded "Things are Changing" (NARA's equal-opportunity campaign song, produced by Phil Spector).

August 27– September 9	The Michigan State Fair.
August 29	*The Dean Martin Show* (NBC).
September	Motown announces that the group is booked through September 1966 (at Flamingo Hotel, Las Vegas, Nevada—rumors that this would be Diana's last engagement with group).
September 2	Rerecorded "Mother Dear" (possibly for single release, cut already on *More Hits*).
September 10	JFK Stadium, Philadelphia, Pennsylvania.
September 13	*Hullabaloo* (NBC).
September 14	Recorded "Noel" (on *Merry Christmas*, 1965).
September 17–26	Safari Room, San Jose, California.
September 30– October 8	European tour.
October	*The Steve Allen Show*.
October 2	Holland's Grand Gala du Disque Festival, Amsterdam.
October 6	"I Hear a Symphony" released (recorded September 22, 1966), #1.
October 7	*Tops of the Pops*, Manchester, England.
October 8	*Ready, Steady, Go!*, London, England.
October 9	*Michigan Chronicle* announces a tour of Vietnam that will run from January 6 to January 22, 1966, with the Four Tops. (Later cancelled.)
October 10	*The Ed Sullivan Show* (CBS), performed "I Hear a Symphony" and "You're Nobody 'til Somebody Loves You."
October 13	Sybil Burton's "Very, Very In," Arthur's, New York, New York.
October 15	Lincoln Center, New York, New York, with the Spinners.
October 18	*Hullabaloo* (NBC).
October 20–25	Boston.
October 27	Recorded "Heaven Must Have Sent You" (unreleased).
October 28– November 3	Latin Quarter, Philadelphia, Pennsylvania.

November	*Live at the Copa*, #11, and *Merry Christmas* released.
November 3	Recorded "Here I Am Alone in Life" (unreleased).
November 7–14	Oklahoma.
November 14	Oklahoma State Fair arena, with the Lovin' Spoonful.
November 14	USO a Go-Go Benefit, Madison Square Garden, New York, New York, with Sammy Davis, Jr., Joan Crawford, Carroll Baker, Johnny Carson, Robert Vaughan.
November 15–16	Recorded *I Hear a Symphony*, Los Angeles, California.
November 18	Dean Martin special (NBC).
November 24	Recorded "(I Know) I'm Losing You" (unreleased).
November 29	Motortown Revue recorded live at Musicorama, Olympia Music Hall, Paris, France, with the Miracles, Martha and the Vandellas, and Stevie Wonder.
December 3	University of Bridgeport winter formal.
December 4–11	Twin Coaches, Pittsburgh, Pennsylvania.
December 6	*Hullabaloo* (NBC).
December 13	*Hullabaloo* (NBC).
December 15	*Where the Action Is* (ABC).
December 16–18	Houston.
December 16	Shamrock Hilton DJ party, Houston, Texas.
December 17	Went Christmas shopping.
December 17	Tape Larry King Show (air date December 18) performed "I Hear a Symphony."
December 17	Opening of the Astrodome, Houston, Texas, with Judy Garland.
December 18	*Larry Kane Show*, performed "I Hear a Symphony."
December 23– January 1, 1966	Pompeii Room, Eden Roc Hotel, Miami, Florida, with Jack E. Leonard.
December 29	"My World Is Empty Without You" released, #5.
December 31	Orange Bowl Parade.

1966

January 9	*The Ed Sullivan Show* (CBS).
January 17–29	Roostertail, Detroit, Michigan.
January 19	Rerecorded "Mother Dear" (possibly for single release, already on *More Hits*).
January 25	*The Red Skelton Show* (CBS).
January 25	Tape Washington Hilton Grand Ballroom performance; CBS to televise gala party.
January 30	Leave for San Juan, El San Juan Hotel.
February	Nominated for Grammy Award for Best Group Vocal Performance, "Stop! In the Name of Love."
February 5	Civic Arena, Pittsburgh, Pennsylvania.
February 9–28*	Tour of West Germany and Scandinavia.
February 11	Recorded "He" (on *We Remember*).
February 12	Holy Cross College, Mount St. James Field House, Massachusetts.
February 12 and/or February 13	Waltham-Branden University, Massachusetts.
February 15	"Anatomy of Pop: The Music Explosion," special (ABC), performed "My World Is Empty Without You."
February 17*	Open at the Copacabana, New York, New York.
February 18	*I Hear a Symphony* released, #8.
February 20	*The Ed Sullivan Show* (CBS), performed "My World Is Empty Without You" and "Somewhere."
February 27	"Anatomy of Pop," rerun as ABC Sunday afternoon special.
March	*What's My Line?* Recorded "Who Can I Turn To" (on *25th Anniversary*, 1986).
March 3–16	Copacabana, New York, New York.
March 4	*Time* Magazine article.
March 4	*The Sammy Davis Show* (NBC), with the Andrews Sisters.

March 11–12*	Recorded in Los Angeles, California, "On a Clear Day You Can See Forever," "The Wheels of the City" (all unreleased), and "Blowin' in the Wind" (on *Cream of the Crop*, 1969).
March 17	Recorded "One Way Out" (unreleased).
March 17	*The Dean Martin Show* (NBC).
March 22–April 3	Blinstraub's, Boston, Massachusetts.
March 23	Recorded two sides for *The Supremes Sing Holland-Dozier-Holland*.
March 24	*The Dean Martin Show* (NBC).
March 24	Supremes White Bread on the market.
April	Press conference at Roostertail, Detroit, Michigan.
April 8	"Love Is like an Itching in My Heart" released, #9.
April 13	Recorded "Deep Inside" (unreleased).
April 19	Recorded "Until You Love Someone" (unreleased).
May	*Look* Magazine.
May 1	*The Ed Sullivan Show* (CBS), performed "Love Is Like an Itching in My Heart."
May 19–June 8	Fairmont Hotel, San Francisco, California.
June 1	Recorded "Together Again" (unreleased).
June 2	Recorded "Hurtin' Again" and "It's Summer" (unreleased).
June 11	Recorded "Hurtin' Bad" (unreleased).
June 14	Recorded/rerecorded five *Holland-Dozier-Holland* sides and "Baby I Need Your Loving" (on *A Go-Go*, 1966).
June 15	Rerecorded "Baby I Need Your Loving" (on *A Go-Go*, 1966).
June 20–25	O'Keefe Center, Toronto, Canada.
June 28	Recorded "Moment of Weakness" (unreleased).
June 30	*The Today Show* (NBC).
June 30	Recorded "Misery Makes Its Home in My Heart" (on *Reflections*, 1968).
July 1	Recorded "Many Good Times," "Mother Tell Me What to Do," "Just a Little

July 1 (*cont.*)	Misunderstanding" (all unreleased), "What Becomes of the Brokenhearted" (on *Let the Sunshine In*, 1969), and "Come On and See Me" (on *25th Anniversary*, 1986).
July 7	*The Mike Douglas Show*, with the Temptations.*
July 8	Recorded "With a Child's Heart" (on *Let the Sunshine In*, 1969).
July 9	Rerecorded "Put Yourself in My Place" (on *A Go-Go*, 1966).
July 11	Recorded "Just a Smile Away" (unreleased).
July 16	Recorded "Here Are the Pieces of My Broken Heart" (unreleased).
July 20	Co-host *The Mike Douglas Show*.
July 24–30	Steele Pier, Atlantic City, New Jersey.
July 24	*The Ed Sullivan Show* (CBS).
July 25	"You Can't Hurry Love" released, #1.
August	17 Magazine. Music Circus, Lambertville, New Jersey. Colonie Summer Theatre, Lathan, New York. Recorded "If I Ruled the World" (on *25th Anniversary*, 1986).
August 9–14	Circle Star Theatre, San Carlos, California.
August 11	Recorded in Los Angeles, California, seven unreleased sides including "The Sound of Music," "If I Ruled the World," (on *25th Anniversary*, 1986), "I've Been Blessed," "Tender Is the Night." Also recorded "Love (Makes Me Do Foolish Things)" (on *Reflections*, 1968).
August 10–16	Rehearsal/taping "Rodgers and Hart Today" special (ABC) Los Angeles, California.
August 18	*The Tonight Show* (NBC).
August 19	Civic Center, Virginia Beach, Virginia.
August 20	Forest Hills Tennis Stadium, Forest Hills, New York, with the Temptations and Stevie Wonder.
August 25	*A Go-Go* released, #1.
August 26–30	State Fair, St. Paul, Michigan.
September	In Los Angeles this month to tape "Rodgers and Hart Today." Mary and Florence visit

September (*cont.*)	the Temptations at The Trip, Los Angeles, California.
September 2	Arrive in Tokyo.
September 3–22	The Far East Tour: Tokyo, Okinawa, Taiwan, Hong Kong, Manila, Philippines.
September *	Yokosukso Naval Base, USS *Coral* (4,000 men).
September 14	Leave for Manila.
September 15	*Soul* Magazine cover story "Surprises from the Supremes."
September 23–25	*The Ed Sullivan Show* (CBS), performed "You Can't Hurry Love."
September 25	Recorded live LP (unreleased) at Roostertail, Detroit, Michigan.
September 29– October 19	Flamingo Hotel, Las Vegas, Nevada.
October	Recorded "Manhattan" and "The Blue Room" (on *25th Anniversary*, 1986).
October 12	"You Keep Me Hangin' On" released (recorded June 30, 1966), #1.
October 13*	Recorded "My Guy" (unreleased).
October 19	Recorded "Leave It in the Hand of Love" (unreleased).
October 21	Taped *The Hollywood Palace* (ABC) (air date October 22 or October 29).
October 21 and 24	Recorded in Los Angeles sides for *Rodgers and Hart* LP (twelve sides were unreleased).
November 27	*The Ed Sullivan Show* (CBS), performed "You Keep Me Hangin' On."
December	Deauville Hotel, Miami, Florida.
December 4	*The Ed Sullivan Show* (CBS), performed "You Keep Me Hangin' On."
December	Helped commemorate the independence of Barbados.
December 25	Open at the Eden Roc Hotel, Miami, Florida.
December 31	New Year's Eve King Orange Jamboree Parade.

1967

January 6–7	Recorded sides for unreleased *Disney* LP in New York, New York.
January 11	"Love Is Here and Now You're Gone" released, #1.
January 12, 14, and 20	Unreleased *Disney* LP recording in New York, New York. Among these recordings is "When You Wish Upon a Star" (on *25th Anniversary*, 1986).
January 22	*The Ed Sullivan Show* (CBS) performed "Love Is Here and Now You're Gone."
January 22	*The Andy Williams Show* (NBC).
January 23	*The Supremes Sing Holland-Dozier-Holland* released, #6.
January 23–27	Elmwood Casino, Windsor, Ontario, Canada.
January	*Playboy* annual reader's poll: voted #1 group (the Beatles, #2; Peter, Paul and Mary, #3).
February 13–25	Roostertail, Detroit, Michigan.
February 13	"Ice Capades" special (NBC).
February 16	*Soul* Magazine cover story "Good Things Come in Threes."
March	Deauville Hotel, Miami, Florida.
March 20	"The Happening" released (recorded March 2, 1967), #1.
March 22	"The Happening" released to coincide with film premiere Adams Theatre, Detroit, Michigan.
April 1*	Opening at Eden Roc, Miami, Florida, with Sonny Sands.
April 29	Hollywood Bowl benefit for UCLA School of Music and United Negro Fund, Los Angeles, California, (first appearance with Cindy Birdsong); receive KHJ Radio award.
May 7	*The Ed Sullivan Show* (CBS) performed "The Happening" and "Millie/Rose/Mame" medley (Florence's last appearance on Sullivan Show).

May 11	"Rodgers and Hart Today" special (ABC) with Bobby Darin, Petula Clark, the Mamas and Papas.
May 11–24	Copacabana, New York, New York.
May 19–20	Recorded live album at Copacabana (unreleased).
May 21*	*The Ed Sullivan Show* (CBS), broadcast from Expo '67 Theatre, Montreal, Canada.
May 22	*The Tonight Show* (NBC), performed "The Happening" and "The Lady Is a Tramp" (Florence's last TV appearance).
May 26	University of Cincinnati, Ohio.
May 27	Southern Illinois University, Carbondale, Illinois.
May 28	Hara Arena, Dayton, Ohio.
May 29	Minneapolis Auditorium, Minnesota.
May 30 and/or May 31	Arena Auditorium, Duluth, Minnesota.
May	*The Supremes Sing Rodgers & Hart* released, #20.
June 1–10	Shoreham, Washington, D.C.
June 8	*Soul* Magazine cover story, "A Smash at the Copa."
June 11	Symphony Hall, Washington, D.C.
June 13–18	Cocoanut Grove, Los Angeles, California.
June 22	Recorded "Lonely Boy" and "Ask the Lonely" (unreleased).
June 23	Presidential Ball, Las Vegas, Nevada, Presidents Club of California, Citizens for Johnson-Humphrey.
June 28–July 19	Flamingo Hotel, Las Vegas, Nevada.
July	Met President Lyndon Johnson. Cocoanut Grove, Los Angeles, California.
July 14	Invited by Johnny and Joanna Carson to party, Las Vegas, Nevada.
July 18	Invited to Milton Berle screening of *Who's Minding the Mint*, Las Vegas, Nevada.
July 24	"Reflections" released (recorded March 2, 1967), #2.
July 29	Forest Hills Stadium, Forest Hills, New York.

August 5–9	Allentown Fair, Allentown, Pennsylvania.
August 8	St. Moritz Hotel, New York, New York.
August 12	*American Bandstand* (ABC), performed "Reflections."
August 13–19	Steele Pier, Atlantic City, New Jersey.
August 20	In Montreal, Canada.
August 21–23	Expo '67 Theatre, Montreal, Canada.
August 25–28	"Showcase '68" Motown's first national sales convention Hotel Pontchartrain, Detroit, Michigan, debuted Supremes' *Greatest Hits*.
August 26	Two-hour "Motown Showcase," Hotel Pontchartrain, Detroit, Michigan, with Stevie Wonder, Gladys Knight and the Pips, the Spinners, Chris Clark, and Earl Van Dyke.
August 27	Recorded live at the Roostertail album, Detroit, Michigan (unreleased).
August 28–30	Ohio State Fair, Columbus, Ohio.
September	*Cosmopolitan* Magazine article "The Supremes: They Make You Believe Again," by Rona Jaffe. Recorded "Heigh-Ho" and "Someday My Prince Will Come" (on *25th Anniversary*, 1986).
September 1–4	Michigan State Fair, Michigan.
September 11–17	Farmington Music Circus, Farmington, Massachusetts.
September 17	Rhode Island Auditorium, Providence, Rhode Island.
September 23	*The Hollywood Palace* (ABC), performed "Reflections," "I've Got You Under My Skin," and "I Get a Kick out of You" (Cindy's TV debut*).
October 29	*Diana Ross and the Supremes Greatest Hits* released (double album), #1.
October*	In Mexico this month to film *Tarzan*.
October 2–14	The Cave, Vancouver, Canada.
October 6*	Recorded "Heaven Must Have Sent You" (unreleased) and "Stay in My Lonely Arms" (on *Motown's Brightest Stars*, 1986).
October 11*	Recorded* "Then" (on *Reflections*, 1968).

October 14	Recorded "Up, Up and Away" and "Ode to Billie Joe" (both on *Reflections*, 1968).
October 25	"In and Out of Love" released (recorded April 20, 1967), #9.
October 27	University of Oregon, Oregon.
October 28	Coliseum, Portland, Oregon.
October 29	Coliseum, Spokane, Washington.
October 30	Arena, Seattle, Washington.
November 3	Coliseum, Oakland, California.
November 4	UCLA Pauley Pavilion, Los Angeles, California, with Hugh Masekela, Sandy Baron.
November 6–12	Rehearsal/taping "The Tennessee Ernie Ford Special" (CBS), Los Angeles, California (air date December 3), with Andy Griffith, Danny Thomas.
November 19	*The Ed Sullivan Show* (CBS), with the Temptations, performed "In and Out of Love."
November 27	Recorded "What a Friend We Have in Jesus" and "Everytime I Feel the Spirit" (both unreleased).
December 3	"The Tennessee Ernie Ford Special" (CBS), performed "Reflections," "The Happening," and medley of hits.
December 18	Recorded "I'm Gonna Make It" (on *Reflections*, 1968) and "Treat Me Nice John Henry" (*25th Anniversary*, 1986).
December 22–31	Deauville Hotel, Miami, Florida.

1968

January 8–9	Milano TV show.
January 10	Lunch with the Duke and Duchess of Bedford, London, England.
January 11	Paris TV show.
January 12	*Tarzan* "The Convert" episode (NBC), with James Earl Jones, airs.

January 13	Berry "Pops" and Bertha Gordy's fiftieth wedding anniversary, renewed vows at Bethel A.M.E. Church, Detroit, Michigan, entire family and Motown artists attended.
January 14	"The Supremes in Berlin" TV show.
January 16	TV show in Amsterdam.
January 17	TV show in Madrid.
January 18	TV show in Paris.
January 19–20	Bal Paree, Munich Bambi Film Festival.
January 21	Miden Festival, Cannes.
January 22– February 3	Talk of the Town, London, England.
January 28– February 9*	In London, England.
January 28	Duke and Duchess of Bedford give party honoring group at the Club Dell'Aretusa, Chelsea, London, England. Guests included Tom Jones, Mick Jagger, Marianne Faithfull, Michael Caine, Lynn Redgrave.
January 28	Palladium TV show.
February 3	"Live at London's Talk of the Town," BBC hour special (shown live*).
February 4	Eamon Andrews TV show.
February 5–11	Berns Restaurant, Stockholm.
February 10	Recorded "Am I Asking Too Much" and "He Loves Me So" (both unreleased).
February 12	TV show in Geneva.
February 13	Recorded "Don't Forget I Love You" (unreleased).
February 17	Recorded "I Can't Shake It Loose" (on *Love Child*, 1968) and "You'll Never Cherish a Love So True" (unreleased).
February 22	Florence signs her general release from Motown, a nine-page settlement.
February 24	Recorded "Can't Take My Eyes Off You" (unreleased, Mary lead).
February 29	Recorded "A Little Breeze" (unreleased).
February 29	"Forever Came Today" released (recorded April 21, 1967), #28. This is the first single

February 29 (*cont.*)	on which no other Supremes except Diane appear.
March	*Reflections* released, #18.
March 6	Florence sings with ABC Records, $15,000 advance, two year exclusive contract.
March 7	Recorded "When It's to the Top" (on *Cream of the Crop*, 1969) and "You Made Me Feel Like Everything Was Alright" (unreleased).
March 9	Recorded "Honey Bee" (on *Love Child*, 1968) and "The Beginning of the End" (on *Cream of the Crop*, 1969).
March 14	Recorded "Sweet Soul Music" and "If You Should Walk Away" (unreleased).
March 15	Recorded "A Place in the Sun" (on *Join the Temptations*, 1969) and "Believe in Me" (unreleased).
March 18	Recorded "Growing," "The Nitty Gritty," "The Boy from Crosstown," "For Once in My Life" (unreleased).
March 24	*The Ed Sullivan Show* (CBS), performed "Forever Came Today" and Fats Waller medley.
April 4*	Copacabana, New York, New York.
April 4	Recorded "Will This Be the Day" (on *Love Child*, 1968).
April 5	*The Tonight Show* (NBC), performed "Somewhere."
April 12	Recorded "You've Been So Wonderful to Me" (on *Love Child*, 1968).
April 20	"Crusade '68" special (CBS).
April 24	Recorded "Touched by the Hand of Love" (unreleased).
April 29	Recorded "Hey Hey" and "Honey Babe" (unreleased).
April 30	Recorded "He's My Sunny Boy" (on *Love Child*, 1968) and "Ain't I Gonna Win Your Love" (unreleased).
May 4	*The Hollywood Palace* (ABC).
May 4*	Open at the Copacabana, New York, New York, with Lewis and Christy, Copa girls.

May 5	*The Ed Sullivan Show* (CBS) performed "Some Things You Never Get Used To."
May 10	Recorded "Uptown" (unreleased).
May 11	ABC Records lists Florence's "It Doesn't Matter How I Say It" as coming product, *Billboard*.
May 13–18	Westbury Music Fair, Long Island, New York.
May 21	"Some Things You Never Get Used To" released (recorded April 15, 1968), #30. Recorded two unreleased sides, rerecorded "Honey Bee" (on *Love Child*, 1968). Appeared at Fisher Theatre, Detroit, Michigan
May 27–31	Fisher Theatre, Detroit, Michigan.
May 31	Recorded "Don't Break These Chains of Love" (on *Love Child*, 1968).
June 20	Recorded *Funny Girl* LP sides in New York, New York.
June 24–30	Carter Barron Amphitheatre, Rock Creek Park, Washington, D.C., with Stevie Wonder, the Little Step Brothers.
July 19	Recorded "Ain't No Sun Since You've Been Gone" (unreleased).
July 20	Forum, Los Angeles, California, with Stevie Wonder, Shorty Long.
July 22–27	Garden State Arts Center, New Jersey, with George Kirby, the Little Step Brothers.
July 23	Endorsed Hubert Humphrey, Waldorf Astoria, New York, New York.
July 24	Waldorf Astoria, New York, New York.
July 25	Recorded "Weak Spot," "Soul Appeal," "Double or Nothing," "Operation Teamwork" (unreleased).
July 26	Recorded "This Is Where I Came In," "It Only Happens When Love Is Gone," "The Girl that Was," "I Feel Love" (unreleased).
July 28	Recorded "How Long Has That Evening Train Been Gone" (on *Love Child*, 1968) and "I Can't Give Back the Love I Feel for You" (same cut that's on Diana's solo *Surrender* LP*).

August 1	Recorded "You Ain't Livin' Until You're Lovin'" (on *Love Child*, 1968).
August 2	Recorded "Make Me Yours" with the Temptations (unreleased) and "This Is Where I Came In" (unreleased).
August 5	Recorded "You've Got the Love" (unreleased), rerecorded "I'll Set You Free" (on *Love Child*, 1968).
August 9	Recorded "Those Precious Memories" (unreleased).
August 19	Recorded "I'm So Glad I Got Somebody (Like You Around)" (on *Let the Sunshine In*, 1969) and "For Us Both I'll Be Concerned" (unreleased).
August	*The Supremes Sing and Perform "Funny Girl"* released, #150.
	Live at London's Talk of the Town released, #57.
September*	Carousel Theatre, Framingham, Maine, with the Temptations, one week engagement.
September 1	Baltimore Civic Center, Maryland.
September 6	Recorded "I Get Lost" (unreleased).
September 12	Recorded "Love for a Lifetime" (unreleased).
September 14	Recorded "Where the People Live," "Won't You Come Fly with Me," "Don't Say You Love Me" (unreleased).
September 17	Rhode Island Auditorium, Providence, Rhode Island, with the Temptations.
September 18	Recorded "Seeing Is Believing" (unreleased).
September 23	Recorded "It Could Have Gone Either Way" (unreleased).
September 29	*The Ed Sullivan Show* (CBS), performed *Funny Girl* medley and "Love Child."
September 30	"Love Child" released (recorded September 17, 1968), #1.
October*	Florence's second 45, "Love Ain't Love," released.
October 1–14	The Grove (Cocoanut Grove), Los Angeles, California.

October 2	Recorded "Does Your Mama Know About Me" (on *Love Child*, 1968).
October 8	Recorded "The Shadows of Society" (on *Cream of the Crop*, 1969) and "Give Back the Good Things" (unreleased).
October 13	Florence gives birth to twin daughters, Michelle Denise and Nicole Rene, at Henry Ford Hospital, Detroit, Michigan.
October 16	Rerecorded "I'm So Glad I Got Somebody (Like You Around)" (on *Let the Sunshine In*, 1969).
October 23	"Bing Crosby Special" (NBC), performed "You Keep Me Hangin' On."
November*	*Soul Illustrated* Magazine cover story (winter '68) "The Beauty, the Soul, the Style of . . ."
November 4	Recorded "My Love for Your Love" (unreleased).
November 5	Recorded "I'm Lost" and "It's Unbelievable" (unreleased).
November 8	*Love Child* released, #14.
November	In Europe.
November 8	Olympia Theatre, Paris, France.
November 11	London Palladium, London, England, meet royalty.
November 12	Stockholm.
November 13	*Diana Ross and the Supremes Join the Temptations* released, #2.
November 13	Copenhagen.
November 14	Malmö, Sweden.
November 16	Brussels, Belgium.
November 16*	Rerecorded "The World Can't See Through the Eyes of Love" (unreleased).
November 17	Royal Command Performance, London, England.
November 18	London Palladium, London, England, members of Royal Family in attendance.
November 21	"I'm Gonna Make You Love Me" (with the Temptations) released, #2.
November 21	Dublin, Ireland.

November 23	Manchester Odeon Free Trade Hall, Manchester, England.
November 24	London Palladium, London, England.
November 26	Hamburg, Germany.
November 29	Munich, Germany.
November 30	Frankfurt, Germany.
December*	Still in Europe.
December 2	*TCB* soundtrack LP (with the Temptations) released, #1.
December 3*	Rerecorded "I'll Set You Free" (already on *Love Child*, 1968).
December 5	Recorded "The Young Folks" (on *Cream of the Crop*, 1969) and "I Just Can't Carry On" (unreleased).
December 6	Rerecorded (for third time*) "I'm So Glad I Got Somebody (Like You Around)" (on *Let the Sunshine In*, 1969).
December 9	"TCB (Takin' Care of Business)" special (NBC) with the Temptations.
December 28	Recorded "Are You Sure Love Is the Name of this Game" (released on *25th Anniversary*, 1986).
December 28	Host *The Hollywood Palace* (ABC).

1969

January 5	*The Ed Sullivan Show* (CBS), performed "Love Child" and "I'm Livin' in Shame."
January 6	"I'm Livin' in Shame" released (recorded December 26, 1968), #10.
January 10	Trinity University Earl C. Sams Memorial Center, San Antonio, Texas.
January 13	Recorded "Sunshine Days" (unreleased).
January 17	Recorded "Why Am I Lovin' You" (unreleased).

January 21	Recorded "Everyday People" and "Western Union Man" (both cuts on *Let the Sunshine In*, 1969), "Hey Jude" (on *Cream of the Crop*, 1969) "Stormy" (unreleased), rerecorded "For Once in My Life" (unreleased).
January 24	Recorded "Son of a Preacher Man," "Chained to Yesterday," "Nothing from Nothing," "Witchi-Tai-To" (unreleased).
January 25	Recorded "I Had a Dream" and "The Onion Song" (unreleased).
January 29	Recorded "You're Gonna Hear from Me," rerecorded "Witchi-Tai-To" (unreleased).
January 30– February 12	Frontier Hotel, Las Vegas, Nevada.
February 15	Recorded "Memories" and "A Little Too Much" (unreleased), rerecorded "For Both of Us I'll Be Concerned" (unreleased).
February 17	"Bob Hope Special" (NBC), performed "Coronet Man" and "Sam, You Made the Pants Too Long" (both from *Funny Girl*).
February 20	"I'll Try Something New" (with the Temptations) released, #25.
February 24	Recorded six sides for *Together* LP with the Temptations.
February 27	Recorded "The Paper Said Rain" (unreleased).
March 8	*The Hollywood Palace* (ABC).
March 18	*The Tonight Show* (NBC).
March 20	Recorded "Discover Me" (on *Let the Sunshine In*, 1969), rerecorded "The Beginning of the End" (on *Cream of the Crop*, 1969).
March 24	Recorded (with the Temptations) "Why (Must We Fall in Love)" (on *Together*, 1969).
March 25 or 27	"The Composer" released (recorded December 28, 1968), #27.
April*	$1,000-a-plate concert/fundraiser to help clear Robert Kennedy's political debts, Beverly Hills, California.
April*	Announced that Diana would make her film debut in Walter Zeltzer's *Darker than Amber*.
April 1	Recorded "Make the Most of It" (unreleased).

April 4–13	Casanova Room, Deauville Hotel, Miami, Florida, with Scoey Mitchell. (Motown artists appearing across the country paid tribute in their concerts to Dr. Martin Luther King, Jr., on this first anniversary of his death.)
April 7	Recorded "I'm Just a Little Bit Nothing When Love Falls" and "Love What Have You Done to Me" (unreleased).
April 10	Recorded "Since You Came Back" (unreleased).
April 13	"Like Hep!" special (NBC) (Diana solo) with Dinah Shore and Lucille Ball.
April 19	Recorded "Will I" (unreleased).
April 22*	O'Keefe Center, Toronto, Canada, with O. C. Smith, the Little Step Brothers.
May 9	"No Matter What Sign You Are" released, #31.
May 11	*The Ed Sullivan Show* (CBS), performed "No Matter What Sign You Are."
May 14*	Waldorf Astoria Empire Room, New York, New York.
May 19	Recorded "Though Love Has Gone," "The Unwanted," "Look at Where We Are" (unreleased).
May 26	*Let the Sunshine In* released, #24.
May 31	*The Hollywood Palace* (ABC).
June*	Jean Terrell signed to Motown as a solo artist.
June 3	Recorded "I Wanna Go Back There Again" (unreleased).
June 10	Recorded "My Heart's on a Trip" and "Mr. Loneliness" (unreleased).
June 23	Recorded with Jean Terrell "Take a Closer Look at Me" (on *New Supremes' Right On*, 1970) and "Standing Ovation," "Baby Don't You Go," and "While They Watch" (unreleased).
June 30–July 6	Carter Barron Amphitheatre, Rock Creek Park, Washington, D.C. with Julius Wechter and the Baja Marimba Band.

July 8–12	Carousel Theatre, Framingham, Massachusetts, with Stevie Wonder.
July 17	Recorded "Honey Take Me" and "I'm Getting Married" (unreleased).
July 18	Recorded "Another Lonely Night" (unreleased).
July 25	Recorded (with the Temptations) "Everyday for a Lifetime" (unreleased).
July 31	Rerecorded "I Wanna Go Back There Again" (unreleased).
July 31	*Top of the Pops* (BBC), London, England, with Donovan, the Rolling Stones, Billy Preston, Cilla Black, host Alan Freeman.
August 11	Daisy Club, Beverly Hills, California, Diana Ross threw a party for Jackson Five.
August 16	Forum, Los Angeles, California, with Edwin Starr, the Edwin Hawkins Singers, Jackson Five.
August 21	"The Weight" (with the Temptations) released, #46.
August 25	Recorded "I'm Going Crazy" (unreleased).
September*	*Together* (with the Temptations) released, #28.
September 7	*The Ed Sullivan Show* (CBS).
September 16	Recorded "Then I Met You" (on New Supremes' *Right On*, 1970).
September 22	Rowan and Martin's *Laugh-In* (NBC).
September 23	*Look* Magazine cover story "The Supreme Supreme" (Diana solo article).
October 12	"Someday We'll Be Together" released, #1. (last 45 release with Diana).
October 18	Hosts *The Hollywood Palace* (ABC), with Sammy Davis, Jr., the Jackson Five, performed "Someday We'll Be Together," Mary solo "Can't Take My Eyes Off You."
November	*Git on Broadway* soundtrack (with the Temptations), #38, and *Cream of the Crop* (last with Diana) released, #33.
November 5	Recorded "These Things Will Keep Me Loving You" (on Diana's first solo LP).

November 8	*Billboard* Magazine carries official confirmation: Diana leaving the Supremes, Jean Terrell her replacement.
November 11	*The Tonight Show* (NBC).
November 12	"Git on Broadway" special (NBC) with the Temptations.
November 14	Recorded "Bill, When Are You Coming Home" (on New Supremes' *Right On*, 1970) and "I Can't Wait 'Til Summer Comes" (unreleased New Supremes cut*).
December 2	Cindy Birdsong kidnapped from her Hollywood, California apartment.
December 18	*Greatest Hits, Volume 3* released, #31.
December 21	*The Ed Sullivan Show* (CBS), performed medley of hits, "I Hear a Symphony" and "Someday We'll Be Together" (last TV appearance with Diane).
December 23– January 14, 1970	Frontier Hotel farewell engagement, Las Vegas, Nevada.
December 31	Recorded "I Got Hurt (Trying to Be the Only Girl in Your Life)" (on New Supremes' *Right On*, 1970) and "The Day Will Come Between Sunday and Monday" (unreleased New Supremes cut).

1970

January 2	Recorded "Up the Ladder to the Roof."
January 6	Recorded "I Wish I Were Your Mirror" (on New Supremes' *New Ways but Love Stays*, 1970) and "Lovin' Country" (on New Supremes' *Right On*, 1970).
January 9	Recorded "Three Day Journey of Me" (unreleased).
January 12	Rerecorded "Then I Met You" (on New Supremes' *Right On*, 1970), recorded "That's How Much You Made Me Love You" and

	"I'll Never Let You Get Away" (unreleased New Supremes*).
January 14	Frontier Hotel, last day, last performance of Diana Ross and the Supremes.
January 15	Recorded "Stepping on a Dream" and "Wasting Time" (both unreleased).
January 16	Recorded "Thank Him for Today" (on New Supremes' *New Ways but Love Stays*, 1970) and "I Almost Had Him (But He Got Away)" (unreleased New Supremes cut*).
January 23	Rerecorded "I Can't Wait 'Til Summer Comes" (unreleased New Supremes cut*).
January 30	Rerecorded "Up the Ladder to the Roof," "Na Na Hey Hey Kiss Him Goodbye" (on New Supremes' *New Ways but Love Stays*, 1970), and "Didn't I Blow Your Mind This Time" (unreleased New Supremes cut*).
February	New Supremes' "Up the Ladder to the Roof" released, #10.
April 13	*Farewell* three-record boxed set released, #46.

APPENDIX II:

SUPREMES DISCOGRAPHY

The following is a discography of all albums and singles by the Supremes—as the Primettes, as the Supremes, and as Diana Ross and the Supremes—up through the departure of Diana Ross from the group in 1970. Solo albums and singles by Florence Ballard and Mary Wilson are included; Diana Ross' are not, because her solo career is well documented in several other sources. Also included is a partial list of songs recorded by the Supremes but never released, as well as a videography. Asterisks indicate information that is missing or unknown.

1959–1960	*The Primettes*
	Florence Ballard
	Betty McGlown
	Diane Ross
	Mary Wilson
1960–1961	*The Primettes*
	Barbara Martin
	Florence Ballard
	Diane Ross
	Mary Wilson
1961–1962	*The Supremes*
	Barbara Martin
	Florence Ballard
	Diane Ross
	Mary Wilson
1962–1967	*The Supremes*
	Florence Ballard
	Diana Ross
	Mary Wilson

1967–1970   *Diana Ross and the Supremes*
                   Cindy Birdsong
                   Diana Ross
                   Mary Wilson

Singles

The Primettes	Label	Released
"Tears of Sorrow"/"Pretty Baby"	Lupine 120	3/59

The Supremes		
"I Want a Guy"/"Never Again"	TAMLA 54038	3/9/61
"Buttered Popcorn"/"Who's Loving You"	TAMLA 54045	7/21/61
"Your Heart Belongs to Me"/"He's Seventeen"	Motown 1027	5/8/62
"Let Me Go the Right Way"/"Time Changes Things"	Motown 1034	11/5/62
"My Heart Can't Take It No More"/ "You Bring Back Memories"	Motown 1040	2/2/63
"A Breath Taking Guy"/"Rock & Roll Banjo Band"	Motown 1044	6/12/63
"When the Lovelight Starts Shining Through His Eyes"/"Standing at the Crossroads of Love"	Motown 1051	10/31/63
"Run, Run, Run"/"I'm Giving You Your Freedom"	Motown 1054	2/7/64
"Where Did Our Love Go"/"He Means the World to Me"	Motown 1054	6/17/64
"Baby Love"/"Ask Any Girl"	Motown 1066	9/17/64
"Come See About Me"/"Always in My Heart"	Motown 1068	10/27/64
"Stop! In the Name of Love"/"I'm in Love Again"	Motown 1074	2/8/65
"Back in My Arms Again"/"Whisper You Love Me Boy"	Motown 1075	4/15/65

"Nothing But Heartaches"/"He Holds His Own"	Motown 1080	7/16/65
"I Hear a Symphony"/"Who Could Ever Doubt My Love"	Motown 1083	10/6/65
"Children's Christmas Song"/ "Twinkle Twinkle Little Me"	Motown 1085	11/18/65
"My World Is Empty Without You"/"Everything's Good About You"	Motown 1089	12/29/65
"Love Is like an Itching in My Heart"/"He's All I Got"	Motown 1094	4/8/66
"You Can't Hurry Love"/"Put Yourself in My Place"	Motown 1097	7/25/66
"You Keep Me Hangin' On"/ "Remove This Doubt"	Motown 1101	10/12/66
"Love Is Here and Now You're Gone"/"There's No Stopping Us Now"	Motown 1103	1/11/67
"The Happening"/"All I Know About You"	Motown 1107	3/20/67

Diana Ross and the Supremes

"Reflections"/"Going Down for the Third Time"	Motown 1111	7/24/67
"In and Out of Love"/"I Guess I'll Always Love You"	Motown 1116	10/28/67
"Forever Came Today"/"Time Changes Things"	Motown 1122	2/24/68
"What the World Needs Now"/ "Your Kiss of Fire"	Motown 1125	1968
"Some Things You Never Get Used To"/"You've Been So Wonderful to Me"	Motown 1126	5/21/68
"Love Child"/"Will This Be the Day"	Motown 1135	9/30/68
"I'm Gonna Make You Love Me"/ "A Place in the Sun" (with the Temptations)	Motown 1137	11/21/68

"I'm Livin' in Shame"/"I'm So Glad I Got Somebody like You Around"	Motown 1139	1/6/69
"I'll Try Something New"/"The Way You Do the Things You Do" (with the Temptations)	Motown 1142	2/20/69
"The Composer"/"The Beginning of the End"	Motown 1146	3/27/69
"No Matter What Sign You Are"/ "The Young Folks"	Motown 1148	5/9/69
"Stubborn Kind of Fellow"/"Try It Baby" (with the Temptations)	Motown 1150	1969
"The Weight"/"For Better or for Worse" (with the Temptations)	Motown 1153	8/29/69
"Someday We'll Be Together"/"He's My Sunny Boy"	Motown 1156	10/14/69

Albums

The Supremes

Meet the Supremes	Motown 606	12/63
Where Did Our Love Go	Motown 621	1/65
A Bit of Liverpool	Motown 623	10/64
Sing Country and Western and Pop	Motown 625	2/65
More Hits by the Supremes	Motown 627	7/65
We Remember Sam Cooke	Motown 629	5/65
At the Copa	Motown 636	11/65
Merry Christmas	Motown 638	11/65
I Hear a Symphony	Motown 643	2/66
A Go-Go	Motown 649	8/66
Sing Holland-Dozier-Holland	Motown 650	1/67
Sing Rodgers & Hart	Motown 659	8/67

Diana Ross and the Supremes

Greatest Hits Volumes I and II	Motown 663	8/67
Reflections	Motown 665	8/68

Love Child	Motown 670	11/68
Sing and Perform "Funny Girl"	Motown 672	8/68
Live at the Talk of the Town	Motown 676	8/68
Join the Temptations	Motown 679	11/68
TCB (with/the Temptations)	Motown 682	12/68
Let the Sunshine In	Motown 689	5/69
Together (with/the Temptations)	Motown 692	9/69
Cream of the Crop	Motown 694	11/69
On Broadway (with the Temptations)	Motown 699	11/69
Greatest Hits Volume 3	Motown 702	12/69
Farewell	Motown 708	4/70
Great Songs and Performances	Motown 5313 ML	1985
Motown Legends	Motown 5361 ML	1985
Sing Motown	Motown 5371 ML	1986
Anthology	Motown 794	5/74

Also:

Live at the Apollo—Volume 1 (1 cut)	Motown 609	4/63
Motortown Revue in Paris (3 cuts)	Tamla 264	1965
In Loving Memory (1 cut)	Motown 642	8/26/68
Motown at the Hollywood Palace (3 cuts)	Motown 703	8/70
From the Vaults (1 cut)	Natural Resources NR4014T1	1979, 1982
Superstar Series—Volume 1	Motown M5-101V1	1979
All the Greatest Hits—Diana Ross (1 medley)	Motown M13-960C2	1981
Motown's Brightest Stars—The 1960's (1 cut)	Motown 538ML	2/86
The Detroit Girl Groups (2 cuts)	Relic Records Lupine 8004	*

Guest Appearances

Four Tops Live! (1 cut)	MS 5654	1966
Temptations—Getting Ready (1 cut)	Gordy 918	1966
"You're the Wonderful One" by Marvin Gaye	*	1964
"You Lost the Sweetest Boy" by Mary Wells	*	1963
"Fancy Passes" by Barbara McNair	*	*

Florence Ballard

"It Doesn't Matter How I Say It"/ "Goin' out of My Head"	ABC 11074	1968
"Love Ain't Love"/"Forever Faithful"	ABC 11144	1968

Mary Wilson

"Red Hot"/"Midnight Dancer"	Motown 1467	1979
Mary Wilson	Motown M7-927R1	8/79

Promotional Singles

"The Only Time I'm Happy"/ "Supremes Interview"	Motown 1079	1965
"What the World Needs Now"/ "Your Kiss of Fire"	Motown 1125	(unreleased)

Unreleased Recordings

Currently Motown has in its vaults countless unreleased recordings. Since no official record of these recordings has ever been released or published by Motown, it is impossible to compile a complete list. However, here are a few more memorable recordings in addition to those listed in the Itinerary.

"Supremes Sing Ballads and Blues"
"Live! Live! Live!"
"There's a Place for Us"
"A Tribute to the Girls"
"Pure Gold"
"Our Day Will Come"
"Can't"
"All I Want to Do"
"Send Him to Me"
"Davy Crockett"
"The Tears"
"I Idolize You"
"Bye Bye Baby"
"Mr. Blues"
"Silent"
"Whistle While You Work"

For the RIAA (the Recording Industry Association of America) to certify a record gold (sales of $1 million wholesale before 1976; 500,000 copies after 1976) or platinum (one million copies; this award established in 1976), a record company must submit its accounts to an audit. Because Motown, among other labels, refused to do this throughout the sixties, only the Supremes three-album set *Anthology* (1974) was ever officially recognized by the RIAA as a gold record. Although no official figures have ever been released by Motown, it is certain that any Supremes release that entered the Top Thirty sold in the millions, and many releases continue to sell today, in some cases, over two decades after their original release.

Videography

The following is a list of all performances or interviews of Mary Wilson or the Supremes currently available on home video.

The Girl Groups, MGM/UA Home Video: interview with Mary Wilson, various clips of performances by the Supremes.

Ready Steady Go: The Sounds of Motown, Sony Video: three performances by the Supremes.

Mellow Memories, USA Home Video: performance of one song by the Supremes.

That Was Rock: The TAMI/TNT Show: performance of four songs by the Supremes.

Motown 25: Yesterday, Today and Forever, MGM/UA Home Video: various performances and clips of the Supremes.

INDEX